W. Inglis

**Book-Keeping by Single and Double-Entry**

with an appendix containing explanations of mercantile terms and transactions,

questions in book-keeping, etc.

W. Inglis

**Book-Keeping by Single and Double-Entry**
*with an appendix containing explanations of mercantile terms and transactions, questions in book-keeping, etc.*

ISBN/EAN: 9783337192655

Printed in Europe, USA, Canada, Australia, Japan

Cover: Foto ©Andreas Hilbeck / pixelio.de

More available books at **www.hansebooks.com**

CHAMBERS'S EDUCATIONAL COURSE—EDITED BY
W. AND R. CHAMBERS.

# BOOK-KEEPING

## BY SINGLE AND DOUBLE ENTRY;

WITH

AN APPENDIX CONTAINING EXPLANATIONS OF MERCANTILE TERMS
AND TRANSACTIONS.

### BY W. INGLIS.

EDINBURGH:
PUBLISHED BY WILLIAM AND ROBERT CHAMBERS.
1850.

EDINBURGH:

PRINTED BY W. AND R. CHAMBERS.

# NOTICE.

In the present Treatise, simplicity is the object chiefly aimed at, and all unnecessary technicalities in the phraseology and complexity in the system of keeping the accounts have been studiously avoided. The principles of Book-Keeping are exhibited, not by means of abstract rules, but by examples of the various transactions common in actual business.

The work embraces Book-Keeping by "Single and Double Entry." Another edition, containing Single Entry alone, is issued for the convenience of those who may not require a knowledge of the entire system.

An Appendix, containing Explanations of Mercantile Terms and Transactions, is subjoined, which will serve in some measure as a guide to the Counting-room.

W. I.

*Edinburgh, August* 1849.

# CONTENTS.

# BOOK-KEEPING.

BOOK-KEEPING is the art of recording and classifying a merchant's or tradesman's daily transactions, and of keeping an account of his property and debts.

The property or capital of persons in business, may be comprised under the following heads :—

I. Stock in trade, including goods, warehouses, machinery, ships, or whatever species of stock is employed in the business.

II. Accounts, or debts owing to the merchant.

III. Bills, „ „

IV. Cash.

A merchant's books ought to exhibit clearly the whole amount of his property, with the particulars of which it is composed ; and also the amount of his debts.

The following are the most important of the books used in Book-Keeping :—

| | | |
|---|---|---|
| DAY-BOOK, | for | Goods *sold* on credit. |
| INVOICE-BOOK, | „ | Goods *bought* on credit. |
| CASH-BOOK, | „ | Cash received and paid. |
| | | Discount received and allowed. |
| BILL-BOOK, | „ | Bills receivable and payable. |
| LEDGER, | to | contain an abstract of the other books. |
| STOCK-BOOK, | „ | contain an inventory of the stock on hand at the time of balancing the books. |

The following subsidiary books are also in general use :—

| | | |
|---|---|---|
| ACCOUNT-BOOK, | to | contain a list of accounts owing to, and owing by, the merchant. |
| WAREHOUSE-BOOK, | „ | contain an account of the *quantities* of goods received, sent out, and on hand. |
| MEMORANDUM-BOOK, | „ | contain temporary memorandums. |
| LETTER-BOOK, | „ | contain copies of letters. |

Various other books are required, according to the nature of the business.

# DAY-BOOK.

The purpose of the Day-Book **is to** keep a daily account of all goods *sold on credit.*

When the goods are sold, the names and addresses of the persons to whom they are sold, with a description of the goods and their prices, are entered in the Day-Book, as shown in the following examples: any other charges are entered in a similar way. The particulars of the entries are filled into the inner money columns; the sums-total into the outer columns :—thus,

> If, on January 1, you sell to George Innes, Liverpool, 20 yards of black silk @ 3s. 6d. per yard, 12 yards of velvet @ 11s., and 15 yards of linen @ 2s. 6d.; and if, besides, you wish to make a charge for packing and commission,

The transaction will be entered in your Day-Book, as in the first of the following examples :—

*January* 1, 1850.

| | Particulars. | | | Sums-Total. | | |
|---|---|---|---|---|---|---|
| | £ | s. | d. | £ | s. | d. |
| George Innes, Liverpool.     *Dr.* | | | | | | |
| To 20 Yards Black Silk.............. @   3/6 | 3 | 10 | 0 | | | |
| „ 12 „ Velvet................... „   11/ | 6 | 12 | 0 | | | |
| „ 15 „ Linen.................... „   2/6 | 1 | 17 | 6 | | | |
| Wrapper and packing.......... | 0 | 3 | 6 | | | |
| Commission...................... | 0 | 12 | 0 | 12 | 15 | 0 |
| *" Dr. To " is a contraction for " Debtor To."* | | | | | | |
| —3d.— | | | | | | |
| Charles Chadwick, Manchester. | | | | | | |
| To 40 Yards Welsh Flannel........ @ 1/10 | | | | 3 | 13 | 4 |
| *When there is only one sum in the entry, it is filled at once into the outer columns.* | | | | | | |
| —4th.— | | | | | | |
| William Wilson, London. | | | | | | |
| To 4 Reams Royal Printing Paper.. @ 21/ | 4 | 4 | 0 | | | |
| „ 1 Edgeworth's Moral Tales............... | 0 | 5 | 0 | 4 | 9 | 0 |
| —6th.— | | | | | | |
| James Brown, Edinburgh. | | | | | | |
| To 10 lbs. Sugar................... @ 6½d. | 0 | 5 | 5 | | | |
| „ 2 „ Tea............................ „ 4/6 | 0 | 9 | 0 | 0 | 14 | 5 |
| James Watt, 60 George Street. | | | | | | |
| To 1 Ream Small Post Paper................ | 1 | 5 | 0 | | | |
| „ 1 Box Steel Pens............................ | 0 | 4 | 6 | 1 | 9 | 6 |

In the Day-Book, instead of " Dr. To," which is the mercantile phrase in full, it is enough to write "To;" and in the Invoice-Book, instead of " Cr. By," it is enough to write " By."

# INVOICE-BOOK.

This book is used for keeping an account of all goods *bought on credit*. It is so called because the entries made in it are copied from the *invoices* (see Appendix) usually sent along with the goods.

When the goods are bought, and have been received, the names and addresses of the persons from whom they are bought, with a description of the goods and their prices, are entered in the Invoice-Book, as below: any other charges are entered in the same way:— thus,

If, on January 1, you receive from James Stewart & Co., Leeds, 180 yards of black cloth @ 13s. 7d., 80 yards of brown cloth @ **14s. 5d.**, 80 yards of olive cloth @ 14s. 10d., and 100 yards of black cloth @ 15s. 2d. ; and if a charge of 9s. 6d. is made for packing, &c.,

You make the entry in your Invoice-Book as in the first of the following examples, the entry being copied from the invoice which you have received from James Stewart & Co.

Instead of copying the *particulars* of the invoices, it is often more convenient to copy the *amount* only, as shown in the entry of J. Miller, Jan. 20.

The invoices are preserved for future reference, if necessary. They may be kept either in a book made for the purpose, or tied up in parcels, having the name, date, and amount marked on each.

*January* 1, 1850.

| | Particulars. | | | Sums-Total. | | |
|---|---|---|---|---|---|---|
| | £ | s. | d. | £ | s. | d. |
| James Stewart & Co., Leeds. Cr. | | | | | | |
| By 9 Pieces Black Cloth, 180 yds.* @ 13/7 | 122 | 5 | 0 | | | |
| „ 3 „ Brown do. 80 „ „ 14/5 | 57 | 13 | 4 | | | |
| „ 4 „ Olive do. 80 „ „ 14/10 | 59 | 6 | 8 | | | |
| „ 5 „ Black do. 100 „ „ 15/2 | 75 | 16 | 8 | | | |
| Wrapper and packing............. | 0 | 9 | 6 | 315 | 11 | 2 |
| * that is, 9 pieces measuring 180 yards, at 13s. 7d. a yard. "Cr. By" is a contraction for "Creditor By." | | | | | | |
| —2d.— | | | | | | |
| Robert Gray, Bradford. | | | | | | |
| By 3 Pieces Black Cloth, 150 yds.. @ 13/6 | 101 | 5 | 0 | | | |
| „ 2 „ Brown do. 90 „ „ 14/6 | 65 | 5 | 0 | | | |
| „ 5 „ Olive do. 125 „ „ 15/ | 93 | 15 | 0 | 260 | 5 | 0 |
| —20th.— | | | | | | |
| John Miller, Edinburgh. | | | | | | |
| By Goods, as per Invoice, January 19...... | | | | 33 | 15 | 6 |
| In practice, instead of copying the particulars of the invoices, it is often more convenient to enter the amount only, with the date of the invoice. | | | | | | |

# CASH-BOOK.

In the Cash-Book is kept an account of all cash received and paid, and of discount received and allowed.

Two pages are always required for the entries; the left-hand page for entering the cash you receive, and the discount allowed *by* you; the right-hand page for the cash you pay, and the discount allowed *to* you.

Each page is ruled with double money columns; the inner columns being used for the discount, the outer for the cash.

When you *receive payment* of an account, enter on the *received* side

### Cash Received.

| 1850. | | | | Discount. | | | Cash. | | |
|---|---|---|---|---|---|---|---|---|---|
| | | | | £ | s. | d. | £ | s. | d. |
| Jan. | 1 | J. Adams—Cash at commencement... | | | | | 1000 | 0 | 0 |
| | | This is the sum with which you commenced business. | | | | | | | |
| | 3 | James Brown, George Street......... | | 0 | 4 | 6 | 4 | 15 | 0 |
| | | Here James Brown settled his account, amounting to £4, 19s. 6d., by paying you £4, 15s. 0d.—4s. 6d. having been allowed to him as discount. | | | | | | | |
| | 5 | Union Bank...................... | | | | | 110 | 0 | 0 |
| | | This sum was received by you from the Bank. | | | | | | | |
| | | Goods—Cash Sales...................... | | | | | 2 | 7 | 6 |
| | | This is an entry for goods which you have sold for ready money. | | | | | | | |
| | 20 | Bills Receivable, No. 1, discounted, £172, 11s. | | 0 | 7 | 6 | 172 | 3 | 6 |
| | | This bill for £172, 11s. 0d., marked No. 1 in your Bill-Book under " Bills Receivable," was sent to the Bank to be discounted; £172, 3s. 6d. was received for it in cash, 7s. 6d. being charged by the Bank for discounting it. | | | | | | | |
| | | BALANCING THE CASH-BOOK.—To ascertain that the sums have been entered correctly, the Cash-Book requires to be balanced at stated times, as explained at page 44.<br>PETTY CASH-BOOK.—See Appendix.<br>CASH-BOOK, DOUBLE ENTRY.—Additional money columns are used in Double Entry: see pages 86 and 87. | | | | | | | | |
| | | | | | | | 1289 | 6 | 0 |

the name of the person from whom you receive the money, and fill the amount of cash and discount into the cash and discount columns.

When you *pay* an account, enter on the *paid* side the name of the person to whom you pay it, and fill the sum and the discount into the cash and discount columns.

Various money transactions are shown in the following example. The nature of every transaction should be distinctly expressed, and the sums paid or received, filled into the money columns opposite each entry.

[It is usual to name the left-hand side the *Dr.* side, and the right-hand the *Cr.* side, prefixing " To " and " By " to the entries; but these have been omitted for the sake of simplicity.]

*Cash Paid.*

| | | | Discount. | | | Cash. | | |
|---|---|---|---|---|---|---|---|---|
| 1850 | | | £ | s. | d. | £ | s. | d. |
| Jan. | 1 | Union Bank................................ | | | | 990 | 0 | 0 |
| | | This sum was paid by you into the Bank. | | | | | | |
| | 3 | Trade Expenses—J. Smith's salary.. | | | | 3 | 10 | 0 |
| | | Do. Carriages............ | | | | 0 | 7 | 6 |
| | 5 | Do. Rent and Taxes... | | | | 33 | 0 | 0 |
| | | The various payments made for the expenses of carrying on the business are entered as above. | | | | | | |
| | | Goods—Cash Purchases................ | | | | 3 | 15 | 0 |
| | | This is an entry for goods which you have bought for ready money. | | | | | | |
| | 20 | Shop-Furniture, J. Anderson's Acct. | | | | 107 | 10 | 0 |
| | | This is a payment for the expense of fitting up your shop, &c. | | | | | | |
| | | Bills Payable, No. 1..................... | | | | 100 | 0 | 0 |
| | | This bill, marked No. 1 in your Bill-Book, under " Bills Payable," having become due, is now paid by you. | | | | | | |
| | 30 | John Adams.............................. | | | | 15 | 0 | 0 |
| | | This sum is received by yourself, or drawn out of the business, for your own use or personal expenses. | | | | | | |
| | | John Miller, Edinburgh................ | 0 | 17 | 0 | 32 | 18 | 6 |
| | | Here you paid J. Miller £32, 18s. 6d. in settlement of his account, 17s. having been allowed to you as discount. | | | | | | |
| | | **Cash** on hand.............................. | | | | 3 | 5 | 0 |
| | | | | | | 1289 | 6 | 0 |

## BILL-BOOK.

In this book is kept an account of all "Bills Receivable"—that is, bills of which you have to receive payment—and "Bills Payable"—that is, bills which you have to pay when they become due. (For an account of bills, see Appendix.)

One portion of the book is kept for "Bills Receivable," and another for "Bills Payable." The names of the persons from whom you have received the bills, or to whom you have granted them, with the sums, dates, and other particulars, are entered as follows:

*Bills Receivable.*

| No. | When Recd. | From whom Received. | Amount. | Date. | Term | When Due. | Entered in Cash-Book |
|---|---|---|---|---|---|---|---|
| | 1850. | | £ s. d. | 1850. | | 1850. | 1850. |
| 1 | Jan. 2 | Geo. Innes, Liverpool. | 100 0 0 | Jan. 1 | 1 mo. | Feb. 4 | January 10 |
| 2 | ,, 12 | J. Lindsay, Aberdeen | 50 0 0 | ,, 10 | 3 ,, | Ap. 13 | March 20 |

These bills were received by you on the dates marked, from G. Innes and J. Lindsay, in settlement of your accounts against them. When you discount the bills at the Bank, or receive payment of them when due, they are entered in the Cash-Book, and the dates of the entries are filled into the column in the Bill-Book, as above. Various other columns used in business, will be seen at pages 51 and 53.

*Bills Payable.*

| No. | When Accep. | To whom Granted.* | Amount. | Date. | Term | When Due. | Entered in Cash-Book |
|---|---|---|---|---|---|---|---|
| | 1850. | | £ s. d. | 1850. | | 1850. | 1850. |
| 1 | Jan. 4 | J. Stewart & Co., Leeds | 300 0 0 | Jan. 4 | 1 mo. | Feb. 7 | February 7 |
| 2 | ,, 8 | R. Gray, Bradford..... | 250 0 0 | ,, 8 | 10 da. | Jan. 21 | January 21 |
| | | *or, By whom Drawn. | | | | | |

These bills were granted by you to J. Stewart & Co. and R. Gray, in settlement of their accounts against you. When you pay the bills, they are entered in the Cash-Book, and the dates of the entries are filled into the column in the Bill-Book, as above.

# THE LEDGER.

In the Ledger is contained an abstract of all the entries made in the other books.

The entries dispersed throughout the Day-Book, Invoice-Book, Cash-Book, and Bill-Book, are collected together in the Ledger, and arranged in the order of their dates, under the names of the various persons to whom they belong.

A page, or such portion of a page as is likely to be required, is assigned to every person's account; and each page being ruled with Dr. and Cr. columns, the amounts of all the Dr. entries belonging to each person, are copied one by one into the Dr. sides, and the amounts of all the Cr. entries into the Cr. sides, of the respective accounts in the Ledger.

The copying of these entries into the Ledger is termed *posting.*

### Example.

#### JAMES BROWN, 75 George Street.

Dr.                  Cr.

| 1850. | | | | £ | s. | d. | 1850. | | | | £ | s. | d. |
|---|---|---|---|---|---|---|---|---|---|---|---|---|---|
| Jan. | 1 | To Goods | 1 | 3 | 10 | 6 | Jan. | 3 | By Cash | 1 | 4 | 15 | 0 |
| | 3 | „ do. | „ | 1 | 9 | 6 | | „ | „ Discount | „ | 0 | 4 | 6 |
| | | | | 4 | 19 | 6 | | | | | 4 | 19 | 6 |

#### THOMAS THOMSON, London.

Dr.                  Cr.

| 1850. | | | | £ | s. | d. | 1850. | | | | £ | s. | d. |
|---|---|---|---|---|---|---|---|---|---|---|---|---|---|
| Feb. | 28 | To Bill due Mar. 31. | 3 | 30 | 0 | 0 | Feb. | 28 | By Goods | 5 | 53 | 13 | 0 |
| | | | | | | | Mar. | 30 | „ do. | 6 | 33 | 10 | 0 |

#### GEORGE INNES, Liverpool.

Dr.                  Cr.

| 1850. | | | | £ | s. | d. | 1850. | | | | £ | s. | d. |
|---|---|---|---|---|---|---|---|---|---|---|---|---|---|
| Jan. | 1 | To Goods | 1 | 172 | 11 | 0 | Jan. | 1 | By Bill due Feb. 4. | 1 | 172 | 11 | 0 |
| Feb. | 6 | „ Do. | 5 | 67 | 3 | 9 | Feb. | 25 | „ Cash | 3 | 65 | 10 | 0 |
| Mar. | 14 | „ Do. | 11 | 15 | 15 | 0 | | | „ Discount | „ | 1 | 13 | 9 |
| | 15 | „ Cash | 6 | 22 | 7 | 0 | Mar. | 1 | „ Goods | 5 | 4 | 10 | 0 |
| | 31 | „ Bill due May 2 | 3 | 100 | 0 | 0 | | 7 | „ Do. | „ | 33 | 12 | 0 |
| | | | | | | | | 20 | „ Do. | 6 | 100 | 0 | 0 |
| | | | | 377 | 16 | 9 | | | | | 377 | 16 | 9 |

The entries of goods on the Dr. side are posted from the Day-Book, and on the Cr. side from the Invoice-Book. The entries of cash and bills are posted from the Cash and Bill-Books.

# SINGLE ENTRY.

---

In Book-Keeping by Single Entry, each entry in the Day-Book, Invoice-Book, Cash-Book, and Bill-Book, is posted or entered *once* to some account in the Ledger; hence the term "*Single* Entry." In "*Double* Entry," each entry is posted to *two* different accounts.

Single Entry is used chiefly by retail dealers, as it is **more** simple, and occupies less time in posting than "Double Entry."

---

## POSTING THE DAY-BOOK.

The posting of the Day-Book into the Ledger, is conducted in the following manner :—

Write the name and address of the person first entered in the Day-Book, along the top of a page in the Ledger; then write below this, on the **Dr.** side, the date, the page of the Day-Book from which the entry is taken, and the amount* of goods to which he is *Dr.*, using the words " To Goods ;" next enter the person's name, and the page of the Ledger, into an Index to be kept of all the names that may be posted ; and finally, mark the page of the Ledger, on the margin of the Day-Book, opposite the entry, to show that the entry has been posted.

The posting of the first entry being now finished, write, in another page of the Ledger, the name of the next person mentioned in the Day-Book, posting the entry as before; and so on with all the other entries in succession, each to the *Dr.* of the various accounts.

When you come to another entry against a person whose name has been already filled into the Ledger, write the second entry immediately below the first, using the words " To ditto," or " To do."

---

* In the Ledger of wholesale merchants the *amount* only of goods is posted; but in Retail Ledgers it is more convenient to copy the particulars, except when they are numerous. For an Example of an Account in a Retail Ledger, see Appendix under " Ledger."

Example.

**If the first entry in the** Day-Book is—

*January* 1, 1850.

| | | £ | s. | d. | £ | s. | d. |
|---|---|---|---|---|---|---|---|
| 1 | George Innes, Liverpool.<br>To 20 Yards Black Silk.................... @ 3/6<br>„ 12 „ Velvet......................... „ 11/ | 3<br>6 | 10<br>12 | 0<br>0 | 10 | 2 | 0 |

You write George Innes's name in a page of the Ledger, and post the entry as follows:—

GEORGE INNES, Liverpool.

| | | | | £ | s. | d. | | | | £ | s. | d. |
|---|---|---|---|---|---|---|---|---|---|---|---|---|
| 1850.<br>Jan. | 1 | To Goods...<br><br>* page of the Day-Book. | *<br>1 | 10 | 2 | 0 | | | | | | |

The figure 1, at the margin of the entry in the Day-Book, indicates the page in the Ledger to which it **is** supposed to be posted.

---

POSTING THE INVOICE-BOOK.

The Invoice-Book is posted in the same way as the **Day-Book**—each entry to its proper account in the Ledger.

All the entries are posted to the *Cr.* of the different persons, using the words "By Goods." Thus, if the first entry in the Invoice-Book is—

*January* 1, 1850.

| | | £ | s. | d. | £ | s. | d. |
|---|---|---|---|---|---|---|---|
| 7 | James Stewart & Co., Leeds.<br>By 50 Yards Black Cloth.................. @ 13/<br>„ 20 „ Brown do..................... „ 12/ | 32<br>12 | 10<br>0 | 0<br>0 | 44 | 10 | 0 |

An account is opened under the name of " James **Stewart** & Co., Leeds," and the entry is posted as follows :—

JAMES STEWART & Co., Leeds.

Dr.     Cr.

| | | | | | | | | | 1850<br>Jan. | 1 | By Goods ...<br><br>* page of the Invoice-Book. | *<br>1 | £<br>44 | s.<br>10 | d.<br>0 |
|---|---|---|---|---|---|---|---|---|---|---|---|---|---|---|---|

## POSTING THE CASH-BOOK.

The **entries,** on the *Received* side of the Cash-Book, are posted to the *Cr.* of the persons from whom, or the transactions on account of **which,** the cash has been received ; and the entries, on the *Paid*

### Cash Received.

| | | | | Discount | | | Cash. | | |
|---|---|---|---|---|---|---|---|---|---|
| | 1850 | | | £ | s. | d. | £ | s. | d. |
| 14 | Jan. | 1 | J. Adams—Cash at commencement | | | | 1000 | 0 | 0 |
| | | | This is posted to the *Cr.* of an account to be opened under your own name, using the words, " By Cash." | | | | | | |
| 1 | | 3 | James Brown, George Street......... | 0 | 4 | 6 | 4 | 15 | 0 |
| | | | This entry for cash and discount is posted to the *Cr.* of J. Brown's account, using the words, " By Cash.........£4, 15s. 0d. ,, Discount.... 4s. 6d." | | | | | | |
| 12 | | 5 | Union Bank............................ | | | | 110 | 0 | 0 |
| | | | This entry is posted to the *Cr.* of the Bank. | | | | | | |
| 14 | | 20 | Goods—Cash Sales..................... | | | | 2 | 7 | 6 |
| | | | The various entries for Cash Sales are, at the end of the month, noted on a piece of paper, and the amount posted to the *Cr.* of an account to be opened under the head of " Goods." See page 71. | | | | | | |
| ✓ | | | Bills Receivable, No.1, £172,11s. discounted | 0 | 7 | 6 | 172 | 3 | 6 |
| | | | This entry is not posted to any account : it requires, however, to be marked in the Bill - Book : see page 10. A mark ✓ is made on the margin to show that this has been done. | | | | | | |
| 14 | | | Discount................................. | 0 | 12 | 0 | | | |
| | | | | | | | 1289 | 6 | 0 |
| | | | The discount columns are added up at the end of the month, and the amount deducted from the *Cr.* of the account for " Goods." See pages 22 and 71. | | | | | | |

side, to the *Dr.* of the persons to whom, or the transactions on account of which, the cash **has** been paid.

The figures on the margin, indicate the pages in the Ledger to which the entries have been posted.

### Cash Paid.

| | 1850 | | | Discount £ | s. | d. | Cash £ | s. | d. |
|---|---|---|---|---|---|---|---|---|---|
| 12 | Jan. | 1 | Union Bank............................. | | | | 990 | 0 | 0 |
| | | | This entry is posted to the *Dr.* of the Bank, using the words, " To Cash." | | | | | | |
| 13 | | 3 | Trade Expenses—J. Smith's salary. | | | | 3 | 10 | 0 |
| | | | Carriages........... | | | | 0 | 7 | 6 |
| | | | Rent and Taxes... | | | | 33 | 0 | 0 |
| | | | These and all similar entries for the expenses of the business, are, at the end of the month, noted on a piece of paper, and the amount posted to an account to be opened under the head of " Trade Expenses," using the words, "To Cash— Rent, Salaries, &c." See page 68. | | | | | | |
| 12 | | 20 | Shop Furniture—J. Anderson's acct. | | | | 107 | 10 | 0 |
| | | | This, and all similar payments, are posted to an account to be opened under the head of " Shop Furniture," using the words, " To Cash." See page 67. | | | | | | |
| 14 | | 30 | John Adams.............................. | | | | 15 | 0 | 0 |
| | | | This sum, received by yourself, is posted to the *Dr.* of your own account. | | | | | | |
| 10 | | | John Miller, Edinburgh................ | 0 | 17 | 0 | 32 | 18 | 6 |
| | | | This entry for cash and discount is posted to the *Dr.* of John Miller, using the words, " To Cash.................£32, 18s. 6d. „ Discount......... 17s. 0d." | | | | | | |
| 14 | | | Goods—Cash Purchases................ | | | | 3 | 15 | 0 |
| | | | The various entries for Cash Purchases are, at the end of the month, noted on a piece of paper, and the amount posted to the *Dr.* of the account for " Goods." | | | | | | |
| ✓ | | | Bills Payable, No. 1..................... | | | | 100 | 0 | 0 |
| | | | This entry is not posted to any account; it requires, however, to be marked in the Bill - Book : see page 10. A mark ✓ is made on the margin to show that this has been done. | | | | | | |
| | | | Cash on hand............... | | | | 3 | 5 | 0 |
| 14 | | | Discount................................ | 0 | 17 | 0 | | | |
| | | | | | | | 1289 | 6 | 0 |
| | | | The discount columns are added up at the end of the month, and the amount deducted from the *Dr.* of the account for " Goods." See pages 22 and 70. | | | | | | |

## POSTING THE BILL-BOOK.

*Bills Receivable.*—Each entry of Bills **Receivable** is posted **to the** *Cr.* of the person from whom the bill has **been** received. Thus, **if** the first entry is—

| No. | | When Recd. | From whom Recd. | Amount. | | | Date. | Term | When Due. | Entered in Cash-Book |
|---|---|---|---|---|---|---|---|---|---|---|
| | | 1850. | | £ | s. | d. | 1850. | | 1850. | 1850. |
| 1 | 1 | Jan. 2. | G. Innes, Liverpool. | 100 | 0 | 0 | Jan. 1. | 1 mo. | Feb. 4. | Jan. 10. |

The entry is posted to the *Cr.* of George Innes, using the **words,** " By Bill due Feb. 4, £100." The page of the Ledger to which **the** entry is posted is marked on the margin.

*Bills Payable.*—Each entry of Bills Payable is posted to the *Dr.* of the person to whom the bill has been granted. Thus, if the first entry is—

| No. | | When Accep. | To whom Granted. | Amount. | | | Date. | Term | When Due. | Entered in Cash-Bk. |
|---|---|---|---|---|---|---|---|---|---|---|
| | | 1850. | | £ | s. | d. | 1850. | | 1850. | 1850. |
| 8 | 1 | Jan. 4. | J. Stewart & Co., Leeds | 300 | 0 | 0 | Jan. 4. | 1 mo. | Feb. 7. | Feb. 7. |

The entry is posted to the *Dr.* of J. Stewart & Co., using the words, " To Bill due Feb. 7, £300."

---

### Miscellaneous Remarks as to Posting.

After **all** the books have been posted, or at any stated convenient time, each entry in the Ledger should be compared with the original entry in the book from which it was taken, to ascertain that it **has been** posted correctly.

When **the page** assigned to any account in the Ledger is filled up, add **the money** columns at the bottom, and transfer the sums to a new **page, where the** person's name must be written as before.

If a **person** who **is** owing an account becomes insolvent, and pays a composition, enter **in** the Cash-**Book** the sum he pays, as a composition of so much **a** pound, and **after** posting it to his credit, carry the balance still **due,** to an **account** to be opened under the head of " Bad Debts." **To** this account are also transferred all other " bad debts"—that **is,** accounts of which you are unable to obtain **payment** from the parties.

It is of little consequence in **what order** the accounts are **posted** into the Ledger; for convenience, however, it is desirable to keep the *Dr.* accounts, being those posted from the Day-Book, in one portion of the Ledger, and the *Cr.* accounts, being those posted from the Invoice-Book, in another portion. When the *Cr.* accounts are numerous, they may be kept in a separate Ledger.

In extensive concerns, it is usual to have several Ledgers, for the different branches of the business, such as a Town Ledger, a Country Ledger, a Foreign Ledger, a Commission Ledger, &c. &c.

## BALANCING THE LEDGER.

To ascertain, at the end of the year, or at any other time that may be most convenient, what is the sum-total of the various accounts owing by you, and owing to you, it is necessary to add up both sides of all the accounts in the Ledger, and to mark how much is the *Dr.* or *Cr.* balance of each. This is termed " Balancing the Ledger."

When it is found that both sides of an account are equal, rule it off as settled. Accounts may also be ruled off as settled, at any time when entries are made which equalise the two sides.

Example.

JAMES BROWN, 75 George Street.

| Dr. | | | | £ | s. | d. | | | Cr. | | | £ | s. | d. |
|---|---|---|---|---|---|---|---|---|---|---|---|---|---|---|
| 1850.<br>Jan. | 1 | To Goods............ | 1 | 3 | 10 | 0 | 1850.<br>Jan. | 3 | By Cash............... | 1 | 4 | 15 | 0 |
| | 3 | ,, do. ............... | ,, | 1 | 9 | 6 | | ,, | ,, Discount.......... | ,, | 0 | 4 | 6 |
| | | | | 4 | 19 | 6 | | | | | 4 | 19 | 6 |

When the *Dr.* side of an account is the greater of the two, enter the *difference* on the *Cr.* side, using the words, " By Balance forward," then rule off the account as balanced, and enter below, on the *Dr.* side, the *Dr.* balance, using the words, " To Balance."

Example.

ALEXANDER PATERSON, London.

| Dr. | | | | £ | s. | d. | | | Cr. | | | £ | s. | d. |
|---|---|---|---|---|---|---|---|---|---|---|---|---|---|---|
| 1850.<br>Jan. | 7 | To Goods............ | 2 | 3 | 6 | 0 | 1850.<br>Jan. | 20 | By Cash............... | 1 | 3 | 3 | 0 |
| Feb. | 9 | ,, do. ............... | 6 | 65 | 2 | 10 | | ,, | ,, Discount.......... | ,, | 0 | 3 | 0 |
| Mar. | 3 | ,, do. ............... | 9 | 2 | 12 | 0 | Mar. | 3 | ,, Balance forward | | 67 | 14 | 10 |
| | | | | 71 | 0 | 10 | | | | | 71 | 0 | 10 |
| Mar. | 3 | To Balance.......... | | 67 | 14 | 10 | | | | | | | |

When the *Cr.* side is the greater of the two, enter the *difference* on the *Dr.* side, using the words, " To Balance forward," then rule off the account as balanced, and enter below, on the *Cr.* side, the *Cr.* balance, using the words, " By Balance."

Example.

THOMAS THOMSON, London.

| 1850. | | | £ | s. | d. | 1850. | | | | £ | s. | d. |
|---|---|---|---|---|---|---|---|---|---|---|---|---|
| Feb. | 28 | To Bill due Mar 31. | 3 | 30 | 0 | 0 | Feb. | 28 | By Goods............ 4 | 53 | 13 | 0 |
| Mar. | 30 | ,, Balance forward | | 57 | 3 | 0 | Mar. | 10 | ,, do. ............ 5 | 33 | 10 | 0 |
| | | | | 87 | 3 | 0 | | | | 87 | 3 | 0 |
| | | | | | | | Mar. | 30 | By Balance............ | 57 | 3 | 0 |

When there are entries on only one side of an account, balance it off, by carrying forward the sum-total to the *Dr.* or *Cr.* of the next account, as the case may be; or the account may be merely added up.

In actual business, it is unnecessary to balance off unsettled accounts in the way now stated. It is sufficient to add up the columns, and mark the *Dr.* and *Cr.* balances in a temporary way with a pencil; ruling off the accounts only when they are actually settled.

After the accounts have been balanced off, the various balances should be carefully examined, to ascertain that they have been correctly brought forward.

It is common, in balancing, when there is a blank space on one side of the account, to draw a diagonal line across it, in the manner shown at page 69.

## TAKING STOCK.

An Inventory of Stock in trade should be taken at least once a year, with the view of ascertaining the state of your affairs.

All the particulars of the goods on hand, for sale, are copied into a book kept for the purpose, termed " The Stock-Book." The goods are valued at cost price, or, when necessary, at a per centage below cost price, to allow for bad stock, or depreciation in value.

Stock of a more permanent nature — such as buildings, shop-furniture, &c.—does not require to be entered in the Stock-Book, as its value is ascertained from the accounts opened in the Ledger under these heads, and is from thence entered into the Balance Sheet. In such accounts, a yearly deduction of 5 or 10 per cent. requires to be made from the original cost, to allow for deterioration, or tear and wear. See Shop Furniture, page 67.

## BALANCE SHEET.

To ascertain the state of affairs at the end of the year, or at any other convenient time, it is necessary to draw out a "Balance Sheet"—that is, a statement showing how much is owing to you, and by you; also the amount of cash, bills, and stock on hand, and what is the balance, if any, in your favour.

To do this, open an account in the Ledger, under the head of Balance Sheet, and make the following entries on the *Dr.* and *Cr.* sides :—

On the *Dr.* side.

> The amount of accounts owing *by* you, as ascertained from the Ledger, deducting the probable amount of discount that will be allowed at settlement.
> The bills owing *by* you, as ascertained from your Bill-Book.

On the *Cr.* side.

> The amount of goods on hand, as per inventory in Stock-Book.
> The value of shop furniture, as per Ledger.
> The amount of accounts owing *to* you, as per Ledger, deducting the discount to be allowed at settlement.
> The amount of bills owing *to* you, as per Bill-Book.
> The amount of cash on hand, and in Bank.

Then add up the two sides, and the *difference* between them will show the amount of your capital at the time of balancing.

This sum is filled into the *Dr.* side, as "Balance, nett capital," and the account is ruled off as balanced.

Example.

BALANCE SHEET OF JOHN ADAMS.

| Dr. | | £ | s. | d. | Cr. | | £ | s. | d. |
|---|---|---|---|---|---|---|---|---|---|
| 1850. | | | | | 1850. | | | | |
| Dec. 31 | To Accounts due by J. Adams...£200 less discount 10 | 190 | 0 | 0 | Dec. 31 | By Goods on hand.. | 410 | 0 | 0 |
| | | | | | | ,, Shop Furniture. 12 | 95 | 0 | 0 |
| | ,, Bills due by J. A. | 160 | 0 | 0 | | ,, Accounts due to J. Adams £300 less discount 15 | 285 | 0 | 0 |
| | ,, Balance, nett capital | 1150 | 0 | 0 | | | | | |
| | | | | | | ,, Bills due to J. A. | 200 | 0 | 0 |
| | The sums-total only of the *Dr.* and *Cr.* accounts are entered in the Balance Sheet: the particulars are filled into the " Account-Book," see p. 72. When the names are numerous, they should be written in alphabetical order. | | | | | ,, Cash in Bank... 12 | 500 | 0 | 0 |
| | | | | | | ,, Do. on hand, per Cash-Book..... | 10 | 0 | 0 |
| | | 1500 | 0 | 0 | | | 1500 | 0 | 0 |

# PROFIT.

To ascertain the profit, if any, that has been gained during the
year, open an account under the head of " Profit," or " Profit and
Loss," and enter as follows :—

On the *Dr.* side.

> The amount of your capital at January 1, being the cash em-
> barked by you in the business, as ascertained from your
> account in the Ledger—or from the previous Balance-Sheet.
>
> Interest at 5 per cent. on the amount of capital.
>
>> The interest is charged, in order to show what is the profit, after allow-
>> ing 5 per cent., on the capital. *Profit*, strictly speaking, being, not the
>> total gain, but only what is gained over and above 5 per cent. on the
>> capital.

On the *Cr.* side.

> The amount of your capital at December 31, as shown by the
> " Balance Sheet."
>
> The amount of cash taken by you for your own use during the
> year, as ascertained from your account in the Ledger.

Then add up the two sides ; and if the *Cr.* amounts to more than
the *Dr.* side, the *difference* is the profit for the year, and is carried
to the *Cr.* of your account as " Profit." The Interest is also
carried to the *Cr.* of your account. If the *Dr.* side is the greater
of the two, the *difference* is the loss, and is carried to the *Dr.* of
your account as " Loss."

Example.

PROFIT (OR, PROFIT AND LOSS).

| Dr. | | | £ | s. | d. | | | Cr. | | £ | s. | d. |
|---|---|---|---|---|---|---|---|---|---|---|---|---|
| 1850. Jan. | 1 | To Capital at this date.............. | 14 | 1000 | 0 | 0 | 1850. Dec. | 31 | By Capital at this date.............. 15 | 1150 | 0 | 0 |
| Dec. | 31 | ,, Interest 5 ʊ ct. ,, Profit.............. | 14 ,, | 50 350 | 0 0 | 0 0 | | | ,, Cash to J. A. in 1850.......... 14 | 250 | 0 | 0 |
| | | | | 1400 | 0 | 0 | | | | 1400 | 0 | 0 |

The *nett* profit is shown above, after paying trade expenses, &c.
By adding to the nett profit the amount of expenses and bad debts,
the *gross* profit will be ascertained ; thus :—

| | | |
|---|---|---|
| Nett Profit............................................£350 | 0 | 0 |
| Trade Expenses, as per Ledger ................. 100 | 0 | 0 |
| Bad Debts, ,, ,, ............... 50 | 0 | 0 |
| **Gross** profits........................... 500 | 0 | 0 |

" Profit and Loss" is the title given to this account, when, as will be seen in
Double Entry, the " Profit" is entered on one side of the account, and the
" Loss "—that is, the expenses, bad debts, &c.—are entered on the other side.

## PRIVATE ACCOUNT.

Your own private account for cash paid into, or drawn from, the business, is kept and balanced in the following manner :

On the *Dr.* side are entered—

The various sums you draw from the business on your own personal account.

On the *Cr.* side are entered—

The sum or capital you embarked in the business at the commencement, and any sums you may pay into the business afterwards.

Interest 5 per cent. on your capital.

The Profit (if any) gained during the year or other given period.

> The Interest and the Profit are brought from the " Profit and Loss" account at the end of the year, or at any other time, when you balance your affairs. The " Profit and Loss" account is balanced off when the transfer is made.

If, instead of a profit, there has been a loss during the year, the loss is carried to the *Dr.* of your account.

### Example.
### JOHN ADAMS.

| | | *Dr.* | | £ | s. | d. | | | *Cr.* | | £ | s. | d. |
|---|---|---|---|---|---|---|---|---|---|---|---|---|---|
| 1850. | | | | | | | 1850. | | | | | | |
| Jan. | 30 | To Cash | 2 | 15 | 0 | 0 | Jan. | 1 | By Cash | 1 | 1000 | 0 | 0 |
| Mar. | 6 | ,, do | 6 | 50 | 0 | 0 | | | | | | | |
| June | 30 | ,, do | 7 | 100 | 0 | 0 | Dec. | 31 | ,, Interest, 1850. | 14 | 50 | 0 | 0 |
| Aug. | 9 | ,, do | 8 | 35 | 0 | 0 | | | ,, Profit, ,, | | 350 | 0 | 0 |
| Dec. | 1 | ,, do | 9 | 50 | 0 | 0 | | | | | | | |
| | 31 | ,, Balance forward | | 1150 | 0 | 0 | | | | | | | |
| | | | | 1400 | 0 | 0 | | | | | 1400 | 0 | 0 |
| | | | | | | | 1851. | | | | | | |
| | | | | | | | Jan. | 1 | By Balance | | 1150 | 0 | 0 |

The Balance Sheet, the Profit and Loss Account, and the Private Account, are usually kept in a separate Ledger, termed " Private Ledger."

## ACCOUNT FOR GOODS BOUGHT AND SOLD.

This is an account which, strictly speaking, belongs not to Single, but to Double Entry. As it is desirable, however, in every business to know the amount of goods bought and sold during the year, or other given period, an account for "Goods" has been embodied in the following Single Entry Ledger, that any one who chooses, may be enabled to adopt it.

Double Entry to the extent required for this account is quite simple, and may be advantageously employed in any retail business with little additional trouble.

### Directions.

*Day-Book.*—Add up the sums-total in the outer columns, at the end of every month, as shown at page 28, and post the amounts, being the total of *goods sold on credit*, to the *Cr.* of an account to be opened under the head of "Goods." See page 71.

*Invoice-Book.*—Add up the sums-total in the outer columns, at the end of every month, as shown at page 39, and post the amounts, being the total of *goods bought on credit*, to the *Dr.* of the "Goods" account. See page 70.

*Cash-Book.*—Add up on a piece of paper, at the end of every month, the entries for Cash Sales and Purchases, and post the amounts, being the sums-total for the month, to the *Dr.* and *Cr.* of the "Goods" account, as shown at pages 70 and 71.

The whole amount of goods sold during any given time is in this way ascertained.

PROFIT.—The Profit may be ascertained from this account as follows :—

Add up the discount columns on both sides of the Cash-Book, at the end of every month, and deduct the amount of discount on the *Received* side, from the *Cr.*, and on the *Paid* side, from the *Dr.* of the "Goods" account, as shown at pages 70 and 71.

Deduct also, at the time of balancing your affairs, the estimated discount on unsettled accounts due *to* you, from the *Cr.* side, and on those due *by* you, from the *Dr.* side of the "Goods" account, as shown at pages 70 and 71.

Enter on the *Dr.* side of the "Goods" account the amount of Trade Expenses and Bad Debts; and on the *Cr.* side the amount of Goods on hand.

Then add up both sides of the account, and if the *Cr.* side be the greater of the two, the difference is the *Profit* gained (including interest on capital). If the *Dr.* side is the greater of the two, the difference shows the *Loss.*

By ascertaining the profit in this way, the accuracy of the other account in the Ledger for Profit (page 68), and also the accuracy of the posting, will be tested, as the result of both accounts will be the same, if no errors have been committed.

# SINGLE ENTRY.

## THE BOOKS

OF

## JOHN ADAMS,

### EDINBURGH.

## DIRECTIONS.

In writing the following course, the pupil should, as far as possible, proceed with the various books simultaneously, as if he were engaged in actual business. It would be inconvenient to do so to the full extent, by writing the entries of each day at a time in the different books : this is done in business, but it will be sufficient here to copy the entries of a month at a time.

The Day-Book, Invoice-Book, Cash-Book, and Bill-Book for January, should first be copied; all the entries in each book on Jan. 1, should then be posted into the Ledger, then those on Jan. 2, and so on with the entries of every succeeding day. The entries for February and March should be copied and posted successively in the same manner.

After the entries for a month have been posted, they should be compared with the corresponding entries in the Ledger, to ascertain that the posting is correct. This is usually done by two individuals. One person calls over, one by one, the entries of the book to be compared—for instance, the Day-Book—and the other turns up the Ledger, and makes a mark $\sqrt{}$ at each entry there, on finding it correctly posted.

The mode of rectifying some of the errors apt to occur in posting will be seen in the accounts of J. Lindsay, page 57 ; D. Falconer and T. Murray, page 58.

In posting, the figures on the margin of the Day-Book, &c. should be written in a slanting position, as shown in the first page of the Day-Book.

Great care should be taken to enter correctly the original sums in the Day-Book, &c., as errors made at first are of course perpetuated in the Ledger, and are not easily detected.

Two books of a foolscap size should be employed for writing out the following set :—

I. The first, consisting of about 36 pages, or 9 sheets, to contain—

| The Day-Book......... 16 pages. | Bill-Book............. 4 pages. |
| --- | --- |
| Invoice-Book.... 9 „ | Stock-Book........ ⎰ 1 „ |
| Cash-Book....... 6 „ | Warehouse-Book ⎱ |

Each page to be ruled with about 36 lines across, exclusive of the head-line.

II. The other, consisting of about 20 pages, or 5 sheets, to contain—

| The Ledger........... 19 pages. | Account-Book.... 1 page. |
| --- | --- |

The first 12 pages of the Ledger should be ruled with *Dr.* and *Cr.* columns, as in the printed pages, being the common form in business, and with about 36 lines across. If, for the sake of more space, the *Dr.* and *Cr.* sides of the accounts are placed in two opposite pages, like the accounts at page 68, the Ledger will occupy about 32 pages, or 8 sheets.

Any one who wishes to shorten the course, can easily do so by transcribing the *amounts* only, instead of the *particulars*, of as many of the entries in the Day-Book, &c. as may be desired.

## THE DAY-BOOK.*

*Edinburgh, January* 1, 1850.

| | | £ | s. | d. | £ | s. | d. |
|---|---|---|---|---|---|---|---|
| | James Brown, 75 George Street. | | | | | | |
| 1 | To Russell's Modern Europe, 4 vols. 8vo. cloth. | 2 | 10 | 0 | | | |
| | „ Byron's Works, 1 vol. royal 8vo. cloth. | 1 | 0 | 0 | 3 | 10 | 0 |
| | | | | | | | |
| | George Innes, Liverpool. | | | | | | |
| | To 6 Pieces Black Silk,*   306 yds. 3/6 | 53 | 11 | 0 | | | |
| 1 | „ 12   „   French Merino, 360   „   5/6 | 99 | 0 | 0 | | | |
| | „ 10   „   Mous. de Laine, 320   „   1/3 | 20 | 0 | 0 | 172 | 11 | 0 |
| | * that is, 6 pieces measuring 306 yards, at 3s. 6d. a yard. | | | | | | |
| | —2d.— | | | | | | |
| | William Hunter, Princes Street. | | | | | | |
| | To 6 lbs. Black Tea...................... 5/ | 1 | 10 | 0 | | | |
| 1 | „ 1   „   Green do...................... 6/ | 0 | 6 | 0 | | | |
| | „ 7   „   Loaf Sugar...................... 8d. | 0 | 4 | 8 | | | |
| | „ 2   „   Coffee ............................ 2/ | 0 | 4 | 0 | 2 | 4 | 8 |
| | | | | | | | |
| | Richard Porteous, Bristol. | | | | | | |
| | To 8 Pieces Black Satin,   240 yds. 8/6 | 102 | 0 | 0 | | | |
| 1 | „ 2   „   Satin Ribbon, 50   „   1/9 | 4 | 7 | 6 | | | |
| | „ 15   „   Gingham,   420   „   1/2 | 24 | 10 | 0 | 130 | 17 | 6 |
| | | | | | | | |
| | —3d.— | | | | | | |
| | James Brown, 75 George Street. | | | | | | |
| 1 | To 1 Ream Small Post Paper.............. | 1 | 5 | 0 | | | |
| | „ 1 Box Steel Pens......................... | 0 | 4 | 6 | 1 | 9 | 6 |
| | | | | | | | |
| | Charles Chadwick, Manchester. | | | | | | |
| 2 | To 10 Pieces Welsh Flannel, 480 yds. 1/10 | 44 | 0 | 0 | | | |
| | „ 24 Pair Blankets.................. 18 | 21 | 12 | 0 | 65 | 12 | 0 |
| | Carried over............ | | | | 376 | 4 | 8 |

* For another form of the Day-Book, see page 37.

### *January* 3, 1850.

| | | £ | s | d | £ | s | d |
|---|---|---|---|---|---|---|---|
| | Brought over.............. | | | | 376 | 4 | 8 |
| | **William Bell, Leeds.** | | | | | | |
| 2 | To 5 Pieces Silk Velvet, 160 yds. 11/6 | 92 | 0 | 0 | | | |
| | „ 8 „ Linen Sheeting, 416 „ 3/2 | 65 | 17 | 4 | 157 | 17 | 4 |
| | *—5th.—* | | | | | | |
| | **Thomas Bladworth, Hull.** | | | | | | |
| 2 | To 12 Pieces Irish Linen, 348 yds. 2/9 | 47 | 17 | 0 | | | |
| | „ 5 „ German Lawn, 65 „ 3/3 | 10 | 11 | 3 | 58 | 8 | 3 |
| | *—6th.—* | | | | | | |
| | **George Innes, Liverpool.** | | | | | | |
| 1 | To 12 Pieces Gingham, 372 yds. 1/6 | 27 | 18 | 0 | | | |
| | „ 10 „ Twilled Cotton, 420 „ 8½d. | 14 | 17 | 6 | 42 | 15 | 6 |
| | **James Lindsay, Aberdeen.** | | | | | | |
| 2 | To 35 Pieces French Cambric, 450 yds. 6/6 | 146 | 5 | 0 | | | |
| | „ 5 „ Mous. de Laine, 160 „ 1/1 | 8 | 13 | 4 | 154 | 18 | 4 |
| | *—7th.—* | | | | | | |
| | **William Bell, Leeds.** | | | | | | |
| 2 | To 6 Dozen India Silk Handkerchiefs.. 54/ | 16 | 4 | 0 | | | |
| | „ 60 Pair Kid Gloves................. 3/ | 9 | 0 | 0 | 25 | 4 | 0 |
| | **Alexander Paterson, London.** | | | | | | |
| | To 1 Silk Umbrella......................... | 0 | 18 | 6 | | | |
| 3 | „ 6 Yards German Lawn............ 3/3 | 0 | 19 | 6 | | | |
| | „ 4 India Silk Handkerchiefs....... 5/3 | 1 | 1 | 0 | | | |
| | „ 2 Pair Kid Gloves................. 3/6 | 0 | 7 | 0 | 3 | 6 | 0 |
| | **David Falconer, Dublin.** | | | | | | |
| | To 6 Reams Demy Printing Paper. 16/ | 4 | 16 | 0 | | | |
| 3 | „ 10 „ Royal do. 18/ | 9 | 0 | 0 | | | |
| | „ 2 „ Wove Foolscap......... 13/ | 1 | 6 | 0 | 15 | 2 | 0 |
| | Carried forward............ | | | | 833 | 16 | 1 |

*January* 10, 1850.

| | | | | | | | |
|---|---|---|---|---|---|---|---|
| | Brought forward.............. | | | | 833 | 16 | 1 . |
| | **Charles Chadwick, Manchester.** | | | | | | |
| 2 | To 5 Pieces Sup. Black Cloth, 100 yds. 19/ | 95 | 0 | 0 | | | |
| | „ 3   „      „    Olive  do.   62  „ 18/6 | 57 | 7 | 0 | | | |
| | „ 4   „      „    Brown do.   83 „ 17/ | 70 | 11 | 0 | | | |
| | Wrapper.................... | 0 | 7 | 6 | 223 | 5 | 6 |
| | **Thomas Murray, Leeds.** | | | | | | |
| 3 | To 25 Pieces Printed Cotton, 750 yds. 10d. | 31 | 5 | 0 | | | |
| | „  5   „   Irish Linen,     140  „   2/2 | 15 | 3 | 4 | 46 | 8 | 4 |
| | *—11th.—* | | | | | | |
| | **Richard Porteous, Bristol.** | | | | | | |
| 1 | To 60 Yards Carpeting................. 2/9 | 8 | 5 | 0 | | | |
| | „ 50   „    Printed Drugget........ 2/7 | 6 | 9 | 2 | 14 | 14 | 2 |
| | **James Brown, 75 George Street.** | | | | | | |
| 1 | To 10 lbs. Sugar...................... 6½d. | 0 | 5 | 5 | | | |
| | „  6  „  White Soap................. 7d. | 0 | 3 | 6 | 0 | 8 | 11 |
| | *—18th.—* | | | | | | |
| | **Charles Smith, Glasgow.** | | | | | | |
| 3 | To 12 Pieces French Merino, 360 yds. 5/6 | 99 | 0 | 0 | | | |
| | „  5   „    Black Satin,   154  „ 9/6 | 73 | 3 | 0 | | | |
| | Wrappers.................... | 0 | 9 | 6 | 172 | 12 | 6 |
| | **William Wilson, London.** | | | | | | |
| 4 | To 6 Cowper's Poems, 18mo., cloth... 2/ | 0 | 12 | 0 | | | |
| | „ 2 Edgeworth's Moral Tales........ 5/ | 0 | 10 | 0 | 1 | 2 | 0 |
| | *—20th.—* | | | | | | |
| | **Thomas Murray, Leeds.** | | | | | | |
| 3 | To 2 Chests Black Tea..... 172 lbs. 4/6 | 38 | 14 | 0 | | | |
| | „ 1 Box Raisins............ **56**  „ 6½d. | 1 | 10 | 4 | | | |
| | „ 2 cwt. White Soap................ 54/ | 5 | 8 | 0 | 45 | 12 | 4 |
| | **Carried over**.............. | | | | 1337 | 19 | 10 |

*January 20, 1850.*

| | | | | | | | |
|---|---|---|---|---|---|---|---|
| | Brought over............... | | | | 1337 | 19 | 10 |
| | **James Taylor, High Street.** | | | | | | |
| 4 | To 12 Yards Welsh Flannel........... 1/9 | 1 | 1 | 0 | | | |
| | „ 6 „ do. ............ 2/6 | 0 | 15 | 0 | | | |
| | „ 6 Pair Cotton Socks.............. 1/6 | 0 | 9 | 0 | 2 | 5 | 0 |
| | **David Anderson, Glasgow.** | | | | | | |
| 4 | To 9 Yards Superfine Black Cloth, 19/6 | 8 | 15 | 6 | | | |
| | „ 15 „ Cotton Shirting......... 8d. | 0 | 10 | 0 | 9 | 5 | 6 |
| | *—25th.—* | | | | | | |
| | **Robert Cook, Liverpool.** | | | | | | |
| 4 | To 12 Reams Royal Brown Paper... 19/ | | | | 11 | 8 | 0 |
| | **William Bell, Leeds.** | | | | | | |
| 2 | To 16 Yards Irish Linen.............. 2/6 | 2 | 0 | 0 | | | |
| | „ 4 „ Muslin.................... 1/6 | 0 | 6 | 0 | 2 | 6 | 0 |
| | *—27th.—* | | | | | | |
| | **William Hunter, Princes Street.** | | | | | | |
| 1 | To 1 Cheese, 21 lbs.................... 9d. | 0 | 15 | 9 | | | |
| | „ 6 lbs. Currants.................... 7d. | 0 | 3 | 6 | | | |
| | „ 2 „ Black Tea.................... 5/6 | 0 | 11 | 0 | 1 | 10 | 3 |
| | **Thomas Bladworth, Hull.** | | | | | | |
| 2 | To 10 Pair Worsted Stockings....... 3/6 | 1 | 15 | 0 | | | |
| | „ 6 „ Cotton do. ....... 2/ | 0 | 12 | 0 | 2 | 7 | 0 |
| | *—31st.—* | | | | | | |
| | **James Taylor, High Street.** | | | | | | |
| 4 | To 1 Dozen Port Wine................... | 1 | 16 | 0 | | | |
| | „ 1 „ Sherry........................ | 2 | 2 | 0 | | | |
| | „ 6 lbs. Tea............................. 5/ | 1 | 10 | 0 | 5 | 8 | 0 |
| 14 | Goods—*Cr. by Credit Sales*................ | | | | 1372 | 9 | 7 |

*February* 1, 1850.

| | | | | | | | | |
|---|---|---|---|---|---|---|---|---|
| 5 | James Durham, Bristol.<br>To 1 Paisley Shawl........................<br>„ 2 Pair Blankets ......................  15/6 | 3 | 15 | 0 | | | | |
| | | 1 | 11 | 0 | 5 | 6 | 0 | |
| 3 | David Falconer, Dublin.<br>To 10 Yards Twilled Cotton......... 7½d.<br>„ 12 Satin Stocks.................... 4/6 | 0 | 6 | 3 | | | | |
| | | 2 | 14 | 0 | 3 | 0 | 3 | |
| | —*5th.*—<br>David Anderson, Glasgow. | | | | | | | |
| 4 | To 6 Dozen India Handkerchiefs.... 42/<br>„ 4 „ do. do. .... 48/<br>„ 6 Pair Cotton Drawers............. 4/6 | 12 | 12 | 0 | | | | |
| | | 9 | 12 | 0 | | | | |
| | | 1 | 7 | 0 | 23 | 11 | 0 | |
| | James Lindsay, Aberdeen. | | | | | | | |
| | To 12 Cotton Umbrellas............... 5/6 | 3 | 6 | 0 | | | | |
| 2 | „ 6 Silk Hats...................... 11/ | 3 | 6 | 0 | | | | |
| | „ 6 do. ........................ 14/ | 4 | 4 | 0 | | | | |
| | Box............................. | 0 | 6 | 0 | 11 | 2 | 0 | |
| | Charles Smith, Glasgow. | | | | | | | |
| 3 | To 12 Reams Wove Post.............. 7/ | 4 | 4 | 0 | | | | |
| | „ 6 „ „ Foolscap.......... 13/ | 3 | 18 | 0 | 8 | 2 | 0 | |
| | —*6th.*—<br>William Hunter, Princes Street. | | | | | | | |
| 1 | To 2 Dozen Silver Table Spoons..... 20/<br>„ 1 „ „ Tea Spoons....... 7/6 | 24 | 0 | 0 | | | | |
| | | 4 | 10 | 0 | 28 | 10 | 0 | |
| | George Innes, Liverpool. | | | | | | | |
| 1 | To 1 Box Raisins, 54 lbs...... 8½d.<br>„ 1 Chest Green Tea, 69 „ ...... 6/6<br>Wharfage.......................... | 1 | 18 | 3 | | | | |
| | | 22 | 8 | 6 | | | | |
| | | 0 | 1 | 6 | 24 | 8 | 3 | |
| | Carried over.............. | | | | 103 | 19 | 6 | |

*February* 6, 1850.

| | | | | | | | |
|---|---|---|---|---|---|---|---|
| | Brought over.................... | | | | 103 | 19 | 6 |
| **4** | Robert Cook, Liverpool. | | | | | | |
| | To 1 Gold Watch, Patent Lever.......... | 15 | 15 | 0 | | | |
| | „ 1 Silver „ do. .......... | 9 | 10 | 0 | 25 | 5 | 0 |
| | *—9th.—* | | | | | | |
| **3** | Alexander Paterson, London. | | | | | | |
| | To 6 Pieces Black Silk, 312 yards 3/6 | 54 | 12 | 0 | | | |
| | „ 8 „ Gingham, 224 „ 11d. | 10 | 5 | 4 | | | |
| | Box.................... | 0 | 5 | 6 | 65 | 2 | 10 |
| | *—11th.—* | | | | | | |
| **5** | James Durham, Bristol. | | | | | | |
| | To 10 Pieces Sup. Black Cloth, 300 yds. 18/ | 270 | 0 | 0 | | | |
| | „ 4 „ Welsh Flannel, 81 „ 2/3 | 9 | 2 | 3 | | | |
| | Wrapper........................ | 0 | 9 | 6 | 279 | 11 | 9 |
| **4** | William Wilson, London. | | | | | | |
| | To Arnot's Physics, 2 vols. cloth...... | 1 | 11 | 6 | | | |
| | „ Macaulay's Essays, 3 vols. „ ...... | 1 | 16 | 0 | 3 | 7 | 6 |
| | *—12th.—* | | | | | | |
| **3** | Daniel Falconer, Dublin. | | | | | | |
| | To 6 Pair Lace Gloves.............. 2/6 | 0 | 15 | 0 | | | |
| | „ 10 „ Cotton Socks............. 1/3 | 0 | 12 | 6 | | | |
| | „ 6 Yards Blue Silk Velvet...... 11/6 | 3 | 9 | 0 | 4 | 16 | 6 |
| **2** | William Bell, Leeds. | | | | | | |
| | To 15 Pieces Scotch Cambric, 180 yds. 1/9 | 15 | 15 | 0 | | | |
| | „ 3 „ French do. 90 „ 11/ | 49 | 10 | 0 | 65 | 5 | 0 |
| | *—17th.—* | | | | | | |
| **5** | William Hunter, Princes Street. | | | | | | |
| | To 8 lbs. Cheese......................... 8d. | 0 | 5 | 4 | | | |
| | „ 1 Dozen Port Wine..................... | 2 | 2 | 0 | 2 | 7 | 4 |
| | **Carried** forward.............. | | | | 549 | 15 | 5 |

*February* 17, 1850.

| | | | | | | | |
|---|---|---|---|---|---|---|---|
| | Brought forward............ | | | | 549 | 15 | 5 |
| | James Brown, George Street. | | | | | | |
| 1 | To 3 lbs. Coffee......................... 2/ | 0 | 6 | 0 | | | |
| | „ 6 „ Loaf-Sugar.................. 8½d. | 0 | 4 | 3 | 0 | 10 | 3 |
| | —18th.— | | | | | | |
| | Charles Smith, Glasgow. | | | | | | |
| 3 | To 12 Yards Black Silk Velvet..... 14/ | 8 | 8 | 0 | | | |
| | „ 15 „ „ Satin............. 10/6 | 7 | 17 | 6 | 16 | 5 | 6 |
| | William Wilson, London. | | | | | | |
| 4 | To 1 Silk Hat............................... | | | | 0 | 15 | 0 |
| | —19th.— | | | | | | |
| | James Watt, Birmingham. | | | | | | |
| 5 | To 15 Yards Printed Cotton......... 10d. | 0 | 12 | 6 | | | |
| | „ 4 „ Irish Linen.............. 2/6 | 0 | 10 | 0 | | | |
| | „ 2 „ Satin Ribbon............ 1/10 | 0 | 3 | 8 | 1 | 6 | 2 |
| | —20th.— | | | | | | |
| | John Alison, 5 Frederick Street. | | | | | | |
| 5 | To 2 Pair Blankets................... 17/6 | 1 | 15 | 0 | | | |
| | „ 10 Yards Superfine Black Cloth, 18/6 | 9 | 5 | 0 | | | |
| | „ 5 „ Doeskin................. 5/6 | 1 | 7 | 6 | 12 | 7 | 6 |
| | Robert Hume, Carlisle. | | | | | | |
| 6 | To 3 Pieces Gingham, 90 yds.1/1 | 4 | 17 | 6 | | | |
| | „ 2 „ do. 60 „ 11d. | 2 | 15 | 0 | | | |
| | „ 6 „ Printed Cotton, 180 „ 1/3 | 11 | 5 | 0 | 18 | 17 | 6 |
| | —22d.— | | | | | | |
| | James Lindsay, Aberdeen. | | | | | | |
| 2 | To 10 Silk Hats....................... 11/6 | 5 | 15 | 0 | | | |
| | „ 6 do. ....................... 15/6 | 4 | 13 | 0 | 10 | 8 | 0 |
| | Carried over............... | | | | 610 | 5 | 4 |

*February* 22, 1850.

| | | | | | | | | |
|---|---|---|---|---|---|---|---|---|
| | Brought over............... | | | | | | 610 | 5 | 4 |

|  |  | £ | s | d | £ | s | d |
|---|---|---|---|---|---|---|---|
| 5 | James Watt, Birmingham.<br>To 2 Pieces Black Silk Velvet, 58 yds. 12/6 | | | | 36 | 5 | 0 |
| | *—23d.—*<br>Charles Smith, Glasgow. | | | | | | |
| 3 | To 10 Pieces French Merino, 320 yds. 4/7 | | | | 73 | 6 | 8 |
| 6 | George Ross, Dublin.<br>To 12 Pieces Muslin, 150 yards...... 1/5 | | | | 10 | 12 | 6 |
| | *—25th.—*<br>James Lindsay, Aberdeen. | | | | | | |
| 2 | To 12 Yards Black Satin............... 5/6 | 3 | 6 | 0 | | | |
| | „ 15 „ „ Silk................ 3/9 | 2 | 16 | 3 | 6 | 2 | 3 |
| | Thomas Murray, Leeds. | | | | | | |
| | To 10 Pieces Cotton Shirting, 380 yds. 8½d. | 13 | 9 | 2 | | | |
| 3 | „ 5 „ Linen Sheeting, 248 „ 1/9 | 21 | 14 | 0 | | | |
| | „ 6 „ Mous. de Laine, 182 „ 1/3 | 11 | 7 | 6 | | | |
| | Wrapper............................. | 0 | 5 | 6 | 46 | 16 | 2 |
| 2 | Thomas Bladworth, Hull.<br>To 1 Chest Black Tea, 85 lbs......... 3/9 | | | | 15 | 18 | 9 |
| | *—28th.—*<br>David Falconer, Dublin. | | | | | | |
| 3 | To 20 Yards Welsh Flannel......... 1/10 | 1 | 16 | 8 | | | |
| | „ 6 India Silk Handkerchiefs.... 4/6 | 1 | 7 | 0 | 3 | 3 | 8 |
| 14 | Goods—*Cr. by Credit Sales*................ | | | | 802 | 10 | 4 |

*March* 1, 1850.

| | | | | | | | | |
|---|---|---|---|---|---|---|---|---|
| 6 | John Lawson, Bristol. | | | | | | | |
| | To 9 Pieces Printed Cotton, 270 yds. 11d. | 12 | 7 | 6 | | | | |
| | „ 2 „ Twilled do. 84 „ 6½d. | 2 | 5 | 6 | 14 | 13 | 0 | |
| 5 | William Hunter, Princes Street. | | | | | | | |
| | To 2 lbs. Coffee......................... 1/10 | 0 | 3 | 8 | | | | |
| | „ 6 „ Sugar......................... 6½d. | 0 | 3 | 3 | 0 | 6 | 11 | |
| | *—2d.—* | | | | | | | |
| 6 | James Cameron, Dundee. | | | | | | | |
| | To 10 Yards Satin Ribbon.............. 1/3 | 0 | 12 | 6 | | | | |
| | „ 6 „ French Cambric......... 6/6 | 1 | 19 | 0 | 2 | 11 | 6 | |
| | *—3d.—* | | | | | | | |
| 3 | Alexander Paterson, London. | | | | | | | |
| | To Sidney Smith's Works, 3 vols. 8vo. cloth | 1 | 16 | 0 | | | | |
| | „ Byron's Poems, 8vo. cloth.............. | 0 | 16 | 0 | 2 | 12 | 0 | |
| 1 | Richard Porteous, Bristol. | | | | | | | |
| | To 6 Pieces German Lawn, 72 yds. 2/9 | 9 | 18 | 0 | | | | |
| | „ 4 „ Irish Linen, 117 „ 1/7 | 9 | 5 | 3 | 19 | 3 | 3 | |
| | *—4th.—* | | | | | | | |
| 7 | W. Edmonds, Newcastle. | | | | | | | |
| |           cwt. qrs. lbs. | | | | | | | |
| | To 1 Hhd. Sugar—gross, 16 3 7 | | | | | | | |
| |          tare, 1 2 3 | | | | | | | |
| |         nett, 15 1 4 @ 53/8 | | | | 41 | 0 | 4 | |
| | *—6th.—* | | | | | | | |
| 4 | David Anderson, Glasgow. | | | | | | | |
| | To 2 Pieces Linen Sheeting, 111 yds. 3/3 | 18 | 0 | 9 | | | | |
| | „ 10 „ Welsh Flannel, 420 „ 1/10 | 38 | 10 | 0 | 56 | 10 | 9 | |
| | Carried over.................. | | | | 136 | 17 | 9 | |

C

### March 7, 1850.

| | | | | | | |
|---|---|---|---|---|---|---|
| | Brought over................... | | | | 136 | 17 | 9 |

| 7 | Thomas Bennett, London. | | | | | | |
|---|---|---|---|---|---|---|---|
| | To 20 Reams Small Post............. 19/6 | | | | 19 | 10 | 0 |

| 6 | James Cameron, Dundee. | | | | | | |
|---|---|---|---|---|---|---|---|
| | To 2 Silk Umbrellas.................. 16/6 | 1 | 13 | 0 | | | |
| | „ 6 Cotton do. .................. 5/9 | 1 | 14 | 6 | 3 | 7 | 6 |

—9th.—

| 7 | Charles Davidson, Charlotte Street. | | | | | | |
|---|---|---|---|---|---|---|---|
| | To 6 lbs. White Soap.................. 7d. | 0 | 3 | 6 | | | |
| | „ 3 „ do. .................. 6d. | 0 | 1 | 6 | 0 | 5 | 0 |

—10th.—

James Milne, London.
To 2 Chests Hyson.

| 7 |       *D. C. 7     76 lbs. | | | | | | |
|---|---|---|---|---|---|---|---|
| |            8      79 | | | | | | |
| |            155 lbs........ 4/2 | | | | 32 | 5 | 10 |

* The letters and numbers marked on the chests.

| 6 | James Cameron, Dundee. | | | | | | |
|---|---|---|---|---|---|---|---|
| | To 1 Pipe of Port Wine..................... | | | | 75 | 0 | 0 |

—12th.—

| 6 | John Lawson, Bristol. | | | | | | |
|---|---|---|---|---|---|---|---|
| | To 5 Pieces French Merino, 150 yds. 4/10 | 36 | 5 | 0 | | | |
| | „ 2 „ Cotton Shirting, 87 „ 9d. | 3 | 5 | 3 | 39 | 10 | 3 |

| 5 | John Alison, Frederick Street. | | | | | | |
|---|---|---|---|---|---|---|---|
| | To 6 lbs. Green Tea..................... 5/6 | 1 | 13 | 0 | | | |
| | „ 8 „ Black do..................... 4/ | 1 | 12 | 0 | | | |
| | „ 6 „ Loaf Sugar.................... 8d. | 0 | 4 | 0 | 3 | 9 | 0 |

| | Carried forward............. | | | | 310 | 5 | 4 |
|---|---|---|---|---|---|---|---|

## *March* 14, 1850.

| | | | | | | | | |
|---|---|---|---|---|---|---|---|---|
| | Brought forward............ | | | | | 310 | 5 | **4** |
| **1** | George Innes, Liverpool.<br>To 12 Pair Blankets.................... 17/ | 10 | 4 | 0 | | | | |
| | „ 6 „ do. .................. 18/6 | 5 | 11 | 0 | | 15 | 15 | 0 |
| **8** | Alexander Morrison, Greenock.<br>To 30 Yards Carpeting ................. 3/6 | 5 | 5 | 0 | | | | |
| | „ 15 „ Printed Drugget........ 2/9 | 2 | 1 | 3 | | | | |
| | „ 6 „ Doeskin................... 4/6 | 1 | 7 | 0 | | 8 | 13 | 3 |
| **7** | —15th.—<br>James Milne, London.<br>To 3 Chests Congou.<br>    C.D.29   gross 102 lbs.   tare 21 lbs.<br>        30       103         22<br>        31        99         20<br>             304       63<br>    deduct tare   63<br>            241 lbs. nett..... 4/2 | | | | | 50 | 4 | 2 |
| **5** | —17th.—<br>James Durham, Bristol.<br>To 20 Reams Printing Demy ....... 18/ | 18 | 0 | 0 | | | | |
| | „ 7 „ do. do. ....... 17/9 | 6 | 4 | 3 | | | | |
| | „ 6 „ do. Royal ....... 21/ | 6 | 6 | 0 | | 30 | 10 | 3 |
| **8** | David Mitchell, Liverpool.<br>To 10 Pieces Irish Linen,   298 yds. 2/10 | 42 | 4 | 4 | | | | |
| | „ 2 „ German Lawn, 120 „ 3/1 | 18 | 10 | 0 | | | | |
| | „ 6 „ Muslin,        71 „ 1/2 | 4 | 2 | 10 | | | | |
| |          Wrapper............................. | 0 | 4 | 6 | | 65 | 1 | 8 |
| **6** | —18th.—<br>Robert Hume, Carlisle.<br>To Wordsworth's Poems................... | 0 | 9 | 0 | | | | |
| | „ Shakspeare, 2 vols. royal 8vo......... | 1 | 16 | 0 | | | | |
| | „ 3 Reams Small Post................ 25/ | 3 | 15 | 0 | | 6 | 0 | 0 |
| |         Carried over............... | | | | | 486 | 9 | 8 |

*March* 22, 1850.

| | | | | cwt | qrs | lbs | £ | s | d |
|---|---|---|---|---|---|---|---|---|---|
| | Brought over............... | | | | | | 486 | 9 | 8 |
| | James Cameron, Dundee. | | | | | | | | |
| | To 4 Hhds. Sugar. | | | | | | | | |
| | | cwt. qrs. lbs. | cwt. qrs. lbs. | | | | | | |
| | G.L. 29 gross 15 2 0 | tare 1 1 3 | | | | | | | |
| 6 | 30 15 3 0 | 1 1 0 | | | | | | | |
| | 31 14 1 7 | 1 1 1 | | | | | | | |
| | 32 16 2 21 | 1 1 3 | | | | | | | |
| | 62 1 0 | 5 0 7 | | | | | | | |
| | deduct tare 5 0 7 | | | | | | | | |
| | nett 57 0 21 .............. 56/ | | | | | | 160 | 2 | 6 |
| | | | | | | | | | |
| | —23d.— | | | | | | | | |
| | James Milne, London. | | | | | | | | |
| 7 | To 4 Pieces French Merino, 88 yds. 5/11 | | | 26 | 0 | 8 | | | |
| | „ 6 Pair Blankets .................... 25/ | | | 7 | 10 | 0 | | | |
| | „ 2 Pieces Gingham, 62 yards .... 1/2 | | | 3 | 12 | 4 | 37 | 3 | 0 |
| | | | | | | | | | |
| | William Edmonds, Newcastle. | | | | | | | | |
| 7 | To 12 Yards Irish Linen ............. 1/10 | | | 1 | 2 | 0 | | | |
| | „ 18 „ Mousseline de Laine .. 1/4 | | | 1 | 4 | 0 | | | |
| | „ 6 „ French Cambric....... 4/8 | | | 1 | 8 | 0 | 3 | 14 | 0 |
| | | | | | | | | | |
| | —24th.— | | | | | | | | |
| | Robert Hume, Carlisle. | | | | | | | | |
| | To 6 Pair Cotton Socks............. 1/3 | | | 0 | 7 | 6 | | | |
| 6 | „ 12 „ Worsted do. .............. 1/8 | | | 1 | 0 | 0 | | | |
| | „ 12 Black Satin Stocks............. 4/7 | | | 2 | 15 | 0 | 4 | 2 | 6 |
| | | | | | | | | | |
| | David Mitchell, Liverpool. | | | | | | | | |
| 3 | To 20 Pieces Cambric, 240 yards... 1/6 | | | 18 | 0 | 0 | | | |
| | „ 12 Silk Hats......................... 10/9 | | | 6 | 9 | 0 | | | |
| | „ 12 Yards Flannel.................. 2/3 | | | 1 | 7 | 0 | 25 | 16 | 0 |
| | **Carried forward**............ | | | | | | 717 | 7 | 8 |

## March 26, 1850.

| | | | | | | | | |
|---|---|---|---|---|---|---|---|---|
| | Brought forward............... | | 7 | 17 | 7 | 8 | | |
| | Charles Davidson, Charlotte Street. | | | | | | | |
| 7 | To 6 Loaves Bread..................... 7½d. | 0 | 3 | 9 | | | | |
| | „ 3 lbs. Coffee.......................... 2/ | 0 | 6 | 0 | | | | |
| | „ 4 „ Tea............................. 4/6 | 0 | 18 | 0 | | | | |
| | „ 6 „ Sugar.......................... 6½d. | 0 | 3 | 3 | 1 | 11 | 0 |
| | *—29th.—* | | | | | | | |
| | George Ross, Dublin. | | | | | | | |
| 6 | To 5 Reams Printing Demy....... 16/6 | 4 | 2 | 6 | | | | |
| | „ 12 „ do. do. ....... 18/ | 10 | 16 | 0 | 14 | 18 | 6 |
| | *—31st.—* | | | | | | | |
| | Charles Chadwick, Manchester. | | | | | | | |
| 2 | To 2 Pieces Doeskin, 38 yds. 4/9 | 9 | 0 | 6 | | | | |
| | „ 6 „ Sup. Black Cloth,122 „ 16/9 | 102 | 3 | 6 | 111 | 4 | 0 |
| 9 | Allan and Bell, London. | | | | | | | |
| | To Commission 10 % on Goods sold, £24, 10s. | | | | 2 | 9 | 0 |
| 14 | Goods—*Cr. by Credit Sales*................... | | | | 847 | 10 | 2 |

*Note.*—The following is the most convenient form of the Day-Book, when the breadth of the page will admit of its use. The word " To " at each entry may be left out.

## March 29, 1850.

| | | | | | | | | |
|---|---|---|---|---|---|---|---|---|
| | George Ross, Dublin. | | | | | | | |
| 6 | 5 Reams Printing **Demy**........... 16/6 | 4 | 2 | 6 | | | | |
| | 12 „ do. do. ........... 18/ | 10 | 16 | 0 | 14 | 18 | 6 |
| | *—31st.—* | | | | | | | |
| | Charles Chadwick, Manchester. | | | | | | | |
| 2 | 2 Pieces Doeskin, 38 yds. 4/9 | 9 | 0 | 6 | | | | |
| | 6 „ Sup. Black Cloth, 122 „ 16/9 | 102 | 3 | 6 | 111 | 4 | 0 |

*Edinburgh, January* 1, 1850.

| | | | | | | | |
|---|---|---|---|---|---|---|---|
| | James Stewart & Co. Leeds. | | | | | | |
| | By 9 Pieces Sup. Black Cloth, 180 **yds.** 13/7 | 122 | 5 | 0 | | | |
| 8 | „ 3 „ „ Brown do. **80** „ 14/5 | 57 | 13 | 4 | | | |
| | „ **4** „ „ Olive do. **80** „ 14/10 | 59 | 6 | 8 | | | |
| | „ **5** „ „ Black do. 100 „ 15/2 | 75 | 16 | 8 | | | |
| | Wrapper............................ | 0 | 9 | 6 | 315 | 11 | 2 |
| | | | | | | | |
| | Edward Johnston & Co., Manchester. | | | | | | |
| | By 26 Pieces Printed Cotton, 825 yds. **7d.** | 24 | 1 | 3 | | | |
| 8 | „ 2 „ do. do. 120 „ 8d. | 4 | 0 | 0 | | | |
| | „ 12 „ Twilled do. 504 „ 7d. | 14 | 14 | 0 | | | |
| | Wrapper............................ | 0 | 2 | 6 | 42 | 17 | 9 |
| | | | | | | | |
| 9 | **Allan and** Bell, London. | | | | | | |
| | By Goods, as per Invoice, **December 30, 1849** | | | | 6 | 10 | 0 |

The *Invoice* containing the particulars is supposed to have been received from Allan and Bell. As formerly mentioned, in actual business it is sufficient to enter the *amount* only of the invoices.

| | | | | | | | |
|---|---|---|---|---|---|---|---|
| | —2d.— | | | | | | |
| | Robert Gray, Bradford. | | | | | | |
| 9 | By 3 Pieces Sup. Black Cloth, **150** yds. 13/6 | 101 | 5 | 0 | | | |
| | „ 2 „ „ Brown do. 90 „ 14/6 | 65 | 5 | 0 | | | |
| | „ 5 „ „ Olive do. 125 „ 15/ | 93 | 15 | 0 | 260 | 5 | 0 |
| | | | | | | | |
| 8 | Edward Johnston & Co., Manchester. | | | | | | |
| | By **Goods,** as **per** Invoice, Jan. 1......... | | | | 70 | 10 | 0 |
| | | | | | | | |
| 9 | A. Jardine & Co., Leith. | | | | | | |
| | By Goods, as per **In**voice, Jan. **2**........ | | | | 25 | 10 | 0 |
| | Carried forward................. | | | | 721 | 3 | 11 |

* For **another form** of the Invoice-Book, see page 43.

*January* 12, 1850.

| | | | | | | | |
|---|---|---|---|---|---|---|---|
| | Brought forward......... | | | | | 721 | 3 11 |
| | **Robertson and Simpson, Glasgow.** | | | | | | |
| 9 | By 16 Pieces Scotch Cambric, 192 yds. 1/5 | 13 12 0 | | | | | |
| | „  3   „   French do.   90  „  8/10 | 39 15 0 | | | | | |
| | „ 11   „    do.    do.   495  „  6/6 | 160 17 6 | | | 214 | 4 | 6 |
| | *—15th.—* | | | | | | |
| | **John Ainslie and Sons, Liverpool.** | | | | | | |
| 10 | By 2 Boxes Raisins, 108 lbs......... 6½d. | 2 18 6 | | | | | |
| | „  2  „   do.   112 „ ......... 5d. | 2  6 8 | | | 5 | 5 | 2 |
| | *—20th.—* | | | | | | |
| | **John Miller, Edinburgh.** | | | | | | |
| | By 24 Reams Wove Pott............. 5/6 | 6 12 0 | | | | | |
| | „ 12   „   „   Foolscap....... 10/3 | 6  3 0 | | | | | |
| 10 | „ 12   „   Royal Crown.......... 16/ | 9 12 0 | | | | | |
| | „  6   „   Printing Demy ....... 12/8 | 3 16 0 | | | | | |
| | „ 10   „    „   Royal....... 15/3 | 7 12 6 | | | 33 | 15 | 6 |
| | *—25th.—* | | | | | | |
| | **James Dalton, London.** | | | | | | |
| | By 6 Dozen Silver Table-Spoons .... 16/ | 57 12 0 | | | | | |
| 10 | „  4  „   „  Tea  do.  .... 6/ | 14  8 0 | | | | | |
| | „  4  „   „  Dessert do.  ... 11/ | 26  8 0 | | | 98 | 8 | 0 |
| | *—31st.—* | | | | | | |
| | **Alexander Jardine & Co., Leith.** | | | | | | |
| | By 4 Chests Congou— | | | | | | |
| | E.F. 42  gross 99 lbs.  tare 20 lbs. | | | | | | |
| | 43      98      24 | | | | | | |
| | 44     100      19 | | | | | | |
| | 45     106      25 | | | | | | |
| | ———     —— | | | | | | |
| | 403      88 | | | | | | |
| | deduct tare  88 | | | | | | |
| 9 | nett 315 lbs........... 3/6 | 55  2 6 | | | | | |
| | „ 4 Tierces Coffee— | | | | | | |
| | cwt. qrs. lbs. | | | | | | |
| | T.D.   gross 23  0  0 | | | | | | |
| | 1 to 4   tare  2  2  0 | | | | | | |
| | nett 20  2  0 £6 10 8 | 133 18 8 | | | | | |
| | „ 2 Pipes Port Wine.......... 65  0  0 | 130  0 0 | | | | | |
| | „ 2  „   do.   .......... 68  0  0 | 136  0 0 | | | 455 | 1 | 2 |
| **14** | Goods—*Dr. to Credit Purchases*.......... | | | | | 1527 | 18 3 |

*February* 1, 1850.

| | | | | | | | | | |
|---|---|---|---|---|---|---|---|---|---|
| **10** | Thomas Graham, Belfast. | | | | | | | | |
| | By 16 Pieces Irish Linen, 456 yards, 2/ | 45 | 12 | 0 | | | | | |
| | „ 6 „ do. 168 „ 1/9 | 14 | 14 | 0 | | | | | |
| | „ 12 „ do. 348 „ 2/2 | 37 | 14 | 0 | 98 | 0 | 0 | | |
| **11** | Walter Kennedy, Paisley. | | | | | | | | |
| | By 6 Shawls.............................. 60/ | | | | 18 | 0 | 0 | | |
| | —4th.— | | | | | | | | |
| | Edward Johnston, Manchester. | | | | | | | | |
| **8** | By 8 Pieces Gingham, 224 yards... 9d. | 8 | 8 | 0 | | | | | |
| | „ 12 „ do. 372 „ ... 1/2 | 21 | 14 | 0 | | | | | |
| | „ 15 „ do. 420 „ ... 11d. | 19 | 5 | 0 | | | | | |
| | „ 12 Dozen Pair Cotton Socks.... 13/ | 7 | 16 | 0 | 57 | 3 | 0 | | |
| **9** | Robertson and Simpson, Glasgow. | | | | | | | | |
| | By 1 Piece Muslin, 20 yds. 1/2 | 1 | 3 | 4 | | | | | |
| | „ 5 „ Mous. de Laine, 160 „ 10d. | 6 | 13 | 4 | | | | | |
| | „ 10 „ do. 320 „ 11d. | 14 | 13 | 4 | 22 | 10 | 0 | | |

—10th.—

John Ainslie & Sons, Liverpool.

By 6 Hhds Sugar—

| | cwt. | qrs. | lbs. | | qrs. | lbs. |
|---|---|---|---|---|---|---|
| C.D. 14 | gross 14 | 2 | 0 | tare 1 | 4 | |
| 15 | 15 | 1 | 0 | 1 | 2 | |
| **16** | 14 | 2 | 14 | 1 | 6 | |
| 17 | 16 | 1 | 14 | 1 | 10 | |
| 18 | 15 | 1 | 7 | 1 | 5 | |
| 19 | 14 | 0 | 21 | 1 | 1 | |

| | | | | | | | | | |
|---|---|---|---|---|---|---|---|---|---|
| | 90 1 0    1 3 0 | | | | | | | | |
| | deduct **tare** 1 3 0 | | | | | | | | |
| | **nett** 88 2 0........... 42/ | 185 | 17 | 0 | | | | | |
| | Wharfage............................... | 0 | 6 | 0 | 186 | 3 | 0 | | |
| | Carried forward............ | | | | 381 | 16 | 0 | | |

## February 10, 1850.

| | | | | | | | | |
|---|---|---|---|---|---|---|---|---|
| | Brought forward............... | | | | | 381 | 16 | 0 |
| 9 | Robert Gray, Bradford.<br>By 2 Pieces Doeskin, 56 yards....... 5/ | | | | | 14 | 0 | 0 |
| | *—16th.—*<br>James Stewart & Co., Leeds. | | | | | | | |
| 8 | By 2 Pieces Black Cloth, 60 yds.... 15/6 | 46 | 10 | 0 | | | | |
| | „ 1 Piece Doeskin,   20 „ .... 4/9 | 4 | 15 | 0 | | 51 | 5 | 0 |
| | *—19th.—*<br>Edward Johnston & Co., Manchester. | | | | | | | |
| 8 | By 2 Pieces Cotton Shirting,   76 yds. 6½d. | 2 | 1 | 2 | | | | |
| | „ 20 „   Black Silk,   996 „   2/9 | 136 | 19 | 0 | | | | |
| | „ 5 „   Black Silk Velvet, 160 „   9/ | 72 | 0 | 0 | | | | |
| | Wrappers.................... | 0 | 9 | 6 | | 211 | 9 | 8 |
| 10 | Thomas Graham, Belfast.<br>By 1 Piece Irish Linen, 28 yards.... 1/9 | | | | | 2 | 9 | 0 |
| | *—20th.—*<br>Allan and Bell, London. | | | | | | | |
| 9 | By   2 Russell's Modern Europe, 4 vols.... 37/6 | 3 | 15 | 0 | | | | |
| | „   2 Byron's Works, 1 vol. 8vo. cloth... 11/6 | 1 | 3 | 0 | | | | |
| | „ 12 Cowper's Poems, 18mo. cloth....... 1/6 | 0 | 18 | 0 | | | | |
| | „ 100 Edgeworth's Moral Tales, 12mo. cl. 3/6 | 17 | 10 | 0 | | | | |
| | Box 3/, wharfage 1/6............ | 0 | 4 | 6 | | 23 | 10 | 6 |
| 8 | Edward Johnston & Co., Manchester.<br>By Goods as per Invoice, Mar. 18th..... | | | | | 84 | 15 | 11 |
| | *—25th.—*<br>Robertson and Simpson, Glasgow. | | | | | | | |
| 9 | By 12 Pieces Linen Sheeting, 624 yds. 2/6 | | | | | 78 | 0 | 0 |
| | *—28th.—*<br>Thomas Thomson, London. | | | | | | | |
| 11 | By Goods as per Invoice, Feb. 26th...... | | | | | 53 | 13 | 0 |
| 14 | Goods—*Dr. to Credit Purchases*........... | | | | | 900 | 19 | 1 |

*March* 1, 1850.

| | | £ | s | d | £ | s | d |
|---|---|---|---|---|---|---|---|
| | George Brooks, London. | | | | | | |
| | By 20 Pieces Black Silk,   358 yds. 3/ | 53 | 14 | 0 | | | |
| | „   6   „   Satinett,   176   „   2/9 | 24 | 4 | 0 | | | |
| 11 | „   4   „   Black Satin, 120   „   7/6 | 45 | 0 | 0 | | | |
| | „   3 Dozen Silk Handkerchiefs.... 36/ | 5 | 8 | 0 | | | |
| | „   4   „   do.    do.    .... 27/ | 5 | 8 | 0 | | | |
| | „   4   „   Satin Stocks............ 42/ | 8 | 8 | 0 | | | |
| | Wrapper and packing......... | 0 | 6 | 0 | 142 | 8 | 0 |
| | | | | | | | |
| | Alexander Hunter, Manchester. | | | | | | |
| | By   8 Pieces Mous. de Laine, 248 yds. 1/1 | 13 | 8 | 8 | | | |
| | „   2   „   do.    do.   78   „   1/ | 3 | 18 | 0 | | | |
| | „   6   „   Printed Cotton, 176   „   9d. | 6 | 12 | 0 | | | |
| 11 | „ 12   „   Gingham,   360   „   10d. | 15 | 0 | 0 | | | |
| | „   4   „   Twilled Cotton, 156   „   6½d. | 4 | 4 | 6 | | | |
| | „   6 Dozen Pair Cotton Socks..... 12/ | 3 | 12 | 0 | | | |
| | Wrappers...................... | 0 | 2 | 6 | 46 | 17 | 8 |
| | | | | | | | |
| | —4th.— | | | | | | |
| | Robert Todd, Glasgow. | | | | | | |
| | By 10 Pieces Cambric,   122 yds. 5d. | 2 | 10 | 10 | | | |
| 12 | „   4   „   Mous. de Laine, 118   „   11d. | 5 | 8 | 2 | | | |
| | „   7   „   Cotton Shirting, 220   „   7½d. | 6 | 17 | 6 | 14 | 16 | 6 |
| | | | | | | | |
| | —10th.— | | | | | | |
| | Thomas Thomson, London. | | | | | | |
| | By   2 Pieces French Merino, 61 yds. 3/6 | 10 | 13 | 6 | | | |
| | „   4   „   Satin Ribbon,   84   „   11d. | 3 | 17 | 0 | | | |
| 11 | „ 54 Yards Satinett.................. 3/3 | 8 | 15 | 6 | | | |
| | „   3 Dozen India Silk Handkerchiefs 33/ | 4 | 19 | 0 | | | |
| | „   2   „   do.    do.   24/ | 2 | 8 | 0 | | | |
| | „   2   „   do.    do.   26/ | 2 | 12 | 0 | | | |
| | Wrapper 3/6, wharfage 1/6......... | 0 | 5 | 0 | 33 | 10 | 0 |
| | | | | | | | |
| | Carried forward................ | | | | 237 | 12 | 2 |

### *March* 15, 1850.

| | | | | | | | | | |
|---|---|---|---|---|---|---|---|---|---|
| | Brought forward............... | | | | | | 237 | 12 | 2 |
| | R. Gray, Bradford. | | | | | | | | |
| 9 | By 4 Pieces Doeskin,       83 yds. 4/ | 16 | 12 | 0 | | | | | |
| | „ 6   „   Sup. Black Cloth, 124 „ 13/ | 80 | 12 | 0 | | | | | |
| | „ 5   „   „ Brown do. 106 „ 14/3 | 75 | 10 | 6 | 172 | 14 | 6 | | |
| | —19th.— | | | | | | | | |
| | Robert Todd, Glasgow. | | | | | | | | |
| 12 | By 30 Yards Muslin.................... 1/2 | 1 | 15 | 0 | | | | | |
| | „ 24   „   Gingham................ 10d. | 1 | 0 | 0 | | | | | |
| | „ 6 Pieces Twilled Cotton, 240 yds. 5½d. | 5 | 10 | 0 | | | | | |
| | „ 3 Dozen Satin Stocks ........... 42/ | 6 | 6 | 0 | 14 | 11 | 0 | | |
| | John Ainslie & Sons, Liverpool. | | | | | | | | |
| |               cwts. qrs. lbs. | | | | | | | | |
| 10 | By 3 Tierces Coffee, gross 17 3 20 | | | | | | | | |
| |           tare   2 0 14 | | | | | | | | |
| |           nett   15 3   6 @ £7 | 110 | 12 | 6 | | | | | |
| |       Wharfage.......................... | 0 | 4 | 6 | 110 | 17 | 0 | | |
| | —25th.— | | | | | | | | |
| | Alexander Hunter, Manchester. | | | | | | | | |
| 11 | By 12 Pieces Black Silk Velvet, 52 yds. 9/ | 23 | 8 | 0 | | | | | |
| | „ 6   „   Crimson Velvet, 25 „ 10/ | 12 | 10 | 0 | | | | | |
| | „ 36 Yards Gingham.................. 1/1 | 1 | 19 | 0 | 37 | 17 | 0 | | |
| | —31st.— | | | | | | | | |
| | George Brooks, London. | | | | | | | | |
| 11 | By 32 Yards Black Silk.............. 2/9 | 4 | 8 | 0 | | | | | |
| | „ 8 Silk Umbrellas.................. 12/6 | 5 | 0 | 0 | | | | | |
| |       Wharfage...................... | 0 | 1 | 6 | 9 | 9 | 6 | | |
| 14 | Goods—*Dr. to Credit Purchases*............ | | | | 583 | 1 | 2 | | |

*Note.*—The following is the most convenient form of the Invoice-Book, when the breadth of the page will admit of its use. The word " By " at each entry may be left out.

### *March* 31, 1850.

| | | | | | | | |
|---|---|---|---|---|---|---|---|
| | George Brooks, London. | | | | | | |
| 11 |       32 Yards Black Silk................. 2/9 | 4 | 8 | 0 | | | |
| |       8 Silk Umbrellas...................... 12/6 | 5 | 0 | 0 | | | |
| |       Wharfage............................. | 0 | 1 | 6 | 9 | 9 | 6 |

| | 1850 | | | Discount. | | | Cash. | | |
|---|---|---|---|---|---|---|---|---|---|
| 13 | Jan. | 1 | J. Adams, Cash at commencement | | | | 1000 | 0 | 0 |
| 14 | | | Goods—Cash Sales, 10/ 8/ 17/ 12/ 8/ 5/6 4/6.. | | | | 3 | 5 | 0 |
| | | | This is a mode of entering small sums, which saves room, and may make it unnecessary to use a " Petty Cash-Book." | | | | | | |
| 1 | | 3 | James Brown, George Street...... | 0 | 4 | 6 | 4 | 15 | 0 |
| 12 | | 5 | Union Bank.......................... | | | | 110 | 0 | 0 |
| 3 | | 7 | D. Falconer, Dublin............... | | | | 15 | 2 | 0 |
| 14 | | ,, | Goods—Cash Sales ................. | | | | 2 | 7 | 6 |
| 1 | | 12 | R. Porteous, Bristol................. | 7 | 5 | 8 | 138 | 6 | 0 |
| 12 | | ,, | Union Bank.......................... | | | | 60 | 0 | 0 |
| 14 | | 14 | Goods—Cash Sales ................. | | | | 3 | 10 | 0 |
| 1 | | 17 | James Brown, George Street...... | 0 | 0 | 5 | 0 | 8 | 6 |
| 3 | | 20 | Alexander Paterson, London ..... | 0 | 3 | 0 | 3 | 3 | 0 |
| 12 | | ,, | Union Bank.......................... | | | | 140 | 0 | 0 |
| 14 | | ,, | Goods—Cash Sales ................. | | | | 5 | 17 | 0 |
| ✓ | | ,, | Bills Receivable, No. 1, discounted,* £172, 11s. | 0 | 7 | 6 | 172 | 3 | 6 |
| 4 | | 21 | William Wilson, London.......... | | | | 1 | 2 | 0 |
| ✓ | | ,, | Bills Receivable, No. 3, discounted . | 2 | 12 | 6 | 286 | 5 | 0 |
| 3 | | 31 | Thomas Murray, Leeds........... | 4 | 12 | 8 | 87 | 8 | 0 |
| | | | * See note as to Bills, page 46. | | | | | | |
| 14 | | | Discount............................. | 15 | 6 | 3 | | | |
| | | | Deducted from the Cr. of the " Goods" acct. | | | | | | |
| | | | | | | | 2033 | 12 | 6 |

BALANCING THE CASH-BOOK.—To ascertain that the sums have been entered correctly, the Cash-Book requires to be *balanced* at stated times. For this purpose, enter on the *paid* side the sum you have on hand at the time of balancing, then add up the cash columns on the *received* and *paid* sides : if there has been no error in the entries, the sums-total of the two sides will be equal to each other, and the columns may be ruled off as settled or balanced. The cash on hand is carried forward to the *received* side, to begin a new account next day. The Cash-Book may be balanced either daily, weekly, or monthly : the cash received and paid ought, how-ever, to be balanced every day, and if the sum on hand is not marked in the Cash-Book itself till the end of the week or month, it must be noted every day in a Memorandum-Book for the purpose.

*Cash Paid.*

| | 1850 | | | Discount. | | | Cash. | | |
|---|---|---|---|---|---|---|---|---|---|
| 12 | Jan. | 1 | Union Bank............................ | | | | 990 | 0 | 0 |
| 14 | " | " | Goods—Cash Purchases............ | | | | 3 | 15 | 0 |
| 13 | | 3 | Trade Expenses—Salaries (or Wages) | | | | 3 | 10 | 0 |
| | | | In actual business, the names of the persons to whom salaries or wages are paid are entered in the Cash-Book: it is, however, unnecessary to do so here. An example is given, in the entry of Jan. 27, " J. Smith's Salary," which applies to all such cases. | | | | | | |
| 13 | | " | Trade Expenses—Carriages....... | | | | 0 | 7 | 6 |
| 13 | | " | " " Poor-rates...... | | | | 3 | 0 | 0 |
| 8 | | 5 | Ed. Johnston & Co., Manchester | 5 | 13 | 9 | 107 | 14 | 0 |
| 13 | | 7 | Trade Expenses—Postage Stamps | | | | | 2 | 6 |
| 9 | | 12 | Robertson & Simpson, Glasgow.. | 10 | 14 | 6 | 203 | 10 | 0 |
| 13 | | 13 | Trade Expenses—Salaries......... | | | | 3 | 13 | 6 |
| 14 | | 17 | Goods—Cash Purchases............ | | | | 4 | 5 | 0 |
| 13 | | 20 | Trade Expenses—Salaries......... | | | | 3 | 18 | 0 |
| 12 | | " | Shop Furniture, J. Anderson's a/c | | | | 107 | 10 | 0 |
| 10 | | " | John Miller, Edinburgh............ | 0 | 17 | 0 | 32 | 18 | 6 |
| 12 | | " | Union Bank............................ | | | | 175 | 0 | 0 |
| ✓ | | 21 | Bills Payable No. 2.................. | | | | 260 | 5 | 0 |
| 13 | | 27 | Trade Expenses—J. Smith's salary for 1 month | | | | 4 | 0 | 0 |
| 13 | | " | John Adams............................ | | | | 20 | 0 | 0 |
| 12 | | " | Union Bank............................ | | | | 90 | 0 | 0 |
| 14 | | 31 | Cash on Hand........................ | | | | 20 | 3 | 6 |
| | | " | Discount.............................. | 17 | 5 | 3 | | | |
| | | | Deducted from the Dr. of the "Goods" acct. | | | | | | |
| | | | | | | | 2033 | 12 | 6 |

NOTE.—Instead of the dates being placed on the margin of the CASH-BOOK, as above, it is usual in business to place them in the centre of the page, as in the Day-Book. The same dates require to be placed opposite each other on the *Received* and *Paid* sides. January 1 opposite January 1, January 2 opposite January 2, and so on.

For an example of this, and of a convenient method of balancing the Cash-Book daily, see Appendix, under the head of "Cash-Book."

PETTY CASH-BOOK.—Besides a Cash-Book, a "Petty Cash-Book" is often used, for entering the various small sums received and paid daily. (See Appendix.)

*Cash Received.*

| | 1850 | | | Discount | | | Cash | | |
|---|---|---|---|---|---|---|---|---|---|
| | Feb. | 1 | Cash on hand................ | | | | 20 | 3 | 6 |
| 14 | | ,, | Goods—Cash Sales............ | | | | 4 | 7 | 6 |
| 1 | | ,, | William Hunter, Princes Street... | | 3 | 11 | 3 | 11 | 0 |
| 2 | | 5 | Thomas Bladworth, Hull.......... | 3 | 0 | 3 | 57 | 15 | 0 |
| 14 | | 7 | Goods—Cash Sales............ | | | | 2 | 9 | 0 |
| 12 | | ,, | Union Bank................. | | | | 320 | 0 | 0 |
| 4 | | ,, | James Taylor, High Street—Composition of 10/ a £1........ | | | | 3 | 16 | 6 |
| ✓ | | ,, | Bills Receivable, No. 2, discounted,* £54, 18s. 4d. | | 9 | 4 | 54 | 9 | 0 |
| 4 | | 12 | David Anderson, Glasgow.......... | 1 | 12 | 6 | 31 | 4 | 0 |
| 12 | | ,, | Union Bank................. | | | | 40 | 0 | 0 |
| 14 | | 16 | Goods—Cash Sales............ | | | | 3 | 19 | 0 |
| 4 | | ,, | Robert Cook, Liverpool.......... | | 18 | 6 | 35 | 14 | 6 |
| 1 | | 25 | George Innes, Liverpool.......... | 1 | 13 | 9 | 65 | 10 | 0 |
| 14 | | ,, | Goods—Cash Sales............ | | | | 2 | 10 | 0 |
| 3 | | 28 | Charles Smith, Glasgow.......... | 4 | 10 | 6 | 176 | 4 | 0 |
| 14 | | | Discount................. | 12 | 8 | 9 | | | |
| | | | | | | | 821 | 13 | 0 |

* BILLS—
The Bills Receivable entered in the Cash-Book are supposed to be discounted at the Bank. Bills are, however, often not discounted, but paid away, sometimes at their full value, to other merchants in settlement of their accounts. In such cases they would be entered thus—

On the Received side—
Bills Receivable, No. 2 ................54 18 4
On the Paid side—
J. Anderson, Hull, Bills
Receivable, No. 2 ....................54 18 4

In business, **the names** as well as the Nos. of the Bills, are marked **in** the Cash-Book. Thus—
Bills Receivable, No. 1, G. Innes,
Liverpool ............................172 11 0
Bills Payable, No. 1, J. Stewart & Co.
Leeds..............................315 11 2

*Cash Paid.*

| | 1850 | | | Discount. | | | Cash. | | |
|---|---|---|---|---|---|---|---|---|---|
| 14 | Feb. | 1 | Goods—Cash Purchases............. | | | | 1 | 15 | 0 |
| 13 | | 3 | Trade Expenses—Salaries........... | | | | 3 | 14 | 6 |
| 12 | | 5 | Union Bank.............................. | | | | 70 | 0 | 0 |
| 13 | | 7 | Trade Expenses—Shop Rent...... | | | | 35 | 0 | 0 |
| 13 | | „ | „    „    Carriages........ | | | | 0 | 8 | 2 |
| 13 | | „ | „    „    Police Tax...... | | | | 1 | 10 | 0 |
| √ | | „ | Bills Payable, No. 1................... | | | | 315 | 11 | 2 |
| 11 | | 9 | Walter Kennedy, Paisley............ | 0 | 9 | 0 | 17 | 11 | 0 |
| 13 | | 10 | Trade Expenses—Salaries........... | | | | 3 | 12 | 0 |
| 10 | | 12 | James Dalton, London................ | 4 | 18 | 6 | 93 | 9 | 6 |
| 13 | | „ | Trade Expenses—Washing Shop.. | | | | 0 | 3 | 2 |
| 14 | | „ | Goods—Cash Purchases............. | | | | 5 | 17 | 0 |
| 12 | | 16 | Union Bank.............................. | | | | 40 | 0 | 0 |
| 13 | | 17 | Trade Expenses—Salaries........... | | | | 4 | 10 | 0 |
| 13 | | 24 | „     „     do. ........... | | | | 4 | 12 | 6 |
| 13 | | 25 | John Adams............................... | | | | 20 | 0 | 0 |
| 13 | | 28 | Trade Expenses — Carriages....... | | | | 0 | 7 | 9 |
| 9 | | „ | Alexander Jardine & Co. Leith ... | 10 | 0 | 0 | 190 | 0 | 0 |
| | | „ | Cash on hand............................ | | | | 13 | 11 | 3 |
| | | | | | | | | | |
| 14 | | | Discount................................ | 15 | 7 | 6 | | | |
| | | | | | | | 821 | 13 | 0 |

*Cash Received.*

| | 1850 | | | Discount. | | | Cash. | | |
|---|---|---|---|---|---|---|---|---|---|
| | Mar. | 1 | Cash on Hand............................ | | | | 13 | 11 | 3 |
| 14 | | ,, | Goods—Cash Sales................... | | | | 3 | 17 | 0 |
| 5 | | ,, | William Hunter, Princes Street... | 1 | 11 | 3 | 29 | 13 | 0 |
| 2 | | ,, | Thomas Bladworth, Hull............ | 0 | 15 | 9 | 15 | 3 | 0 |
| 14 | | 3 | Goods—Cash Sales................... | | | | 5 | 3 | 0 |
| √ | | ,, | Bills Receivable, No. 4, discounted, £157, 17s. 6d. | 1 | 6 | 4 | 156 | 11 | 0 |
| 2 | | 6 | James Lindsay, Aberdeen........... | 0 | 13 | 9 | 26 | 18 | 6 |
| 12 | | ,, | Union Bank.............................. | | | | 20 | 0 | 0 |
| 14 | | ,, | Goods—Cash Sales................... | | | | 3 | 17 | 6 |
| 4 | | 7 | D. Anderson, Glasgow............... | 1 | 8 | 3 | 55 | 2 | 6 |
| 6 | | 8 | George Ross, Dublin.................. | | | | 10 | 12 | 6 |
| 14 | | 10 | Goods—Cash Sales................... | | | | 4 | 15 | 3 |
| 8 | | 15 | Alex. Morrison, Greenock........... | 0 | 4 | 3 | 8 | 9 | 0 |
| 12 | | ,, | Union Bank.............................. | | | | 150 | 0 | 0 |
| 7 | | 21 | Thomas Bennett, London........... | 0 | 10 | 0 | 19 | 0 | 0 |
| √ | | ,, | Bills Receivable, No. 7, discounted, £92, 13s. 0d. | 0 | 7 | 8 | 92 | 7 | 4 |
| 14 | | 25 | Goods—Cash Sales................... | | | | 3 | 10 | 0 |
| 6 | | 30 | George Ross, Dublin................. | 0 | 7 | 6 | 14 | 11 | 0 |
| | | | | | | | | | |
| 14 | | | Discount.............................. | 7 | 4 | 9 | | | |
| | | | | | | | 633 | 1 | 10 |

*Cash Paid.*

| | 1850 | | | Discount. | | | Cash. | | |
|---|---|---|---|---|---|---|---|---|---|
| 14 | Mar. | 1 | Goods—Cash Purchases............. | | | | 12 | 17 | 6 |
| 13 | | „ | Trade Expenses—Carriages........ | | | | 0 | 4 | 9 |
| 13 | | „ | „        „        Salaries.......... | | | | 4 | 3 | 6 |
| 11 | | „ | Alex. Hunter, Manchester.......... | 1 | 3 | 8 | 45 | 14 | 0 |
| 13 | | 3 | John Adams................. | | | | 40 | 0 | 0 |
| 13 | | „ | Trade Expenses — Freight from London..................... | | | | 0 | 12 | 4 |
| 11 | | 6 | George Brooks, London............. | 7 | 2 | 6 | 135 | 5 | 6 |
| 12 | | 7 | Union Bank ........................... | | | | 58 | 0 | 0 |
| 13 | | „ | Trade Expenses—Postage Stamps | | | | 0 | 4 | 7 |
| 14 | | 10 | Goods—Cash Purchases............. | | | | 7 | 10 | 6 |
| √ | | 15 | Bills Payable, No. 3 .................. | | | | 150 | 0 | 0 |
| 13 | | „ | Trade Expenses—Salaries .......... | | | | 4 | 4 | 6 |
| 13 | | „ | „        „        „        Gas.............. | | | | 1 | 15 | 0 |
| 14 | | 17 | Goods—Cash Purchases............. | | | | 3 | 8 | 4 |
| 12 | | 21 | Union Bank ............................. | | | | 80 | 0 | 0 |
| 13 | | 22 | Trade Expenses—Salaries .......... | | | | 4 | 2 | 0 |
| 13 | | 30 | John Adams ........................... | | | | 10 | 0 | 0 |
| √ | | 31 | Bills Payable, No. 6 .................. | | | | 30 | 0 | 0 |
| 9 | | „ | Allan and Bell, London............. | | | | 22 | 1 | 0 |
| | | „ | Cash on **hand** .......................... | | | | 22 | 18 | 4 |
| 14 | | | Discount................. | 8 | 6 | 2 | | | |
| | | | | | | | 633 | 1 | 10 |

D

## Bills

| | No. | When received | From whom Received. | Amount. | | | Date. | Term. | When Due. | Entered in Cash-Bk. |
|---|---|---|---|---|---|---|---|---|---|---|
| | | 1850. | | | | | 1850. | | 1850. | **1850.** |
| 1 | 1 | Jan. 2 | G. Innes, Liverpool. | 172 | 11 | 0 | Jan. 1 | 1 mo. | Feb. 4 | Jan. 20 |
| 2 | 2 | „ 12 | J. Lindsay, Aberdeen. | 54 | 18 | 4 | „ 10 | 3 „ | April 13 | Feb. 7 |
| 2 | 3 | „ 18 | C. Chadwick, Manchester. | 288 | 17 | 6 | „ 17 | 2 „ | Mar. 20 | Jan. 21 |
| 2 | 4 | „ 31 | W. Bell, Leeds. | 157 | 17 | 4 | „ 26 | 3 „ | April 29 | Mar. 3 |
| 2 | 5 | Feb. 10 | J. Lindsay, Aberdeen. | 100 | 0 | 0 | Feb. 7 | 6 „ | Aug. 10 | |
| 5 | 6 | „ 16 | J. Durham, Bristol. | 100 | 0 | 0 | „ 14 | 4 „ | June 17 | |
| 2 | 7 | „ 19 | W. Bell, Leeds. | 92 | 15 | 0 | „ „ | 2 „ | April 17 | Mar. 21 |
| 5 | 8 | „ 25 | J. Durham, Bristol. | 50 | 0 | 0 | „ 22 | 3 „ | May 25 | |
| 3 | 9 | Mar. 1 | T. Murray, Leeds. | 46 | 16 | 2 | „ 28 | 2 „ | May 1 | |
| 3 | 10 | „ 4 | C. Smith, Glasgow. | 89 | 12 | 2 | Mar. 3 | 3 „ | June 6 | |
| 5 | 11 | „ 19 | J. Watt, Birmingham. | 37 | 11 | 2 | „ 18 | 2 „ | May 21 | |
| 6 | 12 | „ 20 | J. Lawson, Bristol. | 54 | 3 | 3 | „ „ | 2 „ | May 21 | |
| 7 | 13 | „ 25 | W. Edmonds, Newcastle. | 44 | 14 | 4 | „ 24 | 1 „ | April 27 | |
| 8 | 14 | „ 27 | D. Mitchell, Liverpool. | 90 | 17 | 8 | „ 26 | 3 „ | June 29 | |

mo. is a contraction for month.
1 mo. means that the bill is due 1 month after its date.

The Bills, when discounted, or otherwise disposed of, are entered in the Cash-Book, see note, page 46, and the dates are filled in here.

### Receivable.

| By whom Drawn. | On whom Drawn. | To whom Payable. | Where Payable. | Jan. | Feb. | March. | April. | May. | June. | July. | August. | Sept. | Oct. | Nov. | Dec. |
|---|---|---|---|---|---|---|---|---|---|---|---|---|---|---|---|
| J. Adams. | G. Innes. | J. Adams. | Liverpool. | 4 | | | | | | | | | | | |
| J. Lindsay. | W. Gray. | J. Lindsay. | Aberdeen. | | | | 13 | | | | | | | | |
| | | | | | | 20 | | | | | | | | | |
| | | | | | | | 29 | | | | | | | | |
| | | | | | | | | | | | 10 | | | | |
| | | | | | | | | | | 17 | | | | | |
| | | | | | | | 17 | | | | | | | | |
| | | | | | | | | 25 | | | | | | | |
| | | | | | | | | 1 | | | | | | | |
| | | | | | | | | | 6 | | | | | | |
| | | | | | | | | 21 | | | | | | | |
| | | | | | | | | 21 | | | | | | | |
| | | | | | | | 27 | | | | | | | | |
| | | | | | | | | | 29 | | | | | | |

These columns are used in business for entering the particulars shown in the above examples: it is unnecessary here, however, to fill up the other blanks.

These columns are used for ascertaining readily the dates when the bills are due.

## Bills

| No. | When Granted* | To whom Granted.* | Amount. | | | Date. | Term. | When Due. | Entered in Cash-Bk. |
|---|---|---|---|---|---|---|---|---|---|
| | 1850. | | | | | 1850. | | 1850. | 1850. |
| 8 | 1 | Jan. 4 | J. Stewart & Co., Leeds. | 315 | 11 | 2 | Jan. 4 | 1 mo. | Feb. 7 | Feb. 7 |
| 9 | 2 | „ 8 | R. Gray, Bradford. | 260 | 5 | 0 | „ 8 | 10 da. | Jan. 21 | Jan. 21 |
| 10 | 3 | Feb. 12 | Ainslie & Sons, Liverpool | 150 | 0 | 0 | Feb.12 | 1 mo. | Mar. 15 | Mar. 15 |
| 8 | 4 | „ 22 | Johnston & Co. Manchest. | 200 | 0 | 0 | „ 22 | 3 „ | May 25 | |
| 8 | 5 | „ 27 | Stewart & Co., Leeds. | 51 | 5 | 0 | „ 27 | 6 „ | Aug. 30 | |
| 11 | 6 | „ 28 | T. Thomson, London. | 30 | 0 | 0 | „ 28 | 1 „ | Mar. 31 | Mar. 31 |
| 9 | 7 | „ „ | A. Jardine & Co., Leith. | 100 | 0 | 0 | „ „ | 2 „ | May 1 | |
| 8 | 8 | Mar. 2 | Johnston & Co. Manchest. | 153 | 8 | 7 | Mar. 2 | 2 „ | May 5 | |
| 10 | 9 | „ 5 | T. Graham, Belfast. | 100 | 9 | 0 | „ 5 | 1 „ | April 8 | |
| 12 | 10 | „ 19 | R. Todd, Glasgow. | 29 | 7 | 6 | „ 19 | 3 „ | June 22 | |
| 10 | 11 | „ 24 | Ainslie & Sons, Liverpool | 100 | 0 | 0 | „ 24 | 2 „ | May 27 | |
| 9 | 12 | „ 30 | R. Gray, Bradford. | 186 | 14 | 6 | „ 30 | 1 „ | May 3 | |

*Or, accepted      *Or, By whom Drawn.

mo. is a contraction for month; da. for days.
10 da. means that the bill is due 10 days after its date.

## Payable.

| To whom Payable. | Where Payable. | Jan. | Feb. | March. | April. | May. | June. | July. | August. | Sept. | Oct. | Nov. | Dec. |
|---|---|---|---|---|---|---|---|---|---|---|---|---|---|
| Stewart & Co. | Union Bank, Edinburgh. | 7 | | | | | | | | | | | |
| J. Brown. | Do. do. | 21 | | | | | | | | | | | |
| | | | | 15 | | | | | | | | | |
| | | | | | | 25 | | | | | | | |
| | | | | | | | | | 30 | | | | |
| | | | | 31 | | | | | | | | | |
| | | | | | | 1 | | | | | | | |
| | | | | | | 5 | | | | | | | |
| | | | | | 8 | | | | | | | | |
| | | | | | | | 22 | | | | | | |
| | | | | | | 27 | | | | | | | |
| | | | | | | 3 | | | | | | | |

These columns are used in business for entering the particulars shown in the above examples: it is unnecessary here, however, to fill up the other blanks.

These columns are used for ascertaining readily the dates when the bills are due.

*Goods* on hand, *March* 31, 1850.

| | £ | s | d |
|---|---|---|---|
| 4 Pieces Superfine Black Cloth, 80 yds. ...... 13/7 | 54 | 6 | 8 |
| 2   „       „     Brown do.   40  „   ...... 14/5 | 28 | 16 | 8 |
| 6   „   Printed Cotton,    180  „   ...... 7d. | 5 | 5 | 0 |
| 5   „   Scotch Cambric,    60  „   ...... 1/5 | 4 | 5 | 0 |
| 1   „   Irish Linen,      28  „   ...... 2/ | 2 | 16 | 0 |
| 3   „   Gingham,       90  „   ...... 9d. | 3 | 7 | 6 |
| 3   „   Welsh Flannel,    60  „   ...... 1/6 | 4 | 10 | 0 |
| 20 Yards Muslin ..................................... 1/2 | 1 | 3 | 4 |
| 20   „   Black Silk .................................. 2/9 | 2 | 15 | 0 |
| 4 Silk Umbrellas.................................... 12/6 | 2 | 10 | 0 |
| 10 Reams Printing Demy Paper................ 12/8 | 6 | 6 | 8 |
| 2 Comstock's Natural Philosophy.............. 3/6 | 0 | 7 | 0 |
| 3 Gibbon's Rome, 5 vols. 8vo...................... 42/ | 6 | 6 | 0 |
| 1 Chest Congou Tea, 80 lbs. ...................... 3/6 | 14 | 0 | 0 |
| 1 Tierce Coffee, 5 cwt............................... 130/8 | 32 | 13 | 4 |
| 1 Pipe Port Wine..................................... | 65 | 0 | 0 |
| 2 Hhds. Sugar, 28 cwt............................... 42/ | 58 | 16 | 0 |
| Sundries    (In a real inventory all the particulars are given.) | 100 | 9 | 0 |
| | 393 | 13 | 2 |

*Goods on Commission from Allan & Bell, London,*
*on hand March* 31, 1850.

| | £ | s | d |
|---|---|---|---|
| Sundries...................................................... | 5 | 10 | 6 |

These goods, all the particulars of which would be given
in a real inventory, are not entered along with John Adams'
own goods, as they belong to Allan & Bell, the parties who
sent them on sale.

The Warehouse-Book **at page** 73, to be written out here, next to the Stock-Book.

# LEDGER.

## INDEX.

## James Brown, 75 George Street.

| 1850. | | | | £ | s. | d. | 1850. | | | | £ | s. | d. |
|---|---|---|---|---|---|---|---|---|---|---|---|---|---|
| Jan. | 1 | To Goods...... | 1 | 3 | 10 | 0 | Jan. | 3 | By Cash........ | 1 | 4 | 15 | 0 |
| | 3 | ,, do......... | ,, | 1 | 9 | 6 | | ,, | ,, Discount.. | ,, | 0 | 4 | 6 |
| | 11 | ,, do........ | 3 | 0 | 8 | 11 | | 17 | ,, Cash....... | ,, | 0 | 8 | 6 |
| Feb. | 17 | ,, do......... | 7 | 0 | 10 | 3 | | ,, | ,, Discount.. | ,, | 0 | 0 | 5 |
| | | | | | | | Mar. | 31 | ,, Balance * | | 0 | 10 | 3 |
| | | | | 5 | 18 | 8 | | | * or, Balance forward. | | 5 | 18 | 8 |
| Mar. | 31 | To Balance † | | 0 | 10 | 3 | | | | | | | |

## George Innes, Liverpool.

| 1850. | | | | £ | s. | d. | 1850. | | | | £ | s. | d. |
|---|---|---|---|---|---|---|---|---|---|---|---|---|---|
| Jan. | 1 | To Goods...... | 1 | 172 | 11 | 0 | Jan. | 2 | By Bill due Feb. 4.... | 1 | 172 | 11 | 0 |
| | 6 | ,, do........ | 2 | 42 | 15 | 6 | Feb. | 25 | ,, Cash....... | 3 | 65 | 10 | 0 |
| Feb. | 6 | ,, do........ | 5 | 24 | 8 | 3 | | ,, | ,, Discount.. | ,, | 1 | 13 | 9 |
| Mar. | 14 | ,, do........ | 11 | 15 | 15 | 0 | Mar. | 31 | ,, Balance... | | 15 | 15 | 0 |
| | | | | 255 | 9 | 9 | | | | | 255 | 9 | 9 |
| Mar. | 31 | To Balance... | | 15 | 15 | 0 | | | | | | | |

## William Hunter, Princes Street.

| 1850. | | | | £ | s. | d. | 1850. | | | | £ | s. | d. |
|---|---|---|---|---|---|---|---|---|---|---|---|---|---|
| Jan. | 2 | To Goods...... | 1 | 2 | 4 | 8 | Feb. | 1 | By Cash....... | 3 | 3 | 11 | 0 |
| | 27 | ,, do........ | 4 | 1 | 10 | 3 | | ,, | ,, Discount.. | ,, | 0 | 3 | 11 |
| Feb. | 6 | ,, do........ | 5 | 28 | 10 | 0 | | | | | | | |
| | | *to page 5* | | 32 | 4 | 11 | | | *to page 5* | | 3 | 14 | 11 |
| | | carried to p. 5, as this space is filled up. | | | | | | | | | | | |

## Richard Porteous, Bristol.

| 1850. | | | | £ | s. | d. | 1850. | | | | £ | s. | d. |
|---|---|---|---|---|---|---|---|---|---|---|---|---|---|
| Jan. | 2 | To Goods...... | 1 | 130 | 17 | 6 | Jan. | 12 | By Cash....... | 1 | 138 | 6 | 0 |
| | 11 | ,, do........ | 3 | 14 | 14 | 2 | | ,, | ,, Discount.. | ,, | 7 | 5 | 8 |
| Mar. | 3 | ,, do........ | 9 | 19 | 3 | 3 | Mar. | 31 | ,, Balance... | | 19 | 3 | 3 |
| | | | | 164 | 14 | 11 | | | | | 164 | 14 | 11 |
| **Mar.** | 31 | To Balance ... | | 19 | 3 | 3 | | | | | | | |

† In business, it is unnecessary to balance off unsettled **accounts** in this way. It is sufficient merely to add up the columns, marking the Dr. or Cr. balances in a temporary way with a pencil, and ruling off the accounts only when they are actually settled.

## CHARLES CHADWICK, Manchester.

| 1850. | | | | £ | s. | d. | 1850. | | | | £ | s. | d. |
|---|---|---|---|---|---|---|---|---|---|---|---|---|---|
| Jan. | 3 | To Goods...... | 1 | 65 | 12 | 0 | Jan. | 18 | By Bill due | | | | |
| | 10 | ,, do. ...... | 3 | 223 | 5 | 6 | | | Mar. 20.. | 1 | 288 | 17 | 6 |
| Mar. | 31 | ,, do. ...... | 13 | 111 | 4 | 0 | Mar. | 31 | ,, Balance... | | 111 | 4 | 0 |
| | | | | 400 | 1 | 6 | | | | | 400 | 1 | 6 |
| Mar. | 31 | To Balance.... | | 111 | 4 | 0 | | | | | | | |

## WILLIAM BELL, Leeds.

| 1850. | | | | £ | s. | d. | 1850. | | | | £ | s. | d. |
|---|---|---|---|---|---|---|---|---|---|---|---|---|---|
| Jan. | 3 | To Goods...... | 2 | 157 | 17 | 4 | Jan. | 31 | By Bill due | | | | |
| | 7 | ,, do. ...... | ,, | 25 | 4 | 0 | | | April 29. | 1 | 157 | 17 | 4 |
| | 25 | ,, do. ...... | 4 | 2 | 6 | 0 | Feb. | 19 | ,, Bill due | | | | |
| Feb. | 12 | ,, do. ...... | 6 | 65 | 5 | 0 | | | April 17. | ,, | 92 | 15 | 0 |
| | | | | 250 | 12 | 4 | | | | | 250 | 12 | 4 |

## THOMAS BLADWORTH, Hull.

| 1850. | | | | £ | s. | d. | 1850. | | | | £ | s. | d. |
|---|---|---|---|---|---|---|---|---|---|---|---|---|---|
| Jan. | 5 | To Goods...... | 2 | 58 | 8 | 3 | Feb. | 5 | By Cash....... | 3 | 57 | 15 | 0 |
| | 27 | ,, do. ...... | 4 | 2 | 7 | 0 | | ,, | ,, Discount.. | ,, | 3 | 0 | 3 |
| Feb. | 25 | ,, do. ...... | 8 | 15 | 18 | 9 | Mar. | 1 | ,, Cash....... | 5 | 15 | 3 | 0 |
| | | | | | | | | ,, | ,, Discount.. | ,, | 0 | 15 | 9 |
| | | | | 76 | 14 | 0 | | | | | 76 | 14 | 0 |

## JAMES LINDSAY, Aberdeen.

| 1850. | | | | £ | s. | d. | 1850. | | | | £ | s. | d. |
|---|---|---|---|---|---|---|---|---|---|---|---|---|---|
| Jan. | 6 | To Goods*.... | 2 | 144 | 18 | 4 | Jan. | 12 | By Bill due | | | | |
| Feb. | 5 | ,, do. ...... | 5 | 11 | 2 | 0 | | | April 13. | 1 | 54 | 18 | 4 |
| | 22 | ,, do. ...... | 7 | 10 | 8 | 0 | Feb. | 10 | ,, Bill due | | | | |
| | 25 | ,, do. ...... | 8 | 6 | 2 | 3 | | | Aug. 10.. | ,, | 100 | 0 | 0 |
| | ,, | ,, do. Jan. 6, underposted | | 10 | 0 | 0 | Mar. | 6 | ,, Cash........ | 5 | 26 | 18 | 6 |
| | | | | | | | | ,, | ,, Discount.. | ,, | 0 | 13 | 9 |
| | | | | 182 | 10 | 7 | | | | | 182 | 10 | 7 |

* Posted incorrectly, to show the mode of rectifying the error. See entry, Feb. 25.

### ALEXANDER PATERSON, London.

| 1850. | | | | | | | 1850. | | | | | | |
|---|---|---|---|---|---|---|---|---|---|---|---|---|---|
| Jan. | 7 | To Goods...... | 2 | 3 | 6 | 0 | Jan. | 20 | By Cash....... | 1 | 3 | 3 | 0 |
| Feb. | 9 | „ do........ | 6 | 65 | 2 | 10 | „ | „ | „ Discount.. | „ | 0 | 3 | 0 |
| Mar. | 3 | „ do........ | 9 | 2 | 12 | 0 | „ | „ | „ Balance... | | 67 | 14 | 10 |
| | | | | 71 | 0 | 10 | | | | | 71 | 0 | 10 |
| Mar. | 31 | To Balance... | | 67 | 14 | 10 | | | | | | | |

### DAVID FALCONER, Dublin.

| 1850. | | | | | | | 1850. | | | | | | |
|---|---|---|---|---|---|---|---|---|---|---|---|---|---|
| Jan. | 7 | To Goods...... | 2 | 15 | 2 | 0 | Jan. | 7 | By Cash ....... | 1 | 15 | 2 | 0 |
| Feb. | 1 | „ do......* | 5 | 13 | 0 | 3 | Mar. | 31 | „ Goods, Feb. 1, overposted.. | „ | 10 | 0 | 0 |
| | 12 | „ do........ | 6 | 4 | 16 | 6 | | | „ „ Balance... | | 11 | 0 | 5 |
| | 28 | „ do........ | 8 | 3 | 3 | 8 | „ | | | | | | |
| | | | | 36 | 2 | 5 | | | | | 36 | 2 | 5 |
| Mar. | 31 | To Balance... | | 11 | 0 | 5 | | | | | | | |

* Posted incorrectly, to show the mode of rectifying the error. See entry on Cr. side.

### THOMAS MURRAY, Leeds.

| 1850. | | | | | | | 1850. | | | | | | |
|---|---|---|---|---|---|---|---|---|---|---|---|---|---|
| Jan. | 10 | To Goods. .... | 3 | 46 | 8 | 4 | Jan. | 31 | By Cash &disc. | 1 | 92 | 0 | 8 |
| | 20 | „ do........ | 3 | 45 | 12 | 4 | Mar. | 1 | „ Bill due May 1... | 1 | 46 | 16 | 2 |
| Feb. | 25 | „ do........ | 8 | 46 | 16 | 2 | | | „ Goods— posted in error, carried to W. Hunter's acct. | 5 | 0 | 6 | 11 |
| Mar. | 1 | „ do......* | 9 | 0 | 6 | 11 | | | | | | | |
| | | | | 139 | 3 | 9 | | | | | 139 | 3 | 9 |

* Posted incorrectly, to show the mode of rectifying the error. See entry on Cr. side.

### CHARLES SMITH, Glasgow.

| 1850. | | | | | | | 1850. | | | | | | |
|---|---|---|---|---|---|---|---|---|---|---|---|---|---|
| Jan. | 18 | To Goods...... | 3 | 172 | 12 | 6 | Feb. | 28 | By Cash....... | 3 | 176 | 4 | 0 |
| Feb. | 5 | „ do........ | 5 | 8 | 2 | 0 | „ | „ | „ Discount.. | „ | 4 | 10 | 6 |
| | 18 | „ do........ | 7 | 16 | 5 | 6 | Mar. | 4 | „ Bill due June 6... | 1 | 89 | 12 | 2 |
| | 23 | „ do........ | 8 | 73 | 6 | 8 | | | | | | | |
| | | | | 270 | 6 | 8 | | | | | 270 | 6 | 8 |

## WILLIAM WILSON, London.

| 1850. | | | | | | 1850. | | | | | | |
|---|---|---|---|---|---|---|---|---|---|---|---|---|
| Jan. | 18 | To Goods...... | 3 | 1 | 2 | 0 | Jan. | 21 | By Cash....... | 1 | 1 | 2 | 0 |
| Feb. | 11 | „ do. ...... | 6 | 3 | 7 | 6 | Mar. | 31 | „ Balance, | | | | |
| | 18 | „ do. ...... | 7 | 0 | 15 | 0 | | | carried to Bad Debts, page 13.... | | 4 | 2 | 6 |
| | | W. Wilson having become insolvent, is able to pay only a part of his a/c. The balance is carried to the d/c for " Bad Debts." | | 5 | 4 | 6 | | | | | 5 | 4 | 6 |

## JAMES TAYLOR, High Street.

| 1850. | | | | | | | 1850. | | | | | | |
|---|---|---|---|---|---|---|---|---|---|---|---|---|---|
| Jan. | 20 | To Goods...... | 4 | 2 | 5 | 0 | Feb. | 7 | By Cash....... | 3 | 3 | 16 | 6 |
| | 31 | „ do. ...... | 4 | 5 | 8 | 0 | | „ | „ Balance, | | | | |
| | | | | | | | | | carried to Bad Debts, page 13.... | | 3 | 16 | 6 |
| | | | | 7 | 13 | 0 | | | | | 7 | 13 | 0 |

## DAVID ANDERSON, Glasgow.

| 1850. | | | | | | | 1850. | | | | | | |
|---|---|---|---|---|---|---|---|---|---|---|---|---|---|
| Jan. | 20 | To Goods...... | 4 | 9 | 5 | 6 | Feb. | 12 | By Cash....... | 3 | 31 | 4 | 0 |
| Feb. | 5 | „ do. ...... | 5 | 23 | 11 | 0 | | „ | „ Discount.. | „ | 1 | 12 | 6 |
| Mar. | 6 | „ do. ...... | 9 | 56 | 10 | 9 | Mar. | 7 | „ Cash....... | 5 | 55 | 2 | 6 |
| | | | | | | | | „ | „ Discount.. | „ | 1 | 8 | 3 |
| | | | | 89 | 7 | 3 | | | | | 89 | 7 | 3 |

## ROBERT COOK, Liverpool.

| 1850. | | | | | | | 1850. | | | | | | |
|---|---|---|---|---|---|---|---|---|---|---|---|---|---|
| Jan. | 25 | To Goods...... | 4 | 11 | 8 | 0 | Feb. | 16 | By Cash....... | 3 | 35 | 14 | 6 |
| Feb. | 6 | „ do. ...... | 6 | 25 | 5 | 0 | | „ | „ Discount.. | „ | 0 | 18 | 6 |
| | | | | 36 | 13 | 0 | | | | | 36 | 13 | 0 |

## James Durham, Bristol.

| 1850. | | | | | | 1850. | | | | | |
|---|---|---|---|---|---|---|---|---|---|---|---|
| Feb. | 1 | To Goods...... | 5 | 5 6 0 | | Feb. | 16 | By Bill due June 17. | 1 | 100 0 0 |
| | 11 | ,, do. ...... | 6 | 279 11 9 | | | 25 | ,, Bill due May 25. | ,, | 50 0 0 |
| Mar. | 17 | ,, do. ...... | 11 | 30 10 3 | | Mar. | 31 | ,, Balance... | | 165 8 0 |
| | | | | 315 8 0 | | | | | | 315 8 0 |
| Mar. | 31 | To Balance... | | 165 8 0 | | | | | | |

## William Hunter, Princes Street.

| 1850. | | | | | | 1850. | | | | | |
|---|---|---|---|---|---|---|---|---|---|---|---|
| | | *from page* 1 | | 32 4 11 | | | | *from page* 1 | | 3 14 11 |
| Feb. | 17 | To Goods...... | 6 | 2 7 4 | | Mar. | 1 | By Cash....... | 5 | 29 13 0 |
| Mar. | 1 | ,, do. ...... | 9 | 0 6 11 | | | ,, | ,, Discount.. | ,, | 1 11 3 |
| | | | | 34 19 2 | | | | | | 34 19 2 |

## James Watt, Birmingham.

| 1850. | | | | | | 1850. | | | | | |
|---|---|---|---|---|---|---|---|---|---|---|---|
| Feb. | 19 | To Goods...... | 7 | 1 6 2 | | | | | | |
| | 22 | ,, do. ...... | 8 | 36 5 0 | | Mar. | 19 | By Bill due May 21. | 1 | 37 11 2 |
| | | | | 37 11 2 | | | | | | |

## John Alison, Frederick Street.

| 1850. | | | | | | 1850. | | | | | |
|---|---|---|---|---|---|---|---|---|---|---|---|
| Feb. | 20 | To Goods...... | 7 | 12 7 6 | | | | | | |
| Mar. | 12 | ,, do. ...... | 10 | 3 9 0 | | Mar. | 31 | By Amount forward. | | 15 16 6 |
| | | | | 15 16 6 | | | | | | |
| Mar. | 31 | To Amount forward. | | 15 16 6 | | | | | | |

## ROBERT HUME, Carlisle.

| 1850. | | | | | | | | 1850. | | | | | | | |
|---|---|---|---|---|---|---|---|---|---|---|---|---|---|---|---|
| Feb. | 20 | To Goods...... | 7 | | 18 | 17 | 6 | | | | | | | | |
| Mar. | 18 | „ do. ...... | 11 | | 6 | 0 | 0 | | | | | | | | |
| | 24 | „ do. ...... | 12 | | 4 | 2 | 6 | | | | | | | | |
| | | | | | — | | | Mar. | 31 | By Amount | | | | | |
| | | | | | 29 | 0 | 0 | | | forward. | | 29 | 0 | 0 | |
| Mar. | 31 | To Amount | | | | | | | | | | | | | |
| | | forward. | | | 29 | 0 | 0 | | | | | | | | |

## GEORGE ROSS, Dublin.

| 1850. | | | | | | | | 1850. | | | | | | | |
|---|---|---|---|---|---|---|---|---|---|---|---|---|---|---|---|
| Feb. | 23 | To Goods...... | 8 | | 10 | 12 | 6 | Mar. | 8 | By Cash........ | 5 | | 10 | 12 | 6 |
| Mar. | 29 | „ do. ..... | 13 | | 14 | 18 | 6 | | 30 | „ do. ...... | „ | | 14 | 11 | 0 |
| | | | | | | | | | „ | „ Discount.. | „ | | 0 | 7 | 6 |
| | | | | | 25 | 11 | 0 | | | | | | 25 | 11 | 0 |

## JOHN LAWSON, Bristol.

| 1850. | | | | | | | | 1850. | | | | | | | |
|---|---|---|---|---|---|---|---|---|---|---|---|---|---|---|---|
| Mar. | 1 | To Goods...... | 9 | | 14 | 13 | 0 | Mar. | 20 | By Bill due | | | | | |
| | 12 | „ do. ...... | 10 | | 39 | 10 | 3 | | | May 21. | 1 | | 54 | 3 | 3 |
| | | | | | 54 | 3 | 3 | | | | | | 54 | 3 | 3 |

## JAMES CAMERON, Dundee.

| 1850. | | | | | | | | 1850. | | | | | | | |
|---|---|---|---|---|---|---|---|---|---|---|---|---|---|---|---|
| Mar. | 2 | To Goods...... | 9 | | 2 | 11 | 6 | | | | | | | | |
| | 7 | „ do. ...... | 10 | | 3 | 7 | 6 | | | | | | | | |
| | 10 | „ do. ...... | „ | | 75 | 0 | 0 | | | | | | | | |
| | 22 | „ do. ...... | 12 | | 160 | 2 | 6 | | | | | | | | |
| | | | | | | | | Mar. | 31 | By Amount | | | | | |
| | | | | | 241 | 1 | 6 | | | forward. | | 241 | 1 | 6 |
| Mar. | 31 | To Amount | | | | | | | | | | | | | |
| | | forward. | | | 241 | 1 | 6 | | | | | | | | |

## WILLIAM EDMONDS, Newcastle.

| 1850. | | | | | | 1850. | | | | | |
|---|---|---|---|---|---|---|---|---|---|---|---|
| Mar. | 4 | To Goods...... | 9 | 41 | 0 | 4 | Mar. | 25 | By Bill due | | |
| | 23 | „ do. ...... | 12 | 3 | 14 | 0 | | | April 27. | 1 | 44 | 14 | 4 |
| | | | | 44 | 14 | 4 | | | | | 44 | 14 | 4 |

## THOMAS BENNETT, London.

| 1850. | | | | | | 1850. | | | | | |
|---|---|---|---|---|---|---|---|---|---|---|---|
| Mar. | 7 | To Goods...... | 10 | 19 | 10 | 0 | Mar. | 21 | By Cash...... | 5 | 19 | 0 | 0 |
| | | | | | | | | | „ „ Discount.. | „ | 0 | 10 | 0 |
| | | | | 19 | 10 | 0 | | | | | 19 | 10 | 0 |

## CHARLES DAVIDSON, Charlotte Street.

| 1850. | | | | | | 1850. | | | | | |
|---|---|---|---|---|---|---|---|---|---|---|---|
| Mar. | 9 | To Goods...... | 10 | 0 | 5 | 0 | | | | | | |
| | 26 | „ do. ...... | 13 | 1 | 11 | 0 | | | | | | |
| | | | | 1 | 16 | 0 | Mar. | 31 | By Amount forward.. | | 1 | 16 | 0 |
| Mar. | 31 | To Amount forward... | | 1 | 16 | 0 | | | | | | |

## JAMES MILNE, London.

| 1850. | | | | | | 1850. | | | | | |
|---|---|---|---|---|---|---|---|---|---|---|---|
| Mar. | 10 | To Goods...... | 10 | 32 | 5 | 10 | | | | | | |
| | 15 | „ do. ...... | 11 | 50 | 4 | 2 | | | | | | |
| | 23 | „ do. ...... | 12 | 37 | 3 | 0 | | | | | | |
| | | | | 119 | 13 | 0 | Mar. | 31 | By Amount forward. | | 119 | 13 | 0 |
| Mar. | 31 | To Amount forward... | | 119 | 13 | 0 | | | | | | |

### ALEXANDER MORRISON, Greenock.

| 1850. | | | | | | 1850. | | | | | | |
|---|---|---|---|---|---|---|---|---|---|---|---|---|
| Mar. | 14 | To Goods...... | 11 | 8 | 13 | 3 | Mar. | 15 | By Cash....... | 5 | 8 | 9 | 0 |
| | | | | | | | " | | " Discount.. | " | 0 | 4 | 3 |
| | | | | 8 | 13 | 3 | | | | | 8 | 13 | 3 |

### DAVID MITCHELL, Liverpool.

| 1850. | | | | | | | 1850. | | | | | | |
|---|---|---|---|---|---|---|---|---|---|---|---|---|---|
| Mar. | 17 | To Goods...... | 11 | 65 | 1 | 8 | Mar. | 27 | By Bill due | | | | |
| | 24 | " do. ....... | 12 | 25 | 16 | 0 | | | June 29.. | 1 | 90 | 17 | 8 |
| | | | | 90 | 17 | 8 | | | | | 90 | 17 | 8 |

### JAMES STEWART & Co., Leeds.

| 1850. | | | | | | | 1850. | | | | | | |
|---|---|---|---|---|---|---|---|---|---|---|---|---|---|
| Jan. | 4 | To Bill due | | | | | Jan. | 1 | By Goods...... | 1 | 315 | 11 | 2 |
| | | Feb. 7... | 3 | 315 | 11 | 2 | Feb. | 16 | " do. ...... | 4 | 51 | 5 | 0 |
| Feb. | 27 | " Bill due | | | | | | | | | | | |
| | | Aug. 30. | " | 51 | 5 | 0 | | | | | | | |
| | | | | 366 | 16 | 2 | | | | | 366 | 16 | 2 |

### EDWARD JOHNSTON & Co., Manchester.

| 1850. | | | | | | | 1850. | | | | | | |
|---|---|---|---|---|---|---|---|---|---|---|---|---|---|
| Jan. | 5 | To Cash ........ | 2 | 107 | 14 | 0 | Jan. | 1 | By Goods...... | 1 | 42 | 17 | 9 |
| | " | " Discount... | " | 5 | 13 | 9 | | 2 | " do. ...... | " | 70 | 10 | 0 |
| Feb. | 22 | " Bill due | | | | | Feb. | 4 | " do. ...... | 3 | 57 | 3 | 0 |
| | | May 5... | 3 | 200 | 0 | 0 | | 19 | " do. ...... | 4 | 211 | 9 | 8 |
| Mar. | 2 | " Bill due | | | | | | 20 | " do. ...... | " | 84 | 15 | 11 |
| | | May 25. | " | 153 | 8 | 7 | | | | | | | |
| | | | | 466 | 16 | 4 | | | | | 466 | 16 | 4 |

### ALLAN & BELL, London.

| 1850 | | | | £ | s | d | 1850 | | | | £ | s | d |
|---|---|---|---|---|---|---|---|---|---|---|---|---|---|
| Mar. | 31 | To Goods on hand.... | | 5 | 10 | 6 | Jan. | 1 | By Goods...... | 1 | 6 | 10 | 0 |
| | | ,, ,, Commission | 13 | 2 | 9 | 0 | Feb. | 20 | ,, do. ...... | 4 | 23 | 10 | 6 |
| | | ,, ,, Cash.......... | 6 | 22 | 1 | 0 | | | | | | | |
| | | | | 30 | 0 | 6 | | | | | 30 | 0 | 6 |
| | | | | | | | Apr. | 1 | By Goods on hand... | | 5 | 10 | 6 |

### ROBERT GRAY, Bradford.

| 1850 | | | | £ | s | d | 1850 | | | | £ | s | d |
|---|---|---|---|---|---|---|---|---|---|---|---|---|---|
| Jan. | 8 | To Bill due Jan. 21. | 3 | 260 | 5 | 0 | Jan. | 2 | By Goods...... | 1 | 260 | 5 | 0 |
| Mar. | 30 | ,, Bill due May 3.. | ,, | 186 | 14 | 6 | Feb. | 10 | ,, do. ...... | 4 | 14 | 0 | 0 |
| | | | | | | | Mar. | 15 | ,, do. ...... | 6 | 172 | 14 | 6 |
| | | | | 446 | 19 | 6 | | | | | 446 | 19 | 6 |

### ALEX. JARDINE & Co., Leith.

| 1850 | | | | £ | s | d | 1850 | | | | £ | s | d |
|---|---|---|---|---|---|---|---|---|---|---|---|---|---|
| Feb. | 28 | To Cash........ | 4 | 190 | 0 | 0 | Jan. | 2 | By Goods...... | 1 | 25 | 10 | 0 |
| | ,, | ,, Discount... | ,, | 10 | 0 | 0 | | 31 | ,, do. ...... | 2 | 455 | 1 | 2 |
| | ,, | ,, Bill due May 1... | 3 | 100 | 0 | 0 | | | | | | | |
| Mar. | 31 | ,, Balance..... | | 180 | 11 | 2 | | | | | | | |
| | | | | 480 | 11 | 2 | | | | | 480 | 11 | 2 |
| | | | | | | | Mar. | 31 | By Balance... | | 180 | 11 | 2 |

### ROBERTSON & SIMPSON, Glasgow.

| 1850 | | | | £ | s | d | 1850 | | | | £ | s | d |
|---|---|---|---|---|---|---|---|---|---|---|---|---|---|
| Jan. | 12 | To Cash........ | 2 | 203 | 10 | 0 | Jan. | 12 | By Goods...... | 2 | 214 | 4 | 6 |
| | ,, | ,, Discount... | ,, | 10 | 14 | 6 | Feb. | 4 | ,, do. ...... | 3 | 22 | 10 | 0 |
| Mar. | 31 | ,, Balance .... | | 100 | 10 | 0 | | 25 | ,, do. ...... | 4 | 78 | 0 | 0 |
| | | | | 314 | 14 | 6 | | | | | 314 | 14 | 6 |
| | | | | | | | Mar. | 31 | By Balance... | | 100 | 10 | 0 |

### JOHN AINSLIE & SONS, Liverpool.

| 1850. | | | | | | | 1850. | | | | | | | |
|---|---|---|---|---|---|---|---|---|---|---|---|---|---|---|
| Feb. | 12 | To Bill due | | | | | Jan. | 15 | By Goods...... | 2 | | 5 | 5 | 2 |
| | | Mar. 15.. | 3 | 150 | 0 | 0 | Feb. | 10 | ,, do. ...... | 3 | | 186 | 3 | 0 |
| Mar. | 24 | ,, do. May 27. | ,, | 100 | 0 | 0 | Mar. | 19 | ,, do. ...... | 6 | | 110 | 17 | 0 |
| | 31 | ,, Balance..... | | 52 | 5 | 2 | | | | | | | | |
| | | | | 302 | 5 | 2 | | | | | | 302 | 5 | 2 |
| | | | | | | | Mar. | 31 | By Balance... | | | 52 | 5 | 2 |

### JOHN MILLER, Edinburgh.

| 1850. | | | | | | | 1850. | | | | | | | |
|---|---|---|---|---|---|---|---|---|---|---|---|---|---|---|
| Jan. | 20 | To Cash........ | 2 | 32 | 18 | 6 | Jan. | 20 | By Goods..... | 2 | | 33 | 15 | 6 |
| | ,, | ,, Discount... | ,, | 0 | 17 | 0 | | | | | | | | |
| | | | | 33 | 15 | 6 | | | | | | 33 | 15 | 6 |

### JAMES DALTON, London.

| 1850. | | | | | | | 1850. | | | | | | | |
|---|---|---|---|---|---|---|---|---|---|---|---|---|---|---|
| Feb. | 12 | To Cash........ | 4 | 93 | 9 | 6 | Jan. | 25 | By Goods...... | 2 | | 98 | 8 | 0 |
| | ,, | ,, Discount... | ,, | 4 | 18 | 6 | | | | | | | | |
| | | | | 98 | 8 | 0 | | | | | | 98 | 8 | 0 |

### THOMAS GRAHAM, Belfast.

| 1850. | | | | | | | 1850. | | | | | | | |
|---|---|---|---|---|---|---|---|---|---|---|---|---|---|---|
| Mar. | 5 | To Bill due | | | | | Feb. | 1 | By Goods...... | 3 | | 98 | 0 | 0 |
| | | April 8... | 3 | 100 | 9 | 0 | | 19 | ,, do ...... | 4 | | 2 | 9 | 0 |
| | | | | 100 | 9 | 0 | | | | | | 100 | 9 | 0 |

E

### WALTER KENNEDY, Paisley.

| 1850. | | | | | | | 1850. | | | | | | |
|---|---|---|---|---|---|---|---|---|---|---|---|---|---|
| Feb. | 9 | To Cash....... | 4 | 17 | 11 | 0 | Feb. | 1 | By Goods....... | 3 | 18 | 0 | 0 |
| " | | " Discount.. | " | 0 | 9 | 0 | | | | | | | |
| | | | | 18 | 0 | 0 | | | | | 18 | 0 | 0 |

### THOMAS THOMSON, London.

| 1850. | | | | | | | 1850. | | | | | | |
|---|---|---|---|---|---|---|---|---|---|---|---|---|---|
| Feb. | 28 | To Bill due | | | | | Feb. | 28 | By Goods..... | 4 | 53 | 13 | 0 |
| | | March 31 | 3 | 30 | 0 | 0 | Mar. | 10 | " do. ..... | 5 | 33 | 10 | 0 |
| Mar. | 31 | " Balance... | | 57 | 3 | 0 | | | | | | | |
| | | | | 87 | 3 | 0 | | | | | 87 | 3 | 0 |
| | | | | | | | Mar. | 31 | By Balance... | | 57 | 3 | 0 |

### GEORGE BROOKS, London.

| 1850. | | | | | | | 1850. | | | | | | |
|---|---|---|---|---|---|---|---|---|---|---|---|---|---|
| Mar. | 6 | To Cash....... | 6 | 135 | 5 | 6 | Mar. | 1 | By Goods....... | 5 | 142 | 8 | 0 |
| " | | " Discount.. | " | 7 | 2 | 6 | | 31 | " do......... | 6 | 9 | 9 | 6 |
| | 13 | " Balance... | | 9 | 9 | 6 | | | | | | | |
| | | | | 151 | 17 | 6 | | | | | 151 | 17 | 6 |
| | | | | | | | Mar. | 31 | By Balance... | | 9 | 9 | 6 |

### ALEXANDER HUNTER, Manchester.

| 1850. | | | | | | | 1850. | | | | | | |
|---|---|---|---|---|---|---|---|---|---|---|---|---|---|
| Mar. | 1 | To Cash....... | 6 | 45 | 14 | 0 | Mar. | 1 | By Goods....... | 5 | 46 | 17 | 8 |
| " | | " Discount.. | " | 1 | 3 | 8 | | 25 | " do. ..... | 6 | 37 | 17 | 0 |
| | 31 | " Balance... | | 37 | 17 | 0 | | | | | | | |
| | | | | 84 | 14 | 8 | | | | | 84 | 14 | 8 |
| | | | | | | | Mar. | 31 | By Balance... | | 37 | 17 | 0 |

## ROBERT TODD, Glasgow.

| 1850. | | | | | | | 1850. | | | | | | | | |
|---|---|---|---|---|---|---|---|---|---|---|---|---|---|---|---|
| Mar. | 19 | To Bill due | | | | | Mar. | 4 | By Goods.... | 5 | | 14 | 16 | 6 |
| | | June 22. | 3 | 29 | 7 | 6 | | 19 | „ do. .... | 6 | | 14 | 11 | 0 |
| | | | | 29 | 7 | 6 | | | | | | 29 | 7 | 6 |

## UNION BANK.

| 1850. | | | | | | | 1850. | | | | | | | | |
|---|---|---|---|---|---|---|---|---|---|---|---|---|---|---|---|
| Jan. | 1 | To Cash...... | 2 | 990 | 0 | 0 | Jan. | 5 | By Cash...... | 1 | | 110 | 0 | 0 |
| | 20 | „ do. ....... | „ | 175 | 0 | 0 | | 12 | „ do. ....... | „ | | 60 | 0 | 0 |
| | 31 | „ do. ....... | „ | 90 | 0 | 0 | | 20 | „ do. ...... | „ | | 140 | 0 | 0 |
| Feb. | 5 | „ do. ...... | 4 | 70 | 0 | 0 | Feb. | 7 | „ do. ...... | 3 | | 320 | 0 | 0 |
| | 16 | „ do. ...... | „ | 40 | 0 | 0 | | 12 | „ do. ...... | „ | | 40 | 0 | 0 |
| Mar. | 7 | „ do. ...... | 6 | 58 | 0 | 0 | Mar. | 6 | „ do. ...... | 5 | | 20 | 0 | 0 |
| | 21 | „ do. ...... | „ | 80 | 0 | 0 | | 15 | „ do. ...... | „ | | 150 | 0 | 0 |
| | | | | | | | | 31 | „ Balance.. | | | 663 | 0 | 0 |
| | | | | 1503 | 0 | 0 | | | | | | 1503 | 0 | 0 |
| Mar. | 31 | To Balance.. | | 663 | 0 | 0 | | | | | | | | |

Interest, when allowed, requires to be charged to the Bank.

## SHOP FURNITURE.

| 1850. | | | | | | | 1850. | | | | | | | |
|---|---|---|---|---|---|---|---|---|---|---|---|---|---|---|
| Jan. | 20 | To Cash...... | 2 | 107 | 10 | 0 | Mar. | 31 | By Depreciation | | | | | |
| | | | | | | | | | 5 ꝑ cent. carried to Trade Expenses, page 13. | | | 5 | 7 | 6 |
| | | This is the sum paid out for furniture. | | | | | | | „ Balance.. | | | 102 | 2 | 6 |
| | | | | 107 | 10 | 0 | | | | | | 107 | 10 | 0 |
| Mar. | 31 | To Balance. | | 102 | 2 | 6 | | | | | | | | |

## BAD DEBTS.

| 1850. | | | | | | | |
|---|---|---|---|---|---|---|---|
| Feb. | 7 | J. Taylor's *a/c*—balance.............................. | 4 | | 3 | 16 | 6 |
| Mar. | 31 | W. Wilson's *a/c*—balance.......................... | „ | | 4 | 2 | 6 |
| | | | | | 7 | 19 | 0 |

## TRADE

| 1850. | | | Rent&Taxes | Salaries. | Sundries. | | | | |
|---|---|---|---|---|---|---|---|---|---|
| Jan. | 31 | To Cash.................. | 3 0 0 | 15 1 6 | 0 10 0 | 2 | 18 | 11 | 6 |
| Feb. | 28 | „ do. .................. | 36 10 0 | 16 9 0 | 0 19 1 | 4 | 53 | 18 | 1 |
| Mar. | 31 | „ do. .................. | | 12 10 0 | 2 16 8 | 6 | 15 | 6 | 8 |
| | „ | „ Shop-Furniture— | | | | | | | |
| | | Depreciation......... | | | | 12 | 5 | 7 | 6 |
| | | | 39 10 0 | 44 0 6 | 4 5 9 | | 93 | 3 | 9 |

The accounts for Trade Expenses and Bad Debts are in Single Entry merely added up, without being balanced by an entry on the opposite side: they may,

## PROFIT (OR, PROFIT AND LOSS).

| 1850. | | | | | | |
|---|---|---|---|---|---|---|
| Jan. | 1 | To Capital at this date, (see J. A.'s *a/c*, Jan. 1)..... | 13 | 1000 | 0 | 0 |
| Mar. | 31 | „ Interest, January to March, carried to J. A.'s *a/c*.. | „ | 12 | 10 | 0 |
| | „ | „ Profit,     „          „      „ .. | „ | 294 | 0 | 10 |
| | | | | 1306 | 10 | 10 |

By adding to the *nett* profit the amount of Trade Expenses and Bad Debts, the *gross* profit is ascertained, as on other side.

## JOHN ADAMS.

| 1850. | | | | | | |
|---|---|---|---|---|---|---|
| Jan. | 27 | To Cash................................................. | 2 | 20 | 0 | 0 |
| Feb. | 25 | „ do. ................................................ | 4 | 20 | 0 | 0 |
| Mar. | 3 | „ do. ................................................ | 6 | 40 | 0 | 0 |
| | 30 | „ do. ................................................ | „ | 10 | 0 | 0 |
| | 31 | „ Balance forward.................................. | | 1216 | 10 | 10 |
| | | | | 1306 | 10 | 10 |

## BAD DEBTS.

| 1850. | | | | |
|---|---|---|---|---|
| Mar. 31 | By Amount, loss—carried to Goods *a/c*......... | | 7 | 19 | 0 |

## EXPENSES.

| 1850. | | | | |
|---|---|---|---|---|
| | In this account is shown the manner of entering some of the particulars of the Trade Expenses, which may be done more or less minutely, according to circumstances. The sum-total of each month is the amount of the entries in the Cash-Book for Trade Expenses, the particulars being noted on a piece of paper and entered as on other side. Care must be taken to see that the amount of the particulars agrees with the sum-total. | | | | |
| Mar. 31 | By Amount, loss—carried to Goods *a/c*......... | | 93 | 3 | 9 |

however, be balanced off, as above, if the account for " Goods " (page 70) is adopted.

## PROFIT (OR, PROFIT AND LOSS).

| 1850. | | | | | |
|---|---|---|---|---|---|
| Mar. 31 | By Capital at this date, (see Balance Sheet)........ | 14 | 1216 | 10 | 10 |
| „ | „ Cash to J. Adams, January to March............ | 13 | 90 | 0 | 0 |
| | | | 1306 | 10 | 10 |

Nett Profit, as above......................................£294  0 10
Trade Expenses, as per Ledger.............................. 93  3  9
Bad Debts,      do.       ........................  7 19  0
      Gross Profit.........................................£395  3  7

## JOHN ADAMS.

| 1850. | | | | | |
|---|---|---|---|---|---|
| Jan. 1 | By Cash..................................... | 1 | 1000 | 0 | 0 |
| Mar. 31 | „ Interest, Jan. to Mar., brought from Profit *a/c* ... | 13 | 12 | 10 | 0 |
| | „ Profit     „     „     „   ... | | 294 | 0 | 10 |
| | | | 1306 | 10 | 10 |
| Mar. 31 | By Balance..................................... | | 1216 | 10 | 10 |
| | This corresponds with the amount of Capital, as per Balance Sheet. | | | | |

## BALANCE SHEET.

*Dr.*            JOHN ADAMS.

| 1850. | | | | |
|---|---|---|---|---|
| Mar. 31 | To Accounts owing by J. A., as per Ledger...<br>This is the sum-total: the particulars are entered in the "Account-Book." See page 72. | 415 | 18 | 0 |
| | „ Bills owing by J. A., as per Bill-Book...... | 921 | 4 | 7 |
| | | 1337 | 2 | 7 |
| | „ BALANCE—NETT CAPITAL...................... | 1216 | 10 | 10 |
| | | 2553 | 13 | 5 |

*(Bought.)*        GOODS.

| 1850 | | | Credit.* | Cash.† | Total | Deduct Discount.‡ | | | |
|---|---|---|---|---|---|---|---|---|---|
| Jan. 31 | To Purchases | | 1527 18 3 | 8 0 0 | 1535 18 3 | 17 5 3 | 1518 | 13 | 0 |
| Feb. 28 | „ do. | | 900 19 1 | 7 12 0 | 908 11 1 | 15 7 6 | 893 | 3 | 7 |
| Mar 31 | „ do. | | 583 1 2 | 23 16 4 | 606 17 6 | 8 6 2 | 598 | 11 | 4 |
| | | | 3011 18 6 | 39 8 4 | 3051 6 10 | 40 18 11 | 3010 | 7 | 11 |
| | *Deduct* Discount on unsettled *a/cts.* due by J. Adams......<br>See "Account-Book," p. 72. | | | | | | 21 | 17 | 10 |
| | | | | | | | 2988 | 10 | 1 |
| | „ Trade Expenses............................................. | | | | | | 93 | 3 | 9 |
| | „ Bad Debts.................................................. | | | | | | 7 | 19 | 0 |
| | „ Profit (including interest)............................. | | | | | | 306 | 10 | 10 |
| | | | | | | | 3396 | 3 | 8 |

Directions for keeping this account are given at page 22.

\* These are the monthly sums-total of the Invoice-Book.

† These are the monthly sums-total of the entries for " Cash Purchases " in the Cash-Book : the particulars being noted on a piece of paper, and the amount then filled in here.

‡ These are the monthly sums-total of the Discount columns on the *Paid* side of the Cash-Book, and are deducted from the amount of Goods, to show the *nett* sum.

In making up a new account, say at December 31, the discount on unsettled accounts, now deducted on each side, must be allowed for, as follows :—If the discount on unsettled accounts, on either side, at December 31 is greater than **at** present, say £45, 10s. 0d. instead of £39, 18s. 1d., the difference

## BALANCE SHEET.

JOHN ADAMS.                                          *Cr.*

| 1850. | | | | | |
|---|---|---|---|---|---|
| Mar. | 31 | By Goods on hand, as per Stock-Book......... | | 393 13 2 | |
| | | „  Shop Furniture............................... | 12 | 102 2 6 | |
| | | | | 495 15 8 | |
| | | „  Accounts owing to J. A., as per Ledger... | | 758 4 8 | |
| | | This is the sum-total: the particulars are entered in the "Account-Book." See page 72. | | | |
| | | „  Bills owing to J. A., as per Bill-Book...... | | 613 14 9 | |
| | | „  Cash in Bank............................. | 12 | 663 0 0 | |
| | | „  Cash on hand, as per Cash-Book............ | | 22 18 4 | |
| | | | | 2553 13 5 | |

GOODS.                                          (*Sold.*)

| 1850 | | | Credit.* | Cash.† | Total. | Deduct Discount.‡ | | |
|---|---|---|---|---|---|---|---|---|
| Jan. | 31 | By Sales...... | 1372 9 7 | 14 19 6 | 1387 9 1 | 15 6 3 | 1372 2 10 | |
| Feb. | 28 | „  do. ...... | 802 10 4 | 13 5 6 | 815 15 10 | 12 8 9 | 803 7 1 | |
| Mar | 31 | „  do. ...... | 847 10 2 | 21 2 9 | 868 12 11 | 7 4 9 | 861 8 2 | |
| | | | 3022 10 1 | 49 7 9 | 3071 17 10 | 34 19 9 | 3036 18 1 | |
| | | *Deduct* Discount on unsettled *a/cts.* due to J. Adams...... | | | | | 39 18 1 | |
| | | See "Account-Book," p. 72. | | | | | | |
| | | | | | | | 2997 0 0 | |
| | | „  Goods on Hand............................. | | | | | 393 13 2 | |
| | | „  do.        do.  on Commission.................. | | | | | 5 10 6 | |
| | | The Goods on Commission require to be entered here, as they are included along with the Credit Purchases on the other side. | | | | | | |
| | | | | | | | 3396 3 8 | |
| | | The Goods on hand require to be carried forward to the Dr. side, to begin a new account on April 1. | | | | | | |

\* These are the monthly sums-total of the Day-Book.

† These are the monthly sums-total of the entries for " Cash Sales " in the Cash-Book: the particulars being noted on a piece of paper, and the amount then filled in here.

‡ These are the monthly sums-total of the Discount columns on the *Received* side of the Cash-Book, and are deducted from the amount of Goods, to show the *nett* sum.

only between the two sums—viz. £5, 11s. 11d.—not the sum itself, must be deducted from the " Goods " account. If, on the other hand, the discount is less at December 31, instead of deducting the discount, the difference between the two sums must be *added* to the " Goods " account.

## Accounts **owing by** J. Adams, March 31, 1850.

| | | £ | s | d | | | |
|---|---|---:|---:|---:|---|---|---|
| Jardine & Co.................................... | 9 | 180 | 11 | 2 | | | |
| Robertson & Simpson, Glasgow.......... | ,, | 100 | 10 | 0 | | | |
| Ainslie & Son, Liverpool.................... | 10 | 52 | 5 | 2 | | | |
| T. Thomson, London........................ | 11 | 57 | 3 | 0 | | | |
| G. Brooks, London............................ | ,, | 9 | 9 | 6 | | | |
| A. Hunter, Manchester...................... | ,, | 37 | 17 | 0 | | | |
| | | | | | | | |
| | | 437 | 15 | 10 | | | |
| Deduct 5 % for Discount at settlement | | 21 | 17 | 10 | | | |
| | | 415 | 18 | 0 | | | |

The Account-Book contains a list of all the Accounts owing to and by J. Adams, as ascertained from the various Accounts in the Ledger.

## Accounts **owing to** J. Adams, March 31, 1850.

| | | £ | s | d | | | |
|---|---|---:|---:|---:|---|---|---|
| James Brown, George Street................ | 1 | 0 | 10 | 3 | | | |
| G. Innes, Liverpool............................ | ,, | 15 | 15 | 0 | | | |
| R. Porteous, Bristol............................ | ,, | 19 | 3 | 3 | | | |
| C. Chadwick, Manchester.................... | 2 | 111 | 4 | 0 | | | |
| A. Paterson, London.......................... | 3 | 67 | 14 | 10 | | | |
| D. Falconer, Dublin............................ | ,, | 11 | 0 | 5 | | | |
| J. Durham, Bristol............................. | 5 | 165 | 8 | 0 | | | |
| J. Alison, Frederick Street................ | ,, | 15 | 16 | 6 | | | |
| R. Hume, Carlisle.............................. | 6 | 29 | 0 | 0 | | | |
| J. Cameron, Dundee.......................... | ,, | 241 | 1 | 6 | | | |
| C. Davidson, Charlotte Street............. | 7 | 1 | 16 | 0 | | | |
| J. Milne, London............................... | ,, | 119 | 13 | 0 | | | |
| | | 798 | 2 | 9 | | | |
| Deduct 5 % for Discount at settlement | | 39 | 18 | 1 | | | |
| | | 758 | 4 | 8 | | | |

When any of the Accounts are paid, the sums are entered in the outer money columns here left blank: it can thus be seen at a glance what accounts are settled.

This book is used for keeping an account of the *quantities* of goods received into, or sent out from the warehouse. It is suitable chiefly in those cases where goods are bought and sold in considerable quantities at a time.

By means of the Warehouse-Book, the *quantity* sold and on hand of any description of goods can be ascertained at once, on turning up the page where the account is kept. It is necessary to have an Index of the different accounts entered.

The mode of keeping the book varies according to the nature of the business. In the following specimen is shown a method adapted to ordinary cases.

The two accounts below are for the Sugar and Tea entered in the Invoice-Book as received from J. Ainslie & Son, and A. Jardine & Co., and which appear in the preceding Day-Book as sold to the various parties mentioned.

The quantities are supposed to be entered on the *Dr.* side, as below, at the time of being received; and on the *Cr.* side when they are sold.

### SUGAR.

| 1850 | | | Hhds. | 1850 | | | Day-Bk page. | Hhds. |
|---|---|---|---|---|---|---|---|---|
| Feb. | 10 | To Received from— J. Ainslie & Son, Liverpool.... | 6 | Mar. | 4 | By Sold to W. Edmonds | 9 | 1 |
| | | | | | 12 | ,, ,, J. Cameron | 12 | 4 |
| | | | | | 31 | ,, On hand, forward | | 1 |
| | | | 6 | | | | | 6 |
| Apr. | 1 | To On hand....... | 1 | | | | | |

### TEA.

| 1850 | | | Chests. | 1850 | | | Day-Bk page. | Chests. |
|---|---|---|---|---|---|---|---|---|
| Jan. | 31 | To Received from— A. Jardine & Co., Leith...... | 4 | Feb. | 25 | By Sold to T. Bladworth | 8 | 1 |
| | | | | Mar. | 15 | ,, ,, J. Milne...... | 11 | 3 |
| | | | 4 | | | | | 4 |

The Warehouse-Book to be written out next to the Stock-Book, page 54.

# DOUBLE ENTRY.

BOOK-KEEPING by Double Entry is so called because all the entries in the Day-Book, Invoice-Book, Cash-Book, and Bill-Book, are posted *twice* into the Ledger.

The entries are *first* posted, as in Single Entry, to the *Dr.* or *Cr.* of their respective accounts, and then a *second* time to the *Dr.* or *Cr.* of some other account. The entries first posted to the *Dr.* side of the Ledger, are posted the second time to the *Cr.* side; and those first posted to the *Cr.* side, are the second time posted to the *Dr.* side.

The system pursued in Double Entry serves the following purposes to persons in business :—

1. To test the accuracy of the posting : the second posting being a check on the first, as will be seen at page 77.

2. To show the amount of goods bought and sold during the year, or for any other given time.

3. To show the profit or loss on the various departments of the business.

4. To keep distinct accounts, under their several heads, of the different branches of stock in trade, and other property.

Double Entry is used chiefly by wholesale merchants and others whose transactions are on a large scale, and who dispose of goods in considerable quantities at a time.

It is less suitable for retail trades, in which there are numerous small entries : it may, however, be used with advantage to a partial extent, by posting the Day-Book, Invoice-Book, and Cash-Book, in the manner described at page 22, under Single Entry.

JOURNAL.—It is usual to employ in Double Entry what is termed a " Journal;" but this book, though useful or necessary in many cases, is not essential, and has been dispensed with in this system.

## POSTING THE DAY-BOOK.

The Day-Book may be posted in two ways—

I. The simplest method is the following, being the same as that employed in Single Entry :—

FIRST POSTING.

Post all the entries to the *Dr.* of the various **persons.**

SECOND POSTING.

> At the end of every month, add up the sum-totals that have been filled into the *outer* columns, and post the amount, being the total of goods sold, to the *Cr.* of an account to be opened in the Ledger under the head of " Goods," using the words, " By Credit Sales."

This mode of Double Entry is suitable for those cases where the merchant wishes to know merely the total amount of goods sold, of whatever kind, and the profit on the whole, without requiring separate accounts of the different kinds of goods, and the profit on each. It is the method already described under Single Entry, p. 22.

**Example.**
*January* 1, 1850.

| | | Particulars | | | Sums-Total | | |
|---|---|---|---|---|---|---|---|
| | John Turner, 10 Charlotte Street. | | | | | | |
| 1 | To 16 Yards Sup. Black Cloth.... 15/6 | 12 | 8 | 0 | | | |
| | „  14  „  „  Brown do. .... 15/9 | 11 | 0 | 6 | 23 | 8 | 6 |
| | *—5th.—* | | | | | | |
| | James Edwards, 20 Princes Street. | | | | | | |
| 1 | To 2 Brown's Moral Philosophy.. 13/6 | 1 | 7 | 0 | | | |
| | „  2 Campbell's Poems. ............ 3/9 | | 7 | 6 | 1 | 14 | 6 |
| | *—27th.—* | | | | | | |
| | Walter Forbes, George Street. | | | | | | |
| 3 | To 6 Pair Kid Gloves ............... 3/6 | 1 | 1 | 0 | | | |
| | „  4  „  Cotton Socks............ 1/ | 0 | 4 | 0 | | | |
| | „ 25 Yards Carpeting............... 2/11 | 3 | 12 | 11 | 4 | 17 | 11 |
| | *—31st.—* | | | | | | |
| 12 | Goods—*Cr.* By Credit Sales.............. | | | | 30 | 0 | 11 |

At the *first* posting, these entries will appear in the Ledger at the *Dr.* of each person's account.

JOHN TURNER, 10 Charlotte Street.

| 1850. Jan. | 1 | To Goods.. | 1 | 23 | 8 | 6 | 1850. | | | | | |
|---|---|---|---|---|---|---|---|---|---|---|---|---|

JAMES EDWARDS, 20 Princes Street.

| 1850. Jan. | 5 | To Goods.. | 1 | 1 | 14 | 6 | 1850. | | | | | |
|---|---|---|---|---|---|---|---|---|---|---|---|---|

WALTER FORBES, George Street.

| 1850. Jan. | 27 | To Goods.. | 3 | 4 | 17 | 11 | 1850. | | | | | |
|---|---|---|---|---|---|---|---|---|---|---|---|---|

At the *second* posting, the sum-total of these entries will appear at the *Cr.* of the account opened under the head of " Goods."

GOODS.

| 1850. | | | | | | 1850. Jan. | 31 | By Credit sales | 4 | 30 | 0 | 11 |
|---|---|---|---|---|---|---|---|---|---|---|---|---|

If the first and second posting be correct, on adding together the sums posted to the *Dr.* of the above accounts, they will be found equal in amount to the sum posted to the *Cr.* of the "Goods" account, it being the same sums that have in this way been posted to the two opposite sides of the Ledger. Hence, as formerly stated, the second posting is a check on the accuracy of the first.

The amount of goods *sold* on credit during the month, is shown by this entry on the *Cr.* side of the account for "Goods."

The amount of goods *bought* on credit is shown in the same way, by posting the monthly amount of the Invoice-Book to the *Dr.* side of the " Goods" account.

The amount of goods bought and sold for cash, is shown by posting these items from the Cash-Book to the " Goods" account.

## POSTING THE DAY-BOOK.

II.—The following is another mode of posting the Day-Book, and is that which is used in the present system :—

In many wholesale concerns, it is necessary to keep *separate* accounts for the different kinds of goods sold, or at least for such as are sold in large quantities, as wine, sugar, coffee, &c. in order that the merchant may know how much is sold, and what is the profit on each article.

For this purpose, in entering goods into the Day-Book of which *separate* accounts are to be kept, the sum-total of each entry is marked in the *inner* columns, immediately below the particulars; and in entering goods, of which no special account is to be kept, but which are to be posted to a general account for " Goods," the sum-total of each entry is extended to the *outer* columns.

This distinction having been carefully attended to, the posting is conducted as follows :—

FIRST POSTING.

Post all the entries to the *Dr.* of the various persons, the same as in Single Entry.

SECOND POSTING.

1. Post the entries for goods, of which *separate* accounts are to be kept (being those of which the sums-total are marked into the inner columns), to the *Cr.* of accounts to be opened under their respective heads, such as Paper, Tea, Sugar, Goods on commission, or whatever title the nature of the entry may require.

2. Add up at the end of every month the sums-total extended to the *outer* columns (being the goods of which no special account is to be kept), and post the amount to the *Cr.* of an account to be opened under the general title of " Goods."

The pages of the Ledger to which the entries have been posted the *first* time, are marked on the margin opposite the *name* of each person; and the pages of the *second* posting, below the others opposite the *goods* of each entry.

A mark $\sqrt{}$ is made against those entries that have been extended to the outer columns, in order to be posted monthly, to show that this has been done; and the page in the Ledger to which the sum-total at the end of the month has been posted, is marked on the margin opposite the addition.

As in the former case, if the posting is correct, the amounts posted to the *Dr.* sides, will be equal to those posted to the *Cr.* sides of the Ledger.

## Example.
### *January* 1, 1850.

| | | | | | | | | |
|---|---|---|---|---|---|---|---|---|
| **1** | | | | | | | | |
| **11** | James Arnold, London. | | | | | | | |
| | To Paper—100 Reams Demy ..... 18/6 | 92 | 10 | 0 | | | | |

As a separate account is to be kept for "Paper," the sum is not extended to the outer columns.

The entry is first posted to the *Dr.* of J. Arnold, and then to the *Cr.* of an account to be opened under the head of "Paper," using the words, "By Amount sold to J. Arnold."

*—5th.—*

| | | | | | | | | |
|---|---|---|---|---|---|---|---|---|
| **1** | John Turner, 10 Charlotte Street. | | | | | | | |
| √ | To 16 Yards Superfine Black Cloth, 15/6 | 12 | 8 | 0 | | | | |
| | „ 14 „ „ Brown do. 15/9 | 11 | 0 | 6 | 23 | 8 | 6 |

As no separate account is to be kept for cloth, the sum-total is extended to the outer columns, a mark √ being made on the margin to show that this has been done.

The entry is first posted to the *Dr.* of J. Turner, and at the end of the month to the *Cr.* of the general account to be opened under the head of "Goods."

*—27th.—*

| | | | | | | | | |
|---|---|---|---|---|---|---|---|---|
| **3** | Walter Forbes, George Street. | | | | | | | |
| √ | To 6 Pair Kid Gloves.............. 3/6 | 1 | 1 | 0 | | | | |
| | „ 4 „ Cotton Socks........... 1/ | 0 | 4 | 0 | | | | |
| | „ 25 Yards Carpeting ............ 2/11 | 3 | 12 | 11 | 4 | 17 | 11 |

This is posted in the same way as the previous entry, to the general account for "Goods."

*—28th.—*

| | | | | | | | | |
|---|---|---|---|---|---|---|---|---|
| **2** | | | | | | | | |
| **14** | Thomas Dundas, Manchester. | | | | | | | |
| | To Tea—454 lbs ....................... 4/9 | 107 | 16 | 6 | | | | |

As a separate account is to be kept for "Tea," the sum is not extended to the outer columns.

The entry is first posted to the *Dr.* of Thomas Dundas, and then to the *Cr.* of an account to be opened under the head of "Tea"—using the words, "By Amount sold to T. Dundas."

| | | | | | | |
|---|---|---|---|---|---|---|
| Carried over.............. | | | | 28 | 6 | 5 |

*January* 31, 1850.

|  |  | £ | s | d | £ | s | d |
|---|---|---|---|---|---|---|---|
|  | Brought over............. |  |  |  | 28 | 6 | 5 |
| 4 | Robert Ireland, London. |  |  |  |  |  |  |
| √ | To 10 Pieces Welsh Flannel, 206 yds. 2/1 | 21 | 9 | 2 |  |  |  |
|  | „ 7 „ Twilled Cotton, 280 „ 7d. | 8 | 3 | 4 | 29 | 12 | 6 |

This is posted in the same way as the entry to John Turner.

| 2 |  |  |  |  |  |  |  |
|---|---|---|---|---|---|---|---|
| 12 | Alexander Gregory, Calcutta. |  |  |  |  |  |  |
|  | To Paper—100 Reams Demy ...... 17/6 | 87 | 10 | 0 |  |  |  |
|  | „ 100 „ Royal ...... 21/6 | 107 | 10 | 0 |  |  |  |
|  | Shipping Charges, &c. | 2 | 10 | 0 |  |  |  |
|  |  | 197 | 10 | 0 |  |  |  |
| 18 | „ Insurance on £220 @ 45/, £4, 19s.— |  |  |  |  |  |  |
|  | Policy and Duty 15/... | 5 | 14 | 0 |  |  |  |
| 18 | „ Commission on £5, 14s.................. | 0 | 5 | 9 |  |  |  |
|  |  | 203 | 9 | 9 |  |  |  |

This entry is first posted in one sum to the *Dr.* of Alexander Gregory, using the words, " To Goods (or To Sundries), £203, 9s. 9d.," and then the separate sums for *Paper, Insurance, Commission,* to the *Cr.* of accounts to be opened under these several heads, as will be seen at page 82.

| 12 | Goods—*Cr.* By Credit Sales............. |  |  |  | 57 | 18 | 11 |
|---|---|---|---|---|---|---|---|

This is the sum-total of those entries that have been extended to the *outer* columns, in order to be posted at the end of the month to the general account for " Goods."

At the *first* posting, these entries will appear in the Ledger at the *Dr.* of the following accounts:—

### JAMES ARNOLD, London.

| 1850. Jan. | 1 | To Goods... | 1 | 92 | 10 | 0 | 1850. | | | | | |
|---|---|---|---|---|---|---|---|---|---|---|---|---|

### JOHN TURNER, Charlotte Street.

| 1850. Jan. | 5 | To Goods.... | 1 | 23 | 8 | 6 | 1850. | | | | |
|---|---|---|---|---|---|---|---|---|---|---|---|

### WALTER FORBES, George Street.

| 1850. Jan. | 27 | To Goods... | 3 | 4 | 17 | 11 | 1850. | | | | |
|---|---|---|---|---|---|---|---|---|---|---|---|

### THOMAS DUNDAS, Manchester.

| 1850. Jan. | 28 | To Goods... | 3 | 107 | 16 | 6 | 1850. | | | | |
|---|---|---|---|---|---|---|---|---|---|---|---|

### ROBERT IRELAND, London.

| 1850. Jan. | 31 | To Goods... | 3 | 29 | 12 | 6 | 1850. | | | | |
|---|---|---|---|---|---|---|---|---|---|---|---|

### ALEXANDER GREGORY, Calcutta.

| 1850. Jan. | 31 | To Goods... or, "To Sundries." | 3 | 203 | 9 | 9 | 1850. | | | | |
|---|---|---|---|---|---|---|---|---|---|---|---|

F

At the *second* posting, the entries will appear at the *Cr.* of the
following accounts :—

GOODS (*General Account*).

| 1850. | | | | | 1850. | | | | | | | |
|---|---|---|---|---|---|---|---|---|---|---|---|---|
| | | | | | Jan. | 31 | By Credit Sales | 3 | | 57 | 18 | 11 |

PAPER.

| 1850. | | | | | 1850. | | | | | | | |
|---|---|---|---|---|---|---|---|---|---|---|---|---|
| | | | | | Jan. | 1 | By Amount sold to J. Arnold | 1 | | 92 | 10 | 0 |
| | | | | | | 31 | By Amount sold to A. Gregory | 3 | | 197 | 10 | 0 |

These and the following entries may be more briefly expressed, "By J. Arnold," "By A. Gregory," and so on; but the nature of the transactions is more clearly seen by entering them as above.

TEA.

| 1850. | | | | | 1850. | | | | | | | |
|---|---|---|---|---|---|---|---|---|---|---|---|---|
| | | | | | Jan. | 28 | By Amount sold to T. Dundas | 3 | | 107 | 16 | 6 |

INSURANCE.

| 1850. | | | | | 1850. | | | | | | | |
|---|---|---|---|---|---|---|---|---|---|---|---|---|
| | | | | | Jan. | 31 | By Amount charged to A. Gregory | 3 | | 5 | 14 | 0 |

COMMISSION.

| 1850. | | | | | 1850. | | | | | | | |
|---|---|---|---|---|---|---|---|---|---|---|---|---|
| | | | | | Jan. | 31 | By Amount charged to A. Gregory | 3 | | 0 | 5 | 9 |

## POSTING THE INVOICE-BOOK.

The Invoice-Book may be posted **by** either of the methods described at pages 76 and 78.

FIRST POSTING.

All the entries are posted to the *Cr.* of the various accounts.

SECOND POSTING.

All the entries **are** posted to the *Dr.* of the various accounts.

### Example.

The following entries **are** posted according to the method described at page 78; separate accounts being kept for Paper, Coffee, Insurance, **and** Commission.

**January 1, 1850.**

| | | | | | | | | |
|---|---|---|---|---|---|---|---|---|
| **5** **11** | John Watson, Edinburgh. By Paper—250 Reams Demy........ 14/ | 175 | 0 | 0 | | | | |
| | This is first posted to the *Cr.* of J. Watson, and then to the *Dr.* of " Paper," using the words, " To Amount Bought from J. Watson." | | | | | | | |
| **6** ✓ | Thomas Johnston, **Leeds.** By 25 Pieces Black **Cloth, 525 yds.** 14/6 „ 10 „ Doeskin 210 „ 3/6 | 380 36 | 12 15 | 6 0 | 417 | 7 | 6 |
| **7** ✓ | —30th.— James Reid, **London.** By 8 Pieces Satinett. 220 yds. 3/2 „ 12 „ French Merino, 370 „ 4/10 | 34 89 | 16 8 | 8 4 | 124 | 5 | 0 |
| | These two entries, after being **posted** to the *Cr.* of T. Johnston, and James **Reid,** are at **the end** of the month, posted the second time to the *Dr.* of the general account for " Goods," using the words, " To Credit Purchases." The sums **are for** this reason extended to the *outer* columns. | | | | | | |
| | **Carried over...........** | | | | 541 | 12 | 6 |

## *January* 31, 1850.

| | | | | | | |
|---|---|---|---|---|---|---|
| | Brought over......... | | | | 541 | 12 | 6 |
| 6 | William Graham, Kingston, Jamaica. | | | | | | |
| | cwt. qrs. lbs. | | | | | | |
| 13 | By Coffee,    30    2    0 @ £5, 7s. 4d. | 163 | 13 | 8 | | | |
| 17 | „ Insurance..................................... | 4 | 5 | 0 | | | |
| 17 | „ Commission on £4, 5s. 0d.............. | 0 | 4 | 3 | | | |
| | | 168 | 2 | 11 | | | |

This entry is first posted in one sum to the *Cr.* of W. Graham, and then the separate sums for *Coffee*, *Insurance*, and *Commission*, to the *Dr.* of accounts under these several heads.

| | | | | |
|---|---|---|---|---|
| 11 | Goods—*Dr.* to Credit Purchases......... | 541 | 12 | 6 |

This is the sum-total of the entries which have been extended to the outer columns, in order to be posted at the end of the month to the general account for " Goods."

# POSTING THE CASH-BOOK.

FIRST POSTING.

All the entries on the *Received* side are posted to the *Cr.* of the persons from whom, or the transactions on account of which, the cash has been received, the same as in Single Entry.

All the entries on the *Paid* side are posted to the *Dr.* of the persons to whom, or the transactions on account of which, the cash has been paid.

The entries on the *Received* side for "Cash Sales" and "Bills Receivable," and on the *Paid* side for "Cash Purchases," "Bills Payable," and "Trade Expenses," are not posted singly: to save room in the Ledger, the sums-total only of these items are posted at the end of each month, to their respective accounts, as shown at pages 86 to 89.

SECOND POSTING.

The sum-total of the CASH on the *Received* side is posted every month to the *Dr.* of an account to be opened under the head of "Cash," using the words, "To Amount Received from Sundries," or more briefly, "To Sundries."

The sum-total of the CASH on the *Paid* side is posted every month to the *Cr.* of the account for "Cash," using the words, "By Amount Paid to Sundries," or more briefly, "By Sundries."

The sum-total of the DISCOUNT on the *Received* side is posted every month to the *Dr.*, and on the *Paid* side to the *Cr.*, of an account to be opened under the head of "Discount," using the words, "To Amount allowed to Sundries," and "By Amount allowed by Sundries," or more briefly, "To" and "By Sundries."

## POSTING

### Cash Received.

| | 1850 Jan | | Cash Sales. | Bills Receivable. | Discount | Cash. |
|---|---|---|---|---|---|---|
| 15 | 1 | J. Hamilton—Cash at commencement..... | | | | 2000 0 0 |
| 15 | ,, | Robert Boyd, do. do. ..... | | | | 2000 0 0 |
| | | These sums, being the capital with which the partners commenced business, are posted to the Cr. of James Hamilton, and Robert Boyd. | | | | |
| √ | 3 | Goods—Cash Sales ...................... | 5 10 0 | | | 5 10 0 |
| | | The various entries for " Cash Sales," besides being entered as usual in the Cash columns, are also filled into the column for Cash Sales (a mark √ being made on the margin to show that this has been done), and posted in one sum at the end of the month. See page 88. | | | | |
| 1 | ,, | James Arnold, London...................... | | | 18 10 0 | 351 0 0 |
| | | The Cash and Discount are posted to the Cr. of J. Arnold. | | | | |
| √ | 10 | Goods—Cash Sales........................... | 7 15 0 | | | 7 15 0 |
| √ | 16 | Bills Receivable, No. 1, discounted.... | | 50 0 0 | 0 4 0 | 49 16 0 |
| | | The various entries for " Bills Receivable," including Cash and Discount, besides being entered as usual in the Cash and Discount columns, are also filled into the column for Bills Receivable (a mark √ being made on the margin to show that this has been done), and posted in one sum at the end of the month. See page 88. | | | | |
| √ | 20 | Goods—Cash Sales........................ | 3 10 6 | | | 3 10 6 |
| | | **Carried over..............** | 16 15 6 | 50 0 0 | 18 14 0 | 4417 11 6 |

## THE CASH-BOOK.

*Cash Paid.*

| | 1850 Jan | | Cash Purchases | Bills Payable. | Trade Expenses. | Discount | Cash. |
|---|---|---|---|---|---|---|---|
| 9 | 1 | Union Bank....................... | | | | | 3700 0 0 |
| | | Posted to the Dr. of the Bank. | | | | | |
| √ | ,, | Goods—Cash Purchases...... | 10 15 0 | | | | 10 15 0 |
| | | The various entries for "Cash Purchases," besides being entered as usual in the Cash columns, are also filled into the column for Cash Purchases (a mark √ being made on the margin to show that this has been done), and posted in one sum at the end of the month.  See page 89. | | | | | |
| 12 | ,, | Counting-House Furniture. | | | | | 125 0 0 |
| | | Entries of this nature are posted to the Dr. of an account to be opened under the head of "Counting-House Furniture," using the words, "To Cash." | | | | | |
| 11 | 4 | Sugar—Duty........£7 0 0  Freight, &c. 3 2 6 | | | | | 10 2 6 |
| | | These payments are posted to the Dr. of "Sugar," using the words, "To Cash." | | | | | |
| √ | 7 | Goods—Cash Purchases...... | 3 7 6 | | | | 3 7 6 |
| √ | 10 | Trade Expenses—Salaries... | | | 5 0 0 | | 5 0 0 |
| | | The various entries for "Trade Expenses," besides being entered as usual in the Cash columns, are also filled into the column for Trade Expenses (a mark √ being made on the margin to show that this has been done), and posted in one sum at the end of the month.  See page 89. | | | | | |
| √ | 13 | Bills Payable, No. 1............ | | 100 0 0 | | | 100 0 0 |
| | | The various entries for "Bills Payable," besides being entered as usual in the Cash columns, are also filled into the column for Bills Payable (a mark √ being made on the margin to show that this has been done), and posted in one sum at the end of the month.  See page 89. | | | | | |
| 5 | 14 | J. Watson, Edinburgh........ | | | | 25 17 6 | 491 16 6 |
| | | The cash and discount are posted to the Dr. of J. Watson. | | | | | |
| √ | 20 | Bills Payable, No. 2........... | | 50 0 0 | | | 50 0 0 |
| √ | 25 | Trade Expenses—Rent & Taxes | | | 30 0 0 | | 30 0 0 |
| 15 | 31 | James Hamilton................ | | | | | 20 0 0 |
| | | Posted to the Dr. of J. Hamilton. | | | | | |
| | | Carried over............ | 14 2 6 | 150 0 0 | 35 0 0 | 25 17 6 | 4546 1 6 |

## POSTING

*Cash Received.*

| | | | Cash Sales. | Bills Receivable | Discount | Cash. |
|---|---|---|---|---|---|---|
| | 1850 Jan | Brought over.............. | 16 15 6 | 50 0 0 | 18 14 0 | 4417 11 6 |
| √ | 28 | Bills Receivable, No. 2, discounted... | | 57 16 6 | 0 7 6 | 57 9 0 |
| 9 | ,, | Union Bank.................... | | | | 100 0 0 |
| | | Posted to the Cr. of the Bank. | | | | |
| 10 | 31 | Goods—Cash Sales.................. | 16 15 6 | | | |
| | | This is the sum-total for the month, and is posted to the Cr. of an account to be opened under the head of "Goods," using the words, "By Cash Sales." | | | | |
| 9 | ,, | Bills Receivable.................. | | 107 16 6 | | |
| | | This is the sum-total for the month, including the Cash and Discount, and is posted to the Cr. of the account for "Bills Receivable" (see page 90), using the words, "By Cash and Discount." | | | | |
| | | | | | | 4575 0 6 |
| | | SECOND POSTING. | | | | |
| 12 | | Discount,     Dr. | | | | |
| | | To Amount allowed to Sundries............................ | | | 19 1 6 | |
| 12 | | Cash,     Dr. | | | | |
| | | To Amount received from Sundries........................... | | | | 4575 0 6 |

The entries to the Bank are commonly posted in one sum at the end of the month, the same as "Cash Sales," &c. by using additional columns.

# THE CASH-BOOK.

*Cash Paid.*

| | | | Cash Purchases | | | Bills Payable. | | | Trade Expenses. | | | Discount. | | | Cash. | | |
|---|---|---|---|---|---|---|---|---|---|---|---|---|---|---|---|---|---|
| | 1850 Jan | Brought over............ | 14 | 2 | 6 | 150 | 0 | 0 | 35 | 0 | 0 | 25 | 17 | 6 | 4546 | 1 | 6 |
| 15 | 31 | Robert Boyd...................... | | | | | | | | | | | | | 20 | 0 | 0 |
| | | Posted to the Dr. of R. Boyd. | | | | | | | | | | | | | | | |
| 10 | ,, | Goods—Cash Purchases...... | 14 | 2 | 6 | | | | | | | | | | | | |
| | | This is the sum-total for the month, and is posted to the Dr. of " Goods," using the words, " To Cash Purchases." | | | | | | | | | | | | | | | |
| 9 | ,, | Bills Payable.................. | | | | 150 | 0 | 0 | | | | | | | | | |
| | | This is the sum-total for the month, and is posted to the Dr. of the account for " Bills Payable" (see page 90), using the words, " To Cash." | | | | | | | | | | | | | | | |
| 13 | ,, | Trade Expenses................. | | | | | | | 35 | 0 | 0 | | | | | | |
| | | This is the sum-total for the month, and is posted to the Dr. of an account to be opened under the head of " Trade Expenses," using the words, " To Cash— Salaries," &c. | | | | | | | | | | | | | | | |
| | ,, | Cash on Hand................... | | | | | | | | | | | | | 8 | 19 | 0 |
| | | | | | | | | | | | | | | | 4575 | 0 | 6 |
| | | SECOND POSTING. | | | | | | | | | | | | | | | |
| 12 | | Discount, Cr. | | | | | | | | | | | | | | | |
| | | By Amount allowed by Sundries.................. | | | | | | | | | | 25 | 17 | 6 | | | |
| 12 | | Cash, Cr. | | | | | | | | | | | | | | | |
| | | By Amount paid to Sundries.................. | | | | | | | | | | | | | 4566 | 1 | 6 |

Viz. sum-total above........................£4575 0 6
Deduct Cash on hand........................ 8 19 0

£4566 1 6

The Cash on hand requires to be **deducted**, as above, from the summation of the cash columns.

## POSTING THE BILL-BOOK.

FIRST POSTING.

Bills Receivable are posted to the *Cr.* of the person from whom they have been received, the same as in Single Entry.

Bills Payable to the *Dr.* of the persons to whom they have been granted.

SECOND POSTING.

Bills Receivable.—Add at the end of every month the amount of bills received, and post the sum-total to the *Dr.* of an account to be opened under the head of "Bills Receivable," using the words, "To Amount received from Sundries," or more briefly, "To Sundries."

Bills Payable.—Add at the end of every month the amount of bills granted, and post the sum-total to the *Cr.* of an account to be opened under the head of "Bills Payable," using the words, "By Amount granted to Sundries," or more briefly, "By Sundries."

*Example.*

*Bills Receivable.*

| | No. | When Recd. | From whom Received. | Amount. | | | Date. | Term. | When Due. | Entered in Cash-Bk. |
|---|---|---|---|---|---|---|---|---|---|---|
| | | 1850. | | | | | 1850. | | 1850. | 1850. |
| 2 | 1 | Jan. 10 | T. Dundas, Manchester........ | 50 | 0 | 0 | Jan. 8 | 1 mo. | Feb. 11 | Jan. 11 |
| 2 | 2 | ,, ,, | do.      do.   ....... | 57 | 16 | 6 | ,, ,, | 2 mo. | ,, ,, | ,, 31 |
| 3 | 3 | ,, 21 | R. Hall, Leeds.................... | 212 | 7 | 11 | ,, 20 | 4 mo. | May 23 | Feb. 2 |
| 3 | 4 | ,, 31 | W. Forbes, George Street..... | 100 | 0 | 0 | ,, 28 | 3 mo. | ,, 1 | Mar. 10 |
| 9 | | | Bills Receivable— *To Amount received from Sundries*.................. | 420 | 4 | 5 | | | | |

*Bills Payable.*

| | No. | When granted | To whom Granted. | Amount. | | | Date. | Term. | When Due. | Entered in Cash-Bk. |
|---|---|---|---|---|---|---|---|---|---|---|
| | | 1850. | | | | | 1850. | | 1850. | 1850. |
| 5 | 1 | Jan. 10 | J. Watson, Edinburgh ........ | 300 | 0 | 0 | Ja. 10 | 10 days | Jan. 23 | Jan. 23 |
| 6 | 2 | ,, 20 | T. Johnston, Leeds............. | 100 | 0 | 0 | ,, 20 | 10 ,, | Feb. 2 | Feb. 2 |
| 6 | 3 | ,, ,, | do.      do............ | 641 | 8 | 0 | ,, 20 | 1 mo. | ,, 23 | ,, 23 |
| 7 | 4 | ,, 25 | Mortimer & Son, Manchester | 572 | 3 | 6 | ,, 25 | 2 mo. | Mar. 28 | ,, 28 |
| 9 | | ,, 31 | Bills Payable— *By Amount granted to Sundries*.................. | 1613 | 11 | 6 | | | | |

## BALANCING THE LEDGER.

**The** Ledger is balanced, as in Single Entry, at the end of the year, or at any other time, when a view of your affairs is required.

NOTE.—After the books have been all posted, or at any stated convenient time, and previous to balancing the Ledger, each entry should be compared with that in the book from which it was taken, to ascertain that it has been posted correctly.

The various personal accounts—that is, those for individuals—are balanced in the same way as in Single Entry (see page 17); all the *Dr.* balances being carried forward to the *Dr.*, and all the *Cr.* balances to the *Cr.* of the next accounts.

The accounts **for** Trade Expenses **and** Bad Debts, and those peculiar to Double Entry, used for showing the profit or the loss on the various transactions—such as for " Goods," " Tea," " Paper," " Commission," &c. are balanced by carrying the balances to the *Dr.* or *Cr.* of the Profit and Loss Account, as shown under their several accounts in the following Ledger, pages 138 to 145.

The accounts for Bills and Cash, also peculiar **to** Double Entry, are balanced in the way shown at pages 137 and **143.**

After the accounts have been balanced, the **operation** should be carefully revised, to ascertain that it has been performed correctly.

TRIAL BALANCE.—As a check **on** the accuracy of the posting and the balancing, and preparatory **to a** final balance, all the accounts on the *Dr.* side of the Ledger **are** added together in one amount, and all those on the *Cr.* side in another. If the entries are posted and the accounts balanced correctly, the two sums will be equal. This statement is termed a " Trial Balance." If the two sums do not agree, some error has been committed, which must be found **out and** rectified. The Trial Balance is made before balancing **the** accounts—for Bad Debts; Trade Expenses; those peculiar to **Double Entry,** used for ascertaining the profit or loss; the account **for Profit** and Loss; and the Private Account. See the **Trial Balance of the** following **set** of books, **page** 146.

## TAKING STOCK.

An inventory of goods or Stock on hand, as mentioned under Single Entry, should be taken at least once a year, with the view of ascertaining the state of your affairs.

The goods are valued either at cost price, or at a per-centage below it, to allow for bad stock or depreciation in value, according to the nature of the case. The inventory is written out in the "Stock-Book."

When the Balance Sheet is to be drawn out, the amounts of the various kinds of goods on hand are entered from the "Stock-Book," either to the general account opened in the Ledger for "Goods," or to the special accounts for "Sugar," "Coffee," "Paper," &c. From thence the respective amounts are copied into the Balance Sheet. See the following Ledger, pages 138 to 141.

Stock of a more permanent nature—such as machinery, buildings, shop-furniture, &c.—does not require to be entered in the Stock-Book, as its value is ascertained from the accounts opened in the Ledger under their respective heads, and is from thence entered into the Balance Sheet. In accounts for machinery, furniture, &c. a yearly deduction of 5 or 10 per cent. requires to be made from the original cost, to allow for deterioration, or tear and wear.

Goods "on commission" are not entered along with the other goods, but in a separate list, as they belong to the parties who have sent them on sale. The amount on hand requires to be entered in the Ledger, to the *Dr.* of the persons from whom they were got. in order to ascertain the balance due to them; and also to the *Cr.* of the account for Goods on Commission. See Ledger, pages 133 and 138.

## PROFIT AND LOSS.

The **Profit**, or the Loss, on the various transactions **for** the year, or any other given time, is ascertained from an **account** to be opened under the head of " Profit **and** Loss."

**This** account is formed by entering—

On the *Dr.* side—

The "Losses"— **as** Bad Debts, **Trade** Expenses, &c.

On the *Cr.* side—

The " Profits"— **as** profit on Goods, Sugar, Paper, Commission, &c.

These profits, or **losses,** are ascertained from the accounts under their respective heads **in** the Ledger, from which they are transferred. The accounts **are** balanced off when the transfer is made.

The Profit and **Loss** account is balanced off **by carrying** the Profit, if any, to **the Cr.** (or the Loss to the *Dr.*) **of the Private** Account. See Profit and Loss Account, page 146.

It will be useful, as a check on the accuracy of this **account, also** to ascertain the Profit **by** the method described **at page 20.**

---

## BALANCE SHEET.

The Balance Sheet **is drawn** out at the **end of the** year, or at any other time when **you wish to** ascertain the state of **your** affairs.

**It** is drawn out in the same way, and embraces **the** same particulars, as in Single Entry (see page 19).

On the *Dr.* **side** are entered—

Your *liabilities*, or the sums you are **owing.**

On the *Cr.* side **are entered—**

Your *assets*—that is, the **sums owing to you,** and your property of every description.

The difference **between** the **two sides shows the nett amount of** your property or capital.

**All the** particulars in the Balance Sheet, are **taken** from the accounts under their respective heads, in the Ledger.

**The Balance** Sheet of **Hamilton** and Boyd, **to** whom the following books are supposed to **belong,** will be seen at page 148.

## PRIVATE ACCOUNT.

This account is kept and balanced in the same manner as in Single Entry.

On the *Dr.* side are entered—

The various sums you draw from the business on your own personal account.

On the *Cr.* side are entered—

The sum or capital you embarked in the business at the commencement, and any sums you may pay into the business afterwards.

Interest 5 per cent. on your capital.

The Profit (if any) gained during the year or other given period.

The Interest and the Profit are brought from the " Profit and Loss" account at the end of the year, or at any other time, when you balance your affairs. The " Profit and Loss" account is balanced off when the transfer is made.

If, instead of a profit, there has been a loss during the year, the loss is carried to the *Dr.* of your account.

The Private Accounts of James Hamilton and Robert Boyd will be seen at page 148.

# DOUBLE ENTRY.

## THE BOOKS

OF

## HAMILTON AND BOYD,

LONDON.

## DIRECTIONS.

In writing the following course, the pupil should proceed as far as possible with the various books simultaneously, as explained at page 24.

Great care should be taken to enter correctly the original sums in the Day-Book, &c., as errors made at first are of course perpetuated in the Ledger, and are not easily detected.

After the entries for a month or other stated period have been posted, they should be compared with the corresponding entries in the Ledger, to ascertain that the posting is correct. (See page 24.)

The mode of rectifying some of the errors apt to occur in posting, will be seen in the accounts of J. Arnold, and J. Edwards, page 128, and T. Dundas, page 129.

The Day-Book and Invoice-Book are posted according to the method described at pages 78 and 83. *Separate* accounts are supposed to be kept by Hamilton and Boyd for Goods on Commission, Paper, Port Wine, Sugar, Tea, Coffee, Insurance, Interest, Commission; all such entries must, therefore, at the second posting, be posted individually to their several accounts. They have the posting marked thus $\frac{2}{6}$

The entries for all other goods are posted in one sum at the end of the month to the general account for "Goods." They have the posting marked thus $\frac{3}{}$

Note.—If Hamilton and Boyd wished to know merely the amount of goods bought and sold without any *separate* accounts, the sums-total of *all* the entries would be extended to the outer columns, and the amounts of the whole posted monthly to the " Goods " account.

Two books of a foolscap size should be employed for the following set :—

I. The first, consisting of about 32 pages, or 8 sheets, to contain—

| | | | |
|---|---|---|---|
| The Day-Book...... 13 pages. | Bill-Book............ 4 pages. |
| Invoice-Book... 7 ,, | Warehouse-Book.. 1 ,, |
| Cash-Book..... 6 ,, | Stock-Book......... 1 ,, |

Each page to be ruled across with about 36 lines, exclusive of the head-line.

II. The second, consisting of about 24 pages, or 6 sheets, to contain—

| | |
|---|---|
| The Ledger......... 23 pages. | Account-Book....... 1 page. |

The first 8 pages of the Ledger should be ruled with *Dr.* and *Cr.* columns, as in the printed pages, and with 36 lines across. The remaining pages, for the sake of more space, should have the *Dr.* and *Cr.* sides of the accounts placed on the two opposite pages. If the first 8 pages are made the same as these last, 8 additional pages will be required, or 8 sheets altogether.

# THE DAY-BOOK.*

*London, January* 1, 1850.

| | | | | | | | | |
|---|---|---|---|---|---|---|---|---|
| 1 | James Arnold, London. | | | | | | | |
| 10 | To Paper,100 Rms. Printing Demy . 18/6 | 92 | 10 | 0 | | | | |
| | " " 75 " do. Royal . 23/ | 86 | 5 | 0 | | | | |
| | " " 100 " do. do. . 22/6 | 112 | 10 | 0 | | | | |
| | " " 50 " do. do. . 23/6 | 58 | 15 | 0 | | | | |
| | " " 20 " Small Post....... 19/6 | 19 | 10 | 0 | | | | |
| | | 369 | 10 | 0 | | | | |
| | For the mode of posting the Day-Book, see pages 78, 79, and 80. | | | | | | | |
| | —2d.— | | | | | | | |
| 1 | John Turner, 10 Charlotte Street. | | | | | | | |
| √ | To 16 Yds. Superfine Black Cloth, 15/6 | 12 | 8 | 0 | | | | |
| | " 14 " " Brown do. 15/9 | 11 | 0 | 6 | | | | |
| | " 8 " Doeskin................. 3/6 | 1 | 8 | 0 | | | | |
| | " 4 " do. ................. 4/0 | 0 | 16 | 0 | 25 | 12 | 6 |
| | —3d.— | | | | | | | |
| 1 | James Pringle, Dublin. | | | | | | | |
| 11 | To Port Wine—2 Pipes.............. £75 | 150 | 0 | 0 | | | | |
| | " " " 1 do. ................... | 72 | 0 | 0 | | | | |
| | | 222 | 0 | 0 | | | | |
| | —5th.— | | | | | | | |
| 1 | James Edwards, 20 Princes Street. | | | | | | | |
| 10 | To Goods on Commission— | | | | | | | |
| | 2 Brown's Moral Philosophy, 1 v. 13/6 | 1 | 7 | 0 | | | | |
| | 4 Comstock's Natural Philosophy.. 3/6 | 0 | 14 | 0 | | | | |
| | 3 Cowper's Poems, 2 vols.12mo. 6/9 | 1 | 0 | 3 | | | | |
| | 2 Campbell's Poems, 18mo...... 3/9 | 0 | 7 | 6 | | | | |
| | | 3 | 8 | 9 | | | | |
| | Carried over............. | | | | 25 | 12 | 6 |

* For another form of the Day-Book, see page 100.

G

*January* 8, 1850.

| | | | | | | | |
|---|---|---|---:|---:|---:|---:|---:|
| | Brought over............ | | | | | 25 | 12 | 6 |

**2 / 11** Thomas Dundas, **Manchester.**

To Tea—(from W. Black, Canton.)

    7 Chests Hyson—

| W. B. | 1 | gross 84 lbs. | tare 19 lbs. | | | |
|---|---|---|---|---|---|---|
| | 2 | 82 | 17 | | | |
| | 3 | 85 | 18 | | | |
| | 4 | 83 | 21 | | | |
| | 5 | 80 | 19 | | | |
| | 6 | 84 | 17 | | | |
| | 7 | 86 | 19 | | | |
| | | 584 | 130 | | | |

*These are the letters and figures marked on the chests.*

    deduct **tare,** 130

        454 lbs............ 4/9    107 | 16 | 6

—*10th.*—

**2 / √** Francis Milner, Dundee.

| To 10 Pieces Black Cloth, | **206** yds. | **18/6** | 190 | 11 | 0 | | | |
|---|---|---|---|---|---|---|---|---|
| „ 2 „ Doeskin, | 42 | 3/10 | 8 | 1 | 0 | | | |
| „ 1 „ Welsh Flannel, 23 | „ | 1/11 | 2 | 4 | 1 | 200 | 16 | 1 |

—*12th.*—

**1 / 11** James Pringle, Dublin.

To Coffee, 12 Tierces—

| | | cwt. qrs. lbs. | | | |
|---|---|---|---|---|---|
| | gross | 66 2 2 | | | |
| W. G. 1 to 12. | tare | 6 2 26 | | | |
| | nett | 59 3 4   @ **£8, 5s. 8d.** | 495 | 4 | 6 |

—*16th.*—.

**2 / 10** Alexander Gregory, Calcutta.

| To Paper—100 Reams Demy....... | **17/6** | 87 | 10 | 0 | | | |
|---|---|---|---|---|---|---|---|
| „ 100 „ Royal....... | **21/** | 105 | 0 | 0 | | | |
| Shipping expenses, &c......... | | 2 | 10 | 0 | | | |
| | | 195 | 0 | 0 | | | |

**13**    „ Insurance on £220 @ 45/, £4, 19s.—

          Policy and Duty, 15/............    5 | 14 | 0

**13**    „ Commission.................................    0 | 5 | 9

     25 Bales, **A.G.,** 1 to 25,
     Shipped **per The Mary.**    200 | 19 | 9

            Carried forward............    226 | 8 | 7

*January* 17, 1850.

|   |   |   |   |   |   |   |   |   |   |
|---|---|---|---|---|---|---|---|---|---|
|   | Brought forward............ |   |   |   |   |   | 226 | 8 | 7 |
| **2** | John Addison, Glasgow. |   |   |   |   |   |   |   |   |
| √ | To 25 Yards Carpeting............... 2/11 | 3 | 12 | 11 |   |   |   |   |   |
|   | „ 30 „ do. ............... 3/2 | 4 | 15 | 0 |   |   |   |   |   |
|   | „ 26 „ do. ............... 3/9 | 4 | 17 | 6 | 13 | 5 | 5 |   |
| **3** | Walter Forbes, George Street. |   |   |   |   |   |   |   |   |
| √ | To 6 Pair Kid Gloves.................. 3/6 | 1 | 1 | 0 |   |   |   |   |   |
|   | „ 4 „ Cotton Socks............... 1/2 | 0 | 4 | 8 | 1 | 5 | 8 |   |

—20*th.*—

**3 / 11**   Richard Hall, Leeds,     (@ 72 *days*).

To Sugar—(from J. Cameron, Demerara.)

6 Hogsheads—

J. C. 1 to 6.

|       | cwt. | qrs. | lbs. |       | cwt. | qrs. | lbs. |
|-------|------|------|------|-------|------|------|------|
| gross | 14   | 2    | 1    | tare  | 1    | 0    | 2    |
|       | 16   | 1    | 7    |       | 1    | 1    | 3    |
|       | 15   | 3    | 8    |       | 1    | 1    | 10   |
|       | 17   | 1    | 4    |       | 1    | 2    | 4    |
|       | 18   | 0    | 6    |       | 1    | 0    | 18   |
|       | 16   | 3    | 1    |       | 1    | 1    | 15   |
|       | 98   | 2    | 27   |       | 7    | 2    | 24   |

deduct tare   7   2   24

    91   0   3   @ £2, 6s. 8d.    | 212 | 7 | 11 |

It is usual in selling goods on consignment, to mark, as above, the time at which they are to be paid. The sugar is supposed to be payable by R. Hall in 72 days; and all the entries for Sugar sold have been marked in this way. See also the "Account - Sales" of Sugar, page 155.

         Carried over.........     | 240 | 19 | 8 |

*January 25, 1850.*

|  |  | | | | | | |
|---|---|---|---|---|---|---|---|
| | Brought over............ | | | 240 | 19 | 8 |
| 3/11 | G. Campbell, Liverpool.<br>To Coffee, 6 Tierces— | | | | | |

|  | cwt. | qrs. | lbs. | | qrs. | lbs. |
|---|---|---|---|---|---|---|
| gross | 5 | 2 | 1 | tare | 2 | 12 |
| | 5 | 3 | 2 | | 2 | 9 |
| | 5 | 0 | 6 | | 2 | 17 |
| | 5 | 1 | 8 | | 2 | 10 |
| | 6 | 1 | 4 | | 2 | 12 |
| | 6 | 0 | 14 | | 2 | 3 |

*(W. G. 13 to 18.)*

|  | | | | | | |
|---|---|---|---|---|---|---|
| | 34 | 0 | 7 | 3 | 2 | 7 |
| deduct tare | 3 | 2 | 7 | | | |
| | 30 | 2 | 0 | @ £8, 3s. 4d. | 249 | 1 | 8 |

—30*th.*—

| | | | | |
|---|---|---|---|---|
| 3/11 | George Smith, Bristol.<br>To Tea—(from W. Black, Canton.)<br>10 Chests Congou— | | | |

*(W. B. 8 to 17.)*

| | | | | | |
|---|---|---|---|---|---|
| gross | 1152 lbs. | | | | |
| tare | 287 | | | | |
| nett | 865 lbs. | @ 3/2 | 136 | 19 | 2 |

—31*st.*—

| | | | | | | |
|---|---|---|---|---|---|---|
| 10 | Goods—*Cr. By Credit Sales*................ | | | 240 | 19 | 8 |

*Note.*—The following is the most convenient form of the Day-Book, when the breadth of the page will admit of its use. The word "To" at each entry may be left out :—

*January 3, 1850.*

| | | | | | | | | |
|---|---|---|---|---|---|---|---|---|
| 1/11 | James Pringle, Dublin.<br>    Port Wine—2 Pipes.................... £75 | 150 | 0 | 0 | | | |
| |     ,,    ,,    1   do. ..................... | 72 | 0 | 0 | | | |
| | | 222 | 0 | 0 | | | |
| | —17*th.*— | | | | | | |
| 3/✓ | Walter Forbes, George Street. | | | | | | |
| |     6 Pair Kid Gloves..................... 3/6 | 1 | 1 | 0 | | | |
| |     4  ,,   Cotton Socks.................. 1/2 | 0 | 4 | 8 | 1 | 5 | 8 |

*February* 1, 1850.

| | | £ | s. | d. | £ | s. | d. |
|---|---|---|---|---|---|---|---|
| 4 | Robert Ireland, London. | | | | | | |
| ✓ | To 10 Pieces Welsh Flannel, 206 **yds.** 2/1 | 21 | 9 | 2 | | | |
| | „ 8 „ Irish Linen, 240 „ 2/9 | 33 | 0 | 0 | | | |
| | „ 6 „ Linen Sheeting 300 „ 2/7 | 38 | 15 | 0 | | | |
| | „ 7 „ Twilled Cotton, 280 „ 7d. | 8 | 3 | 4 | | | |
| | „ 2 „ Mous. de laine, 59 „ 1/1 | 3 | 3 | 11 | | | |
| | „ 3 „ German Lawn, 38 „ 2/8 | 5 | 1 | 4 | 109 | 12 | 9 |
| | *—4th.—* | | | | | | |
| 2 | John Addison, Glasgow. | | | | | | |
| ✓ | To 150 Pair Blankets................. 17/6 | 131 | 5 | 0 | | | |
| | „ 60 „ do. .................. 19/ | 57 | 0 | 0 | | | |
| | „ 20 Pieces Black Silk, 396 **yds.** 4/6 | 89 | 2 | 0 | | | |
| | „ 6 „ Brown Cloth, 124 „ 15/ | 93 | 0 | 0 | | | |
| | „ 4 „ Doeskin, 86 „ 3/10 | 16 | 9 | 8 | 386 | 16 | 8 |
| | *—7th.—* | | | | | | |
| 4/11 | Archibald Logan, Newcastle. | | | | | | |
| | To Port Wine, 1 pipe........................ | 76 | 0 | 0 | | | |
| | „ do. do. 2 „ ................. £73 | 146 | 0 | 0 | | | |
| | „ do. **do.** 1 „ ........................ | 75 | 0 | 0 | | | |
| | | 297 | 0 | 0 | | | |
| | *—9th.—* | | | | | | |
| 3 | George Smith, Bristol. | | | | | | |
| ✓ | To 3 Chests Oranges.................... 45/ | 6 | 15 | 0 | | | |
| | „ 2 Boxes Lemons.................... 87/ | 8 | 14 | 0 | | | |
| | „ 3 Casks Butter, 200 lbs........... 9½d. | 7 | 18 | 4 | | | |
| | cwts. qrs. lbs. | | | | | | |
| | „ 3 „ **Cocoa,** gross 17 1 2 | | | | | | |
| | tare 0 2 26 | | | | | | |
| | nett 16 2 4 @ 63/ | 52 | 1 | 9 | 75 | 9 | 1 |
| | *—14th.—* | | | | | | |
| 3 | Walter Forbes, George Street. | | | | | | |
| ✓ | **To** 6 Pieces Black Satinett, **170** yds. 2/7 | 21 | 19 | 2 | | | |
| | „ 2 „ Silk Velvet, 63 „ 12/ | 37 | 16 | 0 | | | |
| | „ 4 „ French Cambric, 118 „ 9/6 | 56 | 1 | 0 | 115 | 16 | 2 |
| | Carried over........... | | | | 687 | 14 | 8 |

*February* 18, 1850.

| | | £ | s. | d. | £ | s. | d. |
|---|---|---|---|---|---|---|---|
| | **Brought over**............ | | | | 687 | 14 | 8 |
| 2/10 | Alexander Gregory, **Calcutta.** | | | | | | |
| | To Paper—120 Reams Demy...... 17/10 | 107 | 0 | 0 | | | |
| | „ „ 84 „ Royal...... 22/ | 92 | 8 | 0 | | | |
| | „ „ 50 „ do. ..... 22/3 | 55 | 12 | 6 | | | |
| | Shipping expenses, &c......... | 2 | 9 | 6 | | | |
| | | 257 | 10 | 0 | | | |
| 13 | „ **Insurance** on £280 @ 50/, £7— Policy and duty, 14/9.......... | 7 | 14 | 9 | | | |
| 13 | „ Commission.................................. | | 7 | 9 | | | |
| | 30 Bales, A.G., 1 to 30, Shipped per The Amelia. | 265 | 12 | 6 | | | |
| 1/10 | James Arnold, London. | | | | | | |
| | To Goods on Commission— | | | | | | |
| | 6 Campbell's Poems, 18mo....... 3/6 | 1 | 1 | 0 | | | |
| | 4 Gibbon's Rome, 5 vols. 8vo.... 45/ | 9 | 0 | 0 | | | |
| | 6 Russell's Modern Europe, 4 v. 38/ | 11 | 8 | 0 | | | |
| | 2 Shakspeare, 2 vols. roy. 8vo... 26/ | 2 | 12 | 0 | | | |
| | 1 Byron's Poems, royal 8vo...... 12/ | 0 | 12 | 0 | | | |
| | | 24 | 13 | 0 | | | |
| | —19*th.*— | | | | | | |
| 2/11 | Francis Milner, Dundee. | | | | | | |
| | To Coffee, 6 Tierces— | | | | | | |
| | cwt. qrs. lbs. | | | | | | |
| | W. G. 21 to 26. gross 33 1 2 | | | | | | |
| | tare 3 2 0 | | | | | | |
| | nett 29 3 2 @ £8, 3s. 4d. | 243 | 2 | 1 | | | |
| | —20*th.*— | | | | | | |
| 4/11 | Thomas Simpson, Belfast. | | | | | | |
| | To Port Wine—1 pipe........................ | 76 | 0 | 0 | | | |
| | **Carried forward**........... | | | | 687 | 14 | 8 |

*February* 27, 1850.

|  |  |  |  |  |  |  |  |  |
|---|---|---|---|---|---|---|---|---|
| | Brought forward............ | | | | | 687 | 14 | 8 |
| **3** | Richard Hall, Leeds. | | | | | | | |
| ✓ | To 2 Boxes Raisins,   112 lbs...... 5½d. | 2 | 11 | 4 | | | | |
| | „ 20 Dutch Cheeses, 130 „ ...... 5d. | 2 | 14 | 2 | | | | |
| | „   2 Casks Butter,   176 „ ...... 9¼d. | 6 | 15 | 8 | | | | |
| | „   3 Boxes Lemons................. 83/ | 12 | 9 | 0 | | 24 | 10 | 2 |
| | *—28th.—* | | | | | | | |
| **10** | Goods—*Cr. By Credit Sales*............... | | | | | 712 | 4 | 10 |

*March* 1, 1850.

| | | | £ | s | d | £ | s | d |
|---|---|---|---|---|---|---|---|---|
| 5 | William Jerdan, Queen Street. | | | | | | | |
| √ | To 12 Pieces Fr. Merino, 347 yds.. 4/10 | | 83 | 17 | 2 | | | |
| | „ 6 Dozen India Handkerchiefs. 36/ | | 10 | 16 | 0 | | | |
| | „ 3 „ Satin Stocks.......... 45/ | | 6 | 15 | 0 | | | |
| | „ 6 Pair Blankets.................... 16/6 | | 4 | 19 | 0 | 106 | 7 | 2 |
| | | | | | | | | |
| 5 | William Thomson, Aberdeen. | | | | | | | |
| √ | To 12 Silk Hats................. 11/9 | | 7 | 1 | 0 | | | |
| | „ 2 Pieces Satin Ribbon, 42 yds. 1/9 | | 3 | 13 | 6 | | | |
| | „ 3 „ Muslin, 39 „ 1/4 | | 2 | 12 | 0 | | | |
| | „ 6 „ Printed Cotton 170 „ 7d. | | 4 | 19 | 2 | 18 | 5 | 8 |

*—4th.—*

G. Knight, Birmingham, (@ 26 *days*).
(marginal: 5 / 11)

To Sugar—(from J. Cameron, Demerara.)

16 Hogsheads—

| | cwt. | qrs. | lbs. |
|---|---|---|---|
| gross | 245 | 0 | 16 |
| tare | 17 | 1 | 12 |
| nett | 227 | 3 | 4 @ 42/ |

(marginal: J. C. 7 to 22.)

| | | £ | s | d |
|---|---|---|---|---|
| | | 278 | 7 | 0 |

James Arnold, **London.**
(marginal: 1 / 10)

To Goods on Commission—

| | £ | s | d |
|---|---|---|---|
| 12 Campbell's Poems, **12mo**...... 3/7 | 2 | 3 | 0 |
| 6 Gibbon's Rome, 5 vols. **8vo**... 44/ | 13 | 4 | 0 |
| 3 Russell's Modern Europe, **4 v.** 37/ | 5 | 11 | 0 |
| | 20 | 18 | 0 |

*—6th.—*

Thomas Dundas, Manchester.
(marginal: 2 / 11)

To Tea—(from W. Black, Canton.)

6 Chests Hyson—

| | gross | lbs. | tare |
|---|---|---|---|
| | 83 | | 19 |
| | 83 | | 21 |
| | 82 | | 20 |
| | 80 | | 19 |
| | 76 | | 17 |
| | 80 | | 19 |
| | 484 | | 115 |

(marginal: W. B. 18 to 23.)

deduct tare 115

| | | £ | s | d |
|---|---|---|---|---|
| 369......... @ 4/7 | | 84 | 11 | 3 |

| | | £ | s | d |
|---|---|---|---|---|
| Carried **forward**............. | | 124 | 12 | 10 |

*March* 9, 1850.

| | | | | | | | |
|---|---|---|---|---|---|---|---|
| | Brought forward............ | | | | 124 | 12 | 10 |
| **3** | George Campbell, Liverpool. | | | | | | |
| **11** | To Tea—(from W. Black, Canton.) | | | | | | |
| |     9 Chests Congou— | | | | | | |
| |     gross 960 lbs. | | | | | | |
| | W. B. 25 to 34.   tare  198 | | | | | | |
| |     nett  762 ...... @ 3/6 | 133 | 7 | 0 | | | |
| | —11*th.*— | | | | | | |
| **5** | George Knight, Birmingham. | | | | | | |
| ✓ | To 2 Boxes Oranges................. 45/6 | 4 | 11 | 0 | | | |
| |             cwt. qrs. lbs. | | | | | | |
| | „ 1 Cask Cocoa,  gross 4  1  2 | | | | | | |
| |              tare  0  0 27 | | | | | | |
| |              nett  4  0  3 @ 60/8 | 12 | 4 | 3½ | | | |
| | „ 2 Boxes Raisins, 115 lbs......... 6½d. | 3 | 2 | 3½ | 19 | 17 | 7 |
| | —14*th.*— | | | | | | |
| **1** | James Pringle, Dublin. | | | | | | |
| |             cwt. qrs. lbs. | | | | | | |
| ✓ | To 30 Dutch Cheeses,   3  2   6 @ 32/8 | 5 | 16 | 1 | | | |
| | „  3 Casks Cocoa, gross 13  1  4 | | | | | | |
| |              tare  0  3 27 | | | | | | |
| |           **nett** 12  1  5 @ 65/4 | 40 | 3 | 3 | | | |
| | „ 1 Box Lemons............................ | 4 | 7 | 0 | 50 | 6 | 4 |
| **1** | John Turner, Charlotte Street. | | | | | | |
| ✓ | To 10 Pieces Black Cloth, 230 yds. 17/6 | 201 | 5 | 0 | | | |
| | „ 10   „    Doeskin,    210  „  4/10 | 50 | 15 | 0 | 252 | 0 | 0 |
| | —16*th.*— | | | | | | |
| **5** | William Thomson, Aberdeen. | | | | | | |
| ✓ | To 6 Silk Umbrellas ................. 11/7 | 3 | 9 | 6 | | | |
| | „ 4 Cotton  do.   .................. 4/9 | 0 | 19 | 0 | | | |
| | „ 2 Pieces Cotton Shirting, 84 yds. 8½d. | 2 | 19 | 6 | | | |
| | „ 3   „   Linen Sheeting, 146  „  1/9 | 12 | 15 | 6 | 20 | 3 | 6 |
| | Carried over............ | | | | 467 | 0 | 3 |

*March* 16, 1850.

| | | | | | | | |
|---|---|---|---|---|---|---|---|
| | Brought over............ | | | | 467 | 0 | 3 |
| 2/11 | Thomas Dundas, Manchester. | | | | | | |
| | To Coffee, 6 Tierces— | | | | | | |
| | cwt. qrs. lbs. | | | | | | |
| | gross 33 1 2 | | | | | | |
| | tare 3 0 26 | | | | | | |
| | nett 30 0 4 @ £7, 18s. 8d. | 238 | 5 | 8 | | | |
| | —18*th.*— | | | | | | |
| 1/10 | James Arnold, London. | | | | | | |
| | To Paper—105 Reams Demy........ 18/ | 94 | 10 | 0 | | | |
| | " " 73 " Royal........ 24/ | 87 | 12 | 0 | | | |
| | " " 180 " Small Post.. 17/ | 153 | 0 | 0 | | | |
| | | 335 | 2 | 0 | | | |
| | —19*th.*— | | | | | | |
| 4/11 | James Pringle, Dublin. | | | | | | |
| | To Coffee, 6 Tierces— | | | | | | |
| | cwt. qrs. lbs. | | | | | | |
| | gross 40 0 0 | | | | | | |
| | tare 4 0 8 | | | | | | |
| | nett 35 3 20 @ £8, 3s. 4d. | 293 | 8 | 4 | | | |
| | —22*d.*— | | | | | | |
| 4 | Robert Ireland, London. | | | | | | |
| ✓ | To 12 Pieces Irish Linen, 210 yds. 2/8 | 28 | 0 | 0 | | | |
| | " 6 " French Merino 170 " 1/9 | 14 | 17 | 6 | | | |
| | " 8 " Scotch Cambric, 94 " 1/4 | 6 | 5 | 4 | 49 | 2 | 10 |
| | —26*th.*— | | | | | | |
| 5/11 | G. Knight, Birmingham (@ 1 *month*). | | | | | | |
| | To Sugar—(from J. Cameron, Demerara.) | | | | | | |
| | 20 Hogsheads— | | | | | | |
| | cwt. qrs. lbs. | | | | | | |
| | J. C. 23 to 42. gross 311 1 0 | | | | | | |
| | tare 26 1 20 | | | | | | |
| | nett 284 3 8... @ 46/8 | 664 | 11 | 8 | | | |
| | Carried forward........... | | | | 516 | 3 | 1 |

### March 26, 1850.

| | | | | | | | | |
|---|---|---|---|---|---|---|---|---|
| | Brought forward............ | | | | | | 516 | 3 | 1 |

| | | | | | | | | | |
|---|---|---|---|---|---|---|---|---|---|
| **1** | John Turner, Charlotte Street. | | | | | | | | |
| ✓ | To 30 Yds. Superfine Black Cloth, 19/6 | 29 | 5 | 0 | | | | |
| | „ 25 „ „ Olive do. 17/ | 21 | 5 | 0 | | | | |
| | „ 12 „ Doeskin.................. 4/11 | 2 | 19 | 0 | 53 | 9 | 0 |

*—28th.—*

| | | | | | | | | |
|---|---|---|---|---|---|---|---|---|
| **5** | William Jerdan, Queen Street. | | | | | | | |
| ✓ | To 60 Pair Blankets..................... 32/ | 96 | 0 | 0 | | | |
| | „ 50 „ do. .................. 29/ | 72 | 10 | 0 | | | |
| | „ 26 „ do. .................. 33/ | 42 | 18 | 0 | | | |
| | „ 10 Pieces Fr. Merino, 260 yds... 6/1 | 79 | 1 | 8 | 290 | 9 | 8 |

*—29th.—*

**4̲ ̲ ̲** James Pringle, Dublin (@ 1 *month*).

**11̲** To Sugar—(from J. Cameron, Demerara.)

8 Hogsheads—

|  | cwt. | qrs. | lbs. |  | cwt. | qrs. | lbs. |
|---|---|---|---|---|---|---|---|
| gross | 14 | 3 | 7 | tare | 1 | 2 | 8 |
| | 15 | 1 | 9 | | 1 | 2 | 1 |
| | 17 | 3 | 4 | | 1 | 0 | 6 |
| | 16 | 1 | 8 | | 1 | 3 | 7 |
| | 18 | 1 | 1 | | 1 | 1 | 8 |
| | 15 | 2 | 1 | | 1 | 0 | 9 |
| | 16 | 0 | 2 | | 1 | 1 | 5 |
| | 17 | 1 | 5 | | 1 | 3 | 1 |

J. C. 43 to 50.

|  | | | | | | |
|---|---|---|---|---|---|---|
| | 131 | 1 | 9 | 11 | 1 | 17 |
| deduct tare | 11 | 1 | 17 | | | |
| | 119 | 3 | 20 ........ @ 44/4 | 265 | 16 | 10 |

*—31st.—*

| | | | | | |
|---|---|---|---|---|---|
| 9̲ ̲ ̲ | Union Bank. | | | | |
| 12 | To Interest, Jan. 1 to March 31.......... | 21 | 10 | 0 | |
| | **Carried** over............ | | | | 860 | 1 | 9 |

### March 31, 1850.

| | | | | | | | |
|---|---|---|---|---|---|---|---|
| | Brought over........... | | | | 860 | 1 | 9 |
| 6 | J. Wilson, London. | | | | | | |
| 13 | To Commission, 10 % on Sales (£30) ... | 3 | 0 | 0 | | | |
| | This is the charge made against J. Wilson for selling his goods. | | | | | | |
| 11 | Tea—(from W. Black, Canton.) | | | | | | |
| 12 | To Interest, 3 months, on Cash paid for duty, freight,&c.(£277,19s.10d.) | 3 | 9 | 6 | | | |
| 13 | „ Commission, 5 per cent. on Sales (£462, 13s. 11d.)...... | 23 | 2 | 8 | | | |
| 11 | Sugar—(from J. Cameron, Demerara.) | | | | | | |
| 12 | To Interest, 4 months, on Cash paid for duty, freight, &c. (£695, 3s. 2d.) | 11 | 11 | 8 | | | |
| 13 | „ Commission, 5 per cent. on Sales (£1421, 3s. 5d.) ...... | 71 | 1 | 2 | | | |
| | The Tea and Sugar were received from W. Black and J. Cameron to sell on Commission; and when the accounts, showing how much has been sold, are to be made up and sent to them, the Interest and Commission require to be charged as above. | | | | | | |
| 10 | Goods—*Cr. By Credit Sales*................ | | | | 860 | 1 | 9 |

# INVOICE-BOOK.*

### London, January 1, 1850.

| | | | | | | | | |
|---|---|---|---|---|---|---|---|---|
| $\frac{5}{10}$ | John Watson, **Edinburgh**. | | | | | | | |
| | By Paper, 250 **Rms.** Printing Demy | 14/ | 175 | 0 | 0 | | | |
| | „ „ 312 „ do. Royal | 17/ | 265 | 4 | 0 | | | |
| | „ „ 100 „ Small Post..... | 15/6 | 77 | 10 | 0 | | | |
| | | | 517 | 14 | 0 | | | |
| | For the mode of posting the Invoice-Book, see pages 83 and 84. | | | | | | | |
| | | | | | | | | |
| **6** | Thomas Johnston, Leeds. | | | | | | | |
| ✓ | By 25 **Pieces** Black Cloth, 525 yds. | 14/6 | 380 | 12 | 6 | | | |
| | „ 22 „ Brown do. 462 „ | 14/ | 323 | 8 | 0 | | | |
| | „ 10 „ Doeskin, 210 „ | 3/6 | 36 | 15 | 0 | | | |
| | Packing................... | | 0 | 12 | 6 | 741 | 8 | 0 |
| | | | | | | | | |
| $\frac{6}{11}$ | Irving & **Co., Oporto**. | | | | | | | |
| | By Port **Wine**—(per " The Ann.") | | | | | | | |
| | 10 Pipes......................... £35 | | 350 | 0 | 0 | | | |
| **13** | „ Insurance ...................... | | 8 | 18 | 6 | | | |
| **13** | „ Commission on £8, 18s. 6d........... | | 0 | 9 | 0 | | | |
| | | | 359 | 7 | 6 | | | |
| | **—6th.—** | | | | | | | |
| **6** | John Wilson, London. | | | | | | | |
| $\overline{10}$ | By Goods on Commission— | | | | | | | |
| | 6 Brown's Moral Philosophy, 8vo. 12/ | | 3 | 12 | 0 | | | |
| | 6 Cowper's Poems, 2 vols. 12mo. 6/ | | 1 | 16 | 0 | | | |
| | 4 Comstock's Natural Philosophy.... 3/ | | 0 | 12 | 0 | | | |
| | 8 Campbell's Poems, 18mo. ....... 3/4 | | 1 | 6 | 8 | | | |
| | Box........................ | | 0 | 3 | 6 | | | |
| | | | 7 | 10 | 2 | | | |
| | Carried over............ | | | | | 741 | 8 | 0 |

* For another form of the Invoice-Book, see page 111.

*January* 12, 1850.

| | | | | | | | |
|---|---|---|---|---|---|---|---|
| | Brought over............ | | | | 741 | 8 | 0 |

**6 / 11** Wm. Graham, Kingston, Jamaica.
By Coffee, 18 Tierces—(per " The Mary.")

|  |  | cwt. | qrs. | lbs. | | | |
|---|---|---|---|---|---|---|---|
| W. G. 1 to 12. | gross | 66 | 2 | 2 | | | |
| | tare | 6 | 2 | 26 | | | |
| | nett | 59 | 3 | 4 @ £5, 9s. 8d. | 327 | 16 | 6 |
| W. G. 13 to 18. | gross | 34 | 0 | 7 | | | |
| | tare | 3 | 2 | 7 | | | |
| | nett | 30 | 2 | 0 @ £5, 7s. 4d. | 163 | 13 | 8 |

|  | | | | |
|---|---|---|---|---|
| | | 491 | 10 | 2 |
| **13** „ Insurance ..................................... | | 12 | 10 | 0 |
| **13** „ Commission on £12, 10s................ | | 0 | 12 | 6 |
| | | 504 | 12 | 8 |

—15*th.*—

**7 / ✓** D. Mortimer and Son, Manchester.
By Goods, as per Invoice, January 13..      572 | 3 | 6

As formerly mentioned, it is sufficient in actual business to enter merely the *amount* of the Invoice.

—16*th.*—

**7 / 13** Marine Insurance Company.
By Insurance, on Goods to A. Gregory, Calcutta    5 | 14 | 0

**5 / 10** John Watson, Edinburgh.

| By Paper—175 Reams Demy ...... 14/ | 122 | 10 | 0 |
|---|---|---|---|
| „ „ 220 „ Royal ...... 17/ | 187 | 0 | 0 |
| „ „ 100 „ Small Post 14/9 | 73 | 15 | 0 |
| | 383 | 5 | 0 |

—18*th.*—

**7 / ✓** James Reid, London.
By Goods, as per Invoice, January 18..      117 | 8 | 6

| | Carried forward......... | | | 1431 | 0 | 0 |
|---|---|---|---|---|---|---|

l3rr3rr3rr3rr3r

*January 25, 1850.*

|  |  |  |  |  |  |  |
|---|---|---|---:|---:|---:|---:|
|  | Brought forward......... |  |  | 1431 | 0 | 0 |
| 7 / 11 | Alex. Robertson & Co., Glasgow. | | | | | |
|  | By Coffee, 6 Tierces— | | | | | |

```
                      cwt. qrs. lbs.      qrs. lbs.
              gross 7   2   1     tare 3   1
                    5   3   4          2  20
   D. R. 1 to 6.    6   2  20          2  27
                    7   1   3          3   3
                    6   3   1          2   7
                    5   3  27          2   6

                   40   0   0         4   0   8
    deduct tare     4   0   8
```

| | | | | | | |
|---|---|---:|---:|---:|---:|---:|
|  | 35  3  20 @ £6, 10s. 8d. | | 234 | 14 | 8 | |
|  | —31st.— | | | | | |
| 10 | Goods—*Dr. To Credit Purchases*........ | | | 1431 | 0 | 0 |

*Note.*—The following is the most convenient form of the Invoice-Book, when the breadth of the page will admit of its use. The word " By " at each entry may be left out :—

*January 1, 1850.*

| | | | | | | | | | |
|---|---|---:|---:|---:|---:|---:|---:|---:|---:|
| 6 ✓ | Thomas Johnston, Leeds. | | | | | | | | |
|  | 25 Pieces Black Cloth, 525 yards. 14/6 | 380 | 12 | 6 | | | | | |
|  | 22  „  Brown do. 462  „  14/ | 323 | 8 | 0 | | | | | |
|  | 10  „  Doeskin, 210  „  3/6 | 36 | 15 | 0 | | | | | |
|  | Packing........................ | 0 | 12 | 6 | 741 | 8 | 0 | | |
|  | —16th.— | | | | | | | | |
| 5 / 10 | John Watson, Edinburgh. | | | | | | | | |
|  | Paper—175 Reams Demy............ 14/ | 122 | 10 | 0 | | | | | |
|  | „  220  „  Royal............ 17/ | 187 | 0 | 0 | | | | | |
|  | „  100  „  Small Post.... 14/9 | 73 | 15 | 0 | | | | | |
|  |  | 383 | 5 | 0 | | | | | |

### February 1, 1850.

| | | | | | | | | |
|---|---|---|---|---|---|---|---|---|
| **7** | David Mortimer & Son, Manchester. | | | | | | | |
| ✓ | By 60 Pieces Mousseline de Laine, 1800 yds. 1/1 | 97 | 10 | 0 | | | |
| | „ 25 „ Printed Cotton 775 „ 7d. | 22 | 12 | 1 | | | |
| | „ 20 „ Twilled do. 840 „ 6½d. | 22 | 15 | 0 | 142 | 17 | 1 |
| | —6th.— | | | | | | |
| **7** | Alexander Robertson & Co. Glasgow. | | | | | | |
| ✓ | By Goods, as per Invoice, Feb. 5 ......... | | | | 206 | 7 | 6 |
| | —12th.— | | | | | | |
| **6** | William Graham, Kingston, Jamaica. | | | | | | |
| **11** | By Coffee, 12 Tierces—(per " The Jane.") | | | | | | |
| | gross 66 2 4 | | | | | | |
| | tare 6 3 5 | | | | | | |
| | nett 59 2 27 @ £5, 2s. 8d. | 306 | 13 | 5 | | | |
| **13** | „ Insurance ....................... | 8 | 10 | 0 | | | |
| **13** | „ Commission on £8, 10s. ............... | 0 | 8 | 6 | | | |
| | | 315 | 11 | 11 | | | |
| | —16th.— | | | | | | |
| **7** | James Reid, London. | | | | | | |
| ✓ | By 8 Pieces Satinett, 220 yds. 3/2 | 34 | 16 | 8 | | | |
| | „ 12 „ French Merino, 370 „ 4/10 | 89 | 8 | 4 | | | |
| | Packing and Wharfage | 0 | 9 | 6 | 124 | 14 | 6 |
| | —17th.— | | | | | | |
| **6** | John Wilson, London. | | | | | | |
| **10** | By Goods on Commission— | | | | | | |
| | 6 Gibbon's Rome, 5 vols. 8vo... 35/ | 10 | 10 | 0 | | | |
| | 8 Russell's Modern Europe, 4 v. 30/6 | 12 | 4 | 0 | | | |
| | 2 Shakspeare, 2 vols. roy. 8vo. 24/ | 2 | 8 | 0 | | | |
| | 1 Byron's Poems, 8vo.................. | 0 | 12 | 0 | | | |
| | Box....................... | 0 | 5 | 6 | | | |
| | | 25 | 19 | 6 | | | |
| | —24th.— | | | | | | |
| **8** | John Anderson, Glasgow. | | | | | | |
| ✓ | By Goods, as per Invoice, Feb. 23........ | | | | 73 | 6 | 7 |
| | —28th.— | | | | | | |
| **10** | Goods—*Dr. To Credit Purchases*.......... | | | | 547 | 5 | 8 |

*March* 1, 1850.

| | | | | | | | |
|---|---|---:|---:|---:|---:|---:|---:|
| 7 | James Reid, London. | | | | | | |
| ✓ | By 15 Pieces Black Silk, 720 yds. 3/2 | 114 | 0 | 0 | | | |
| | „ 8 „  do. Satin, 248 „ 4/3 | 52 | 14 | 0 | | | |
| | „ 6 „  Silk Velvet,180 „ 12/6 | 112 | 10 | 0 | | | |
| | „ 2 Dozen Satin Stocks……… 38/ | 3 | 16 | 0 | | | |
| |     Packing, &c. …………… | | 13 | 6 | 283 | 13 | 6 |
| | | | | | | | |
| | *—4th.—* | | | | | | |
| 6 | John Wilson, London. | | | | | | |
| 10 | By Goods on Commission— | | | | | | |
| |   20 Campbell's Poems, 12mo… 3/ | 3 | 0 | 0 | | | |
| |   30 Gibbon's Rome, 5 v. 8vo… 35/ | 52 | 10 | 0 | | | |
| |   20 Russell's Modern Europe, 4 v. 30/6 | 30 | 10 | 0 | | | |
| |      Box……………………… | 0 | 9 | 6 | | | |
| | | 86 | 9 | 6 | | | |
| | *—13th.—* | | | | | | |
| 6 | Thomas Johnston, Leeds. | | | | | | |
| ✓ | By 36 Pieces Black Cloth, 838 yds. 15/ | 628 | 10 | 0 | | | |
| | „ 30 „  Doeskin,  630 „ 4/1 | 128 | 12 | 6 | | | |
| |     Packing, &c. …………… | 0 | 15 | 0 | 757 | 17 | 6 |
| | | | | | | | |
| | *—16th.—* | | | | | | |
| 8 | Robert Cunningham, Leeds. | | | | | | |
| ✓ | By 6 Pieces Black Cloth, 120 yds. 14/ | 84 | 0 | 0 | | | |
| | „ 2 „  Brown do.  42 „ 13/6 | 28 | 7 | 0 | | | |
| | „ 3 „  Doeskin,  61 „ 3/9 | 11 | 8 | 9 | 123 | 15 | 9 |
| | | | | | | | |
| | *—20th.—* | | | | | | |
| 7 | James Reid, London. | | | | | | |
| ✓ | By 20 Pieces French Merino, 520 yds. 5/2 | 134 | 6 | 8 | | | |
| | „ 8 Dozen Silk Handkerchiefs.. 30/ | 12 | 0 | 0 | 146 | 6 | 8 |
| | | | | | | | |
| | *—26th.—* | | | | | | |
| 7 | David Mortimer, Manchester. | | | | | | |
| ✓ | By 30 Pieces Printed cotton 990 yds. 6½d. | 26 | 16 | 3 | | | |
| | „ 45 „ Cotton Shirting, 1666 „ 7¼d. | 52 | 1 | 3 | | | |
| | „ 25 „ Twilled cotton, 950 „ 5d. | 19 | 15 | 10 | 98 | 13 | 4 |
| | | | | | | | |
| | *—31st.—* | | | | | | |
| 10 | Goods—*Dr.* *To Credit Purchases*……… | | | | 1410 | 6 | 9 |

*Cash Received.*

| | 1850 Jan. | | Cash Sales. | Bills Receivable | Discount. | Cash. |
|---|---|---|---|---|---|---|
| 15 | 1 | J. Hamilton—Cash at commencement. | | | | 2000 0 0 |
| 15 | ,, | Robert Boyd do. do. | | | | 2000 0 0 |
| ✓ | ,, | Goods—Cash Sales | 7 10 6 | | | 7 10 6 |
| 1 | 3 | James Arnold, London | | | 18 10 0 | 351 0 0 |
| 1 | 4 | James Pringle, Dublin | | | 11 2 0 | 210 18 0 |
| ✓ | ,, | Goods—Cash Sales | 9 11 0 | | | 9 11 0 |
| 1 | 5 | J. Turner, Charlotte Street | | | 0 12 6 | 25 0 0 |
| ✓ | ,, | Goods—Cash Sales | 10 2 0 | | | 10 2 0 |
| 9 | 6 | Union Bank | | | | 150 0 0 |
| 1 | 9 | James Edwards, Princes Street | | | 0 3 3 | 3 5 6 |
| ✓ | ,, | Goods—Cash Sales | 7 16 0 | | | 7 16 0 |
| ✓ | 11 | Bills Receivable, No. 1, discounted * | | 50 0 0 | 0 4 0 | 49 16 0 |
| 9 | 12 | Union Bank | | | | 200 0 0 |
| 2 | 15 | F. Milner, Dundee | | | 10 1 1 | 190 15 0 |
| 2 | 20 | J. Addison, Glasgow | | | 0 6 5 | 12 19 0 |
| ✓ | 22 | Goods—Cash Sales | 14 10 6 | | | 14 10 6 |
| 9 | 23 | Union Bank | | | | 375 0 0 |
| ✓ | 31 | Goods—Cash Sales | 7 11 9 | | | 7 11 9 |
| ✓ | ,, | Bills Receivable, No. 2, discounted | | 57 16 6 | 0 7 6 | 57 9 0 |
| 10 | ,, | Goods—Cash Sales | 57 1 9 | | | |
| 9 | ,, | Bills Receivable | | 107 16 6 | | |
| | | (Cash and Discount.) | | | | |

*Note.*—Instead of the dates being placed on the margin of the CASH-BOOK, as above, it is usual in business to place them in the centre of the page, as in the Day-Book. The same dates require to be placed opposite each other on the *Received* and *Paid* sides. January 1 opposite January 1, January 2 opposite January 2, and **so on.**

For an example of this, **and of a** convenient method of balancing the Cash-Book **daily, see Appendix,** under the head of "Cash-Book."

For the mode of posting the **Cash-**Book, see pages 85 to 89.

\* See note as to Bills, page 116.

| | | | | | | 5683 4 3 |

SECOND POSTING.

| | | | | | | |
|---|---|---|---|---|---|---|
| 12 | Discount— To Amount allowed to Sundries | | | | 41 6 9 | |
| 12 | Cash— To Amount received from Sundries | | | | | 5683 4 3 |

## Cash Paid.

| | 1850 Jan. | | Cash Purchases. | Bills Payable. | Trade Expenses. | Discount. | Cash. |
|---|---|---|---|---|---|---|---|
| 9 | 1 | Union Bank........................... | | | | | 2700 0 0 |
| ✓ | ,, | Goods—Cash Purchases........ | 10 15 0 | | | | 10 15 0 |
| 12 | ,, | Counting-House Furniture... | | | | | 125 0 0 |
| 11 | ,, | Sugar—(☞ "The Jane.") | | | | | |
| | |    Duty................ £506 9 10 | | | | | |
| | |    Freight............ 177 15 0 | | | | | |
| | |    Shore Dues, &c.   2 3 4 | | | | | |
| | |    Cooperage, Por- | | | | | |
| | |     terage, &c...... 8 15 0 | | | | | 695 3 2 |
| ✓ | ,, | Trade Expenses—Carriages... | | | 1 13 6 | | 1 13 6 |
| 11 | ,, | Port Wine, (☞ "The Ann") | | | | | |
| | |   —Duty, Freight, &c.... | | | | | 345 10 6 |
| 5 | 4 | J. Watson, Edinburgh.......... | | | | 25 17 6 | 491 16 6 |
| ✓ | 5 | Trade Expenses—Poor-rates.. | | | 5 7 6 | | 5 7 6 |
| 11 | 6 | Tea, (☞ "The Mary")— | | | | | |
| | |   Duty, Freight, &c....... | | | | | 277 19 10 |
| 9 | 11 | Union Bank...................... | | | | | 123 0 0 |
| ✓ | ,, | Goods—Cash Purchases......... | 15 2 0 | | | | 15 2 0 |
| ✓ | 12 | Trade Exp.—Shipping charges... | | | 2 10 0 | | 2 10 0 |
| 11 | ,, | Coffee, (☞ "The Mary")— | | | | | |
| | |   Duty, Freight, &c............ | | | | | 202 8 6 |
| 9 | 15 | Union Bank...................... | | | | | 180 0 0 |
| 7 | 18 | Marine Insurance Co............ | | | | | 5 14 0 |
| ✓ | 19 | Trade Expenses—Salaries*... | | | 21 2 0 | | 21 2 0 |
| 5 | 23 | Bills Payable, No. 1.............. | | 300 0 0 | | | 300 0 0 |
| 5 | 25 | J. Watson, Edinburgh.......... | | | | 4 3 0 | 79 2 0 |
| 15 | 30 | James Hamilton................ | | | | | 30 0 0 |
| 15 | ,, | Robert Boyd.................... | | | | | 25 0 0 |
| 10 | 31 | Goods—Cash Purchases........ | 25 17 0 | | | | |
| 9 | ,, | Bills Payable..................... | | 300 0 0 | | | |
| 13 | ,, | Trade Expenses................. | | | 30 13 0 | | |
| | ,, | Cash on Hand.................... | | | | | 45 19 9 |
| | | * In actual business, the names of the persons to whom the salaries are paid, are entered. See page 45. | | | | | 5683 4 3 |
| | | Second Posting. | | | | | |
| 12 | | Discount— | | | | | |
| | |   By Amount allowed by Sundries............................... | | | | 30 0 6 | |
| 12 | | Cash— | | | | | |
| | |   By Amount paid to Sundries.................................... | | | | | 5637 4 6 |
| | |      Viz. sum-total above.................£5683 4 3 | | | | | |
| | |      Deduct Cash on Hand................. 45 19 9 | | | | | |
| | |      £5637 4 6 | | | | | |

*Cash Received.*

| 1850 Feb. | | | Discount. | | | Cash. | | |
|---|---|---|---|---|---|---|---|---|
| | 1 | Cash on hand.............................. | | | | 45 | 19 | 9 |
| ✓ | " | Goods—Cash Sales..................... | | | | 6 | 15 | 0 |
| 1 | " | James Pringle, Dublin.................. | 24 | 15 | 6 | 470 | 9 | 0 |
| ✓ | 2 | Bills Receivable, No. 3, discounted*... | 0 | 17 | 11 | 211 | 10 | 0 |
| 3 | " | W. Forbes, George Street............ | 0 | 1 | 2 | 1 | 4 | 6 |
| ✓ | " | Goods—Cash Sales..................... | | | | 7 | 12 | 6 |
| 4 | 9 | Robert Ireland, London.............. | 5 | 9 | 9 | 104 | 3 | 0 |
| 9 | 12 | Union Bank.............................. | | | | 50 | 0 | 0 |
| ✓ | 17 | Bills Receivable, No. 4, discounted.... | 1 | 8 | 2 | 114 | 8 | 0 |
| ✓ | " | Goods—Cash Sales..................... | | | | 9 | 4 | 3 |
| 3 | 20 | George Smith, Bristol................. | 3 | 15 | 7 | 71 | 13 | 6 |
| ✓ | " | Goods—Cash Sales..................... | | | | 8 | 7 | 6 |
| 9 | 23 | Union Bank.............................. | | | | 600 | 0 | 0 |
| ✓ | 25 | Bills Receivable, No. 5, discounted.... | 0 | 9 | 2 | 136 | 10 | 0 |
| 2 | " | John Addison, Glasgow.............. | | | | 200 | 0 | 0 |
| ✓ | " | Goods—Cash Sales..................... | | | | 9 | 17 | 4 |
| ✓ | 28 | Bills Receivable, No. 7, discounted ... | 1 | 0 | 1 | 242 | 2 | 0 |
| 9 | " | Union Bank.............................. | | | | 350 | 0 | 0 |
| 10 | " | Goods—Cash Sales...... ‖ 41|16| 7 | | | | | | |
| 9 | " | Bills Receivable.......... ‖ 708| 5| 4 | | | | | | |

These are the sums-total for the month.

*BILLS—
The Bills Receivable entered in the Cash-Book are supposed to be discounted at the Bank. Bills are, however, often not discounted, but paid away, sometimes at their full value, to other merchants in settlement of their accounts. In such cases they would be entered thus—

On the Received side—
   Bills Receivable, No. 2....................57 16 6

On the Paid side—
   J. Watson, Edinburgh, Bills
     Receivable, No. 2....................57 16 6

In business, the names as well as the Nos. of the Bills, are marked in the Cash-Book. Thus—
   Bills Receivable, No. 1, T. Dundas,
     Manchester................... 50 0 0
   Bills Payable, No. 1, J. Watson,
     Edinburgh.........................300 0 0

| | | | | | | 2639 | 16 | 4 |
|---|---|---|---|---|---|---|---|---|

SECOND POSTING.

| 12 | | Discount— | | | | | | |
|---|---|---|---|---|---|---|---|---|
| | | To *Amount allowed to Sundries*......... | 37 | 17 | 4 | | | |
| 12 | | Cash— | | | | | | |
| | | To *Amount received from Sundries*.... | | | | 2593 | 16 | 7 |

Viz. sum-total above,  £2639 16 4
Deduct Cash on Hand, Feb. 1,   45 19 9

                    £2593 16 7

This page to be written out, with additional columns, in the same form as page 114.

## Cash Paid.

| | 1850 Feb. | | Discount. | | | Cash. | | |
|---|---|---|---|---|---|---|---|---|
| 9 | 1 | Union Bank........................ | | | | 390 | 0 | 0 |
| 7 | ,, | James Reid, London ................. | 5 | 17 | 6 | 111 | 11 | 0 |
| √ | 2 | Trade Expenses—Salaries........... | | | | 8 | 5 | 0 |
| 9 | ,, | Union Bank........................ | | | | 80 | 0 | 0 |
| √ | ,, | Bills Payable, No. 2.................... | | | | 100 | 0 | 0 |
| √ | ,, | Goods—Cash Purchases ............. | | | | 17 | 6 | 0 |
| √ | 9 | **Trade** Expenses—Salaries........... | | | | 7 | 4 | 0 |
| ., | ,, | ,,     ,,     Postage Stamps. | | | | 0 | 13 | 6 |
| 15 | 10 | Robert Boyd ....................... | | | | 15 | 0 | 0 |
| √ | ,, | Trade Expenses—Police **Tax**....... | | | | 2 | 9 | 6 |
| 11 | 12 | Coffee—(℔ "The Jane.") | | | | | | |
| | | Duty........................ £111 10 4 | | | | | | |
| | | Freight..................... 15 15 0 | | | | | | |
| | | Shore Dues, &c....... ..... 0 3 6 | | | | | | |
| | | Cooperage, Porterage, &c.. 1 16 0 | | | | 129 | 4 | 10 |
| √ | 14 | **Trade** Expenses—Brown Paper.... | | | | 0 | 8 | 6 |
| √ | 15 | ,,     ,,     Salaries........... | | | | 7 | 8 | 0 |
| 15 | 17 | James Hamilton ...................... | | | | 30 | 0 | 0 |
| √ | ,, | **Goods—Cash** Purchases............. | | | | 16 | 19 | 0 |
| 9 | ,, | Union Bank........................ | | | | 75 | 0 | 0 |
| 13 | 18 | Insurance, on Goods to A. Gregory, Calcutta... | | | | 7 | 14 | 9 |
| √ | 23 | Bills Payable, No. 3.................... | | | | 641 | 8 | 0 |
| 9 | 25 | Union Bank........................ | | | | 350 | 0 | 0 |
| √ | 28 | Bills Payable, No. 4................... | | | | 572 | 3 | 6 |
| 7 | ,, | D. Mortimer and Son, Manchester. | 2 | 2 | 1 | 40 | 15 | 0 |
| 10 | ,, | Goods—Cash Purchases* | 34 5 0 | | | | | |
| 9 | ,, | Bills Payable............ * | 1313 11 6 | | | | | |
| 13 | ,, | Trade Expenses........ * | 26 8 6 | | | | | |
| | ,, | Cash **on** Hand....................... | | | | 36 | 5 | 9 |
| | | | | | | 2639 | 16 | 4 |

\* These are the sums-total for the **month.**

| | | SECOND POSTING. | | | | | | |
|---|---|---|---|---|---|---|---|---|
| 12 | | Discount— | | | | | | |
| | | By Amount allowed by Sundries......... | 7 | 19 | 7 | | | |
| 12 | | Cash— | | | | | | |
| | | By Amount paid to Sundries............ | | | | 2603 | 10 | 7 |
| | | Viz. sum-total above, £2639 16 4 | | | | | | |
| | | Deduct Cash on Hand, 36 5 9 | | | | | | |
| | | £2603 10 **7** | | | | | | |

This page to be written out, with additional columns, in the same form as page 115.

## Cash Received.

| | 1850 Mar. | | Discount. | | | Cash. | | |
|---|---|---|---|---|---|---|---|---|
| | 1 | Cash on hand.................... | | | | 36 | 5 | 9 |
| ✓ | ,, | Bills Receivable, No. 8, discounted ... | 0 | 5 | 6 | 75 | 14 | 6 |
| ✓ | ,, | Goods—Cash Sales..................... | | | | 4 | 15 | 0 |
| 5 | 4 | Thomas Thomson, Aberdeen...... | 0 | 9 | 2 | 17 | 16 | 6 |
| 9 | ,, | Union Bank............................ | | | | 375 | 0 | 0 |
| ✓ | ,, | Goods—Cash Sales..................... | | | | 4 | 15 | 1 |
| ✓ | 5 | Bills Receivable, No. 10, discounted.. | 0 | 13 | 0 | 119 | 7 | 0 |
| 2 | 7 | T. Dundas, Manchester.............. | | | | 84 | 11 | 3 |
| ✓ | ,, | Goods—Cash Sales..................... | | | | 4 | 13 | 2 |
| 9 | 11 | Union Bank........................... | | | | 75 | 0 | 0 |
| 4 | 15 | James Pringle, Dublin.............. | 2 | 10 | 4 | 47 | 16 | 0 |
| ✓ | ,, | Goods—Cash Sales..................... | | | | 1 | 12 | 6 |
| ✓ | 20 | Bills Receivable, No. 11, discounted.. | 1 | 0 | 0 | 119 | 0 | 0 |
| ✓ | 22 | Goods—Cash Sales..................... | | | | 2 | 12 | 8 |
| 2 | ,, | J. Addison, Glasgow— | | | | | | |
| | | Composition of 10/ a £......... | | | | 93 | 8 | 4 |
| 9 | 23 | Union Bank.......................... | | | | 230 | 0 | 0 |
| 5 | 30 | George Knight, Birmingham...... | | | | 298 | 4 | 7 |
| ✓ | ,, | Goods—Cash Sales.................... | | | | 4 | 19 | 9 |
| 2 | ,, | A. Gregory, Calcutta— | | | | | | |
| | | Drawback on Paper............. | | | | 63 | 16 | 10 |
| 10 | 31 | Goods—Cash Sales...... ‖ 23 8 2 | | | | | | |
| 9 | ,, | Bills Receivable......... ‖ 316 0 0 | | | | | | |
| | | | | | | 1659 | 8 | 11 |

SECOND POSTING.

| | | | | | | | | |
|---|---|---|---|---|---|---|---|---|
| 12 | | Discount— | | | | | | |
| | | To *Amount allowed to Sundries*......... | 4 | 18 | 0 | | | |
| 12 | | Cash— | | | | | | |
| | | To *Amount received from Sundries*.... | | | | 1623 | 3 | 2 |

Viz. sum-total above,   £1659   8   11
Deduct Cash on Hand, March 1,   36   5   9

£1623   3   2

This page to be written out, with additional columns, in the same form as page 114.

## Cash Paid.

| | 1850 Mar. | | | Discount. | | | Cash. | | |
|---|---|---|---|---|---|---|---|---|---|
| 9 | 1 | Union Bank................... | | | | | 100 | 0 | 0 |
| ✓ | ,, | Trade Expenses—Salaries......... | | | | | 5 | 16 | 0 |
| 7 | 4 | James Reid, London................ | 7 | 10 | 0 | | 142 | 10 | 0 |
| ✓ | ,, | Bills Payable, No. 5............... | | | | | 250 | 0 | 0 |
| 15 | 5 | Robert Boyd...................... | | | | | 40 | 0 | 0 |
| 15 | ,, | James Hamilton.................. | | | | | 35 | 0 | 0 |
| ✓ | 8 | Trade Expenses—Rent............. | | | | | 85 | 0 | 0 |
| ✓ | ,, | ,,      ,,      Salaries......... | | | | | 7 | 12 | 0 |
| ✓ | 10 | Goods—Cash Purchases.......... | | | | | 5 | 17 | 0 |
| ✓ | 11 | Bills Payable, No. 8............... | | | | | 100 | 0 | 0 |
| ✓ | 15 | Trade Expenses—Salaries......... | | | | | 7 | 11 | 0 |
| ✓ | ,, | ,,      ,,      Rope and twine | | | | | 0 | 14 | 6 |
| 9 | 20 | Union Bank...................... | | | | | 150 | 0 | 0 |
| 9 | 22 | do.   do. ...................... | | | | | 100 | 0 | 0 |
| 7 | 23 | Robertson & Co. Glasgow.......... | 5 | 3 | 6 | | 201 | 4 | 0 |
| ✓ | 24 | Goods—Cash Purchases........... | | | | | 10 | 17 | 0 |
| 6 | 31 | J. Wilson, London................ | | | | | 27 | 0 | 0 |
| ✓ | ,, | Trade Expenses—Salaries......... | | | | | 7 | 10 | 0 |
| ✓ | ,, | ,,      ,,      Freight......... | | | | | 0 | 5 | 5 |
| 9 | ,, | Union Bank...................... | | | | | 316 | 0 | 0 |
| 15 | ,, | Robert Boyd .................... | | | | | 15 | 0 | 0 |
| 10 | ,, | Goods—Cash Purchases 16 14 0 | | | | | | | |
| 9 | ,, | Bills Payable............ 350 0 0 | | | | | | | |
| 13 | ,, | Trade Expenses......... 114 8 11 | | | | | | | |
| | ,, | **Cash** on Hand................. | | | | | 51 | 12 | 0 |
| | | | | | | | 1659 | 8 | 11 |

### SECOND POSTING.

| | | | | | | | | | |
|---|---|---|---|---|---|---|---|---|---|
| 12 | | Discount— | | | | | | | |
| | | By **Amount** allowed by Sundries....... | | 12 | 13 | 6 | | | | |
| 12 | | Cash— | | | | | | | |
| | | By Amount paid to Sundries........... | | | | | 1607 | 16 | 11 |

Viz. sum-total above, £1659  8 11
Deduct Cash on Hand,   51 12  0

£1607 16 11

This page to be written out, with additional columns, in the same form as page 115.

## Bills

| | No. | When received | From whom Received. | Amount. | | | Date. | Term. | When Due. | Entered in Cash-Bk. |
|---|---|---|---|---|---|---|---|---|---|---|
| | | 1850. | | | | | 1850. | | 1850. | 1850. |
| 2 | 1 | Jan. 10 | T. Dundas,    Manchester. | 50 | 0 | 0 | Jan. 8 | 1 mo. | Feb. 11 | Jan. 11 |
| 2 | 2 | ,,   ,, | do.       do. | 57 | 16 | 6 | ,,   ,, | 2  ,, | Mar. 11 | ,,   31 |
| 3 | 3 | ,,   31 | R. Hall,      Leeds. | 212 | 7 | 11 | ,,   29 | 2  ,, | April 1 | Feb.   2 |
| 9 | | | Bills Receivable—<br>*To Amount received from*<br>*Sundries*............... | 320 | 4 | 5 | | | | |
| 3 | 4 | Feb. 14 | W. Forbes,    George Street | 115 | 16 | 2 | Feb.14 | 3  ,, | May 17 | Feb.   17 |
| 3 | 5 | ,,   ,, | G. Smith,     Bristol. | 136 | 19 | 2 | ,,   ,, | 1  ,, | Mar. 17 | ,,   25 |
| 4 | 6 | ,,   20 | A. Logan,    Newcastle. | 297 | 0 | 0 | ,,   18 | 3  ,, | May 21 | |
| 2 | 7 | ,,   26 | F. Milner,    Dundee. | 243 | 2 | 1 | ,,   20 | 1  ,, | Mar. 23 | ,,   28 |
| 9 | | ,,   28 | Bills Receivable—<br>*To Amount received from*<br>*Sundries*............... | 792 | 17 | 5 | | | | |
| 4 | 8 | Mar. 2 | T. Simpson,    Belfast. | 76 | 0 | 0 | Mar. 1 | 1  ,, | April 4 | Mar.   1 |
| 5 | 9 | ,,   7 | W. Jerdan,    Queen Street | 106 | 7 | 2 | ,,   7 | 4  ,, | July 10 | |
| 1 | 10 | ,,   20 | J. Arnold,    London. | 120 | 0 | 0 | ,,   19 | 1  ,, | April 22 | ,,   5 |
| 1 | 11 | ,,   ,, | do.       **do.** | 120 | 0 | 0 | ,,   ,, | 2  ,, | May 22 | ,,   20 |
| 1 | 12 | ,,   ,, | do.       do. | 140 | 13 | 0 | ,,   ,, | 3  ,, | June 22 | |
| 3 | 13 | ,,   ,, | G. Campbell,    Liverpool. | 182 | 0 | 2 | ,,   17 | 2  ,, | May 20 | |
| 3 | 14 | ,,   ,, | do.       do. | 200 | 8 | 6 | ,,   ,, | 3  ,, | June 20 | |
| 9 | | ,,   31 | Bills Receivable—<br>*To Amount received from*<br>*Sundries*............... | 945 | 8 | 10 | | | | |

mo. is a contraction for month.

1 mo. means that the bill is due 1 month after its date.

The Bills, when discounted, or otherwise disposed of, are entered in the Cash-Book, see note, page 116, and the dates are filled in here.

For the mode of posting the Bill-Book, see page 90.

## Receivable.

| By whom Drawn. | On whom Drawn. | To whom Payable. | Where Payable. | Jan. | Feb. | March. | April. | May. | June. | July. | August. | Sept. | Oct. | Nov. | Dec. |
|---|---|---|---|---|---|---|---|---|---|---|---|---|---|---|---|
| Hamilton & Boyd. | T. Dundas. | Hamilton & Boyd. | Manchester. | 11 | | | | | | | | | | | |
| T. Dundas. | A. Brown. | T. Dundas. | Leeds. | | 11 | | | | | | | | | | |
| | | | | | | 1 | | | | | | | | | |
| | | | | | | 17 | | | | | | | | | |
| | | | | | 17 | | 21 | | | | | | | | |
| | | | | | 23 | | | | | | | | | | |
| | | | | | | 4 | | | | | | | | | |
| | | | | | | | | | 10 | | | | | | |
| | | | | | | 22 | | | | | | | | | |
| | | | | | | | 22 | | | | | | | | |
| | | | | | | | | 22 | | | | | | | |
| | | | | | | | 20 | | | | | | | | |
| | | | | | | | | 20 | | | | | | | |

These columns are used in business for entering the particulars shown in the above examples: it is unnecessary here, however, to fill up the other blanks.

These columns are used for ascertaining readily the dates when the bills are due.

## Bills

| | No. | When Granted* | To whom Granted.* | Amount. | Date. | Term. | When Due. | Entered in Cash-Bk. |
|---|---|---|---|---|---|---|---|---|
| | | 1850. | | | 1850. | | 1850. | 1850. |
| 5 | 1 | Jan. 10 | J. Watson,   Edinburgh. | 300 0 0 | Jan.10 | 10 da. | Jan. 23 | Jan. 23 |
| 6 | 2 | ,, 20 | T. Johnston,   Leeds. | 100 0 0 | ,, 20 | 10 ,, | Feb. 2 | Feb. 2 |
| 6 | 3 | ,, ,, | do.   do. | 641 8 0 | ,, ,, | 1 mo. | ,, 23 | ,, 23 |
| 7 | 4 | ,, 25 | Mortimer & Son, Manchester | 572 3 6 | ,, 25 | 1 ,, | ,, 28 | ,, 28 |
| 9 | | ,, 31 | Bills Payable— *By Amount granted to Sundries*.............. | 1613 11 6 | | | | |
| 6 | 5 | Feb. 1 | T. Johnston,   Leeds. | 250 0 0 | Feb. 1 | 1 ,, | Mar. 4 | Mar. 4 |
| 6 | 6 | ,, ,, | do.   do. | 300 0 0 | ,, ,, | 2 ,, | April 4 | |
| 7 | 7 | ,, 2 | A. Robertson,   Glasgow. | 234 14 8 | ,, 2 | 2 ,, | ,, 5 | |
| 7 | 8 | ,, 8 | Mortimer & Son, Manchester | 100 0 0 | ,, 8 | 1 ,, | Mar. 11 | ,, 11 |
| 7 | 9 | ,, 20 | J. Reid,   London. | 124 14 6 | ,, 20 | 3 ,, | May 23 | |
| 9 | | ,, 28 | Bills Payable— *By Amount granted to Sundries*.............. | 1009 9 2 | | | | |
| 6 | 10 | Mar. 3 | W. Graham,   Kingston.+ | 200 0 0 | Mar. 3 | 30 days sight | | |
| 6 | 11 | ,, ,, | do.   do. + | 200 0 0 | ,, ,, | 60 days sight | | |
| 8 | 12 | ,, 10 | J. Anderson,   Glasgow. | 73 6 7 | ,, 10 | 1 mo. | April 13 | |
| 9 | | ,, 31 | Bills Payable— *By Amount granted to Sundries*.............. | 473 6 7 | | | | |

* Or, accepted

* Or, **By whom Drawn.**

+ These two bills are supposed to be drawn by Hamilton and Boyd upon a person in Kingston who is owing them money, and to be payable to W. Graham at 30 and 60 days' sight— that is, **30** and 60 days after having **been** sighted or seen by **the** person who is to pay **them** to W. Graham.

*(Term column note, vertical): mo. is a contraction for month; da. for days. 10 da. means that the bill is due 10 days after its date.*

## *Payable.*

| To whom Payable. | Where Payable. | Jan. | Feb. | March. | April. | May. | June. | July. | August. | Sept. | Oct. | Nov. | Dec. |
|---|---|---|---|---|---|---|---|---|---|---|---|---|---|
| J. Watson. | Union Bank, Edinburgh. | 23 | | | | | | | | | | | |
| R. Russell. | Bank of England. | | 2 | | | | | | | | | | |
| | | | 23 | | | | | | | | | | |
| | | | 28 | | | | | | | | | | |
| | | | | 4 | | | | | | | | | |
| | | | | | 4 | | | | | | | | |
| | | | | | 5 | | | | | | | | |
| | | | 11 | | | | | | | | | | |
| | | | | | | 23 | | | | | | | |
| | | | | 13 | | | | | | | | | |

These columns are used for ascertaining readily the dates when the bills are due.

# WAREHOUSE-BOOK.

This book is used for keeping an account of the *quantities* of goods received into, or sent out from the warehouse. It is suitable chiefly in those cases where goods are bought and sold in considerable quantities at a time.

By means of the Warehouse-Book, the *quantity* sold and on hand of any description of goods can be ascertained at once, on turning up the page where the account is kept. It is necessary to have an Index of the different accounts entered.

The mode of keeping the book varies according to the nature of the business. In the following specimen is shown a method adapted to ordinary cases.

The two accounts entered below are for the Sugar and Tea received on Commission from James Cameron and William Black, and which appear in the preceding Day-Book as sold to the various parties mentioned.

The quantities are supposed to be entered on the *Dr.* side, as below, at the time of being received; and on the *Cr.* side when they are sold.

## SUGAR.

| 1850 | | | Hhds. | 1850 | | | Day-Bk page. | H |
|---|---|---|---|---|---|---|---|---|
| Jan. | 1 | To Received from— J. Cameron, Demerara, per "The Jane" .... | 50 | Jan. Mar. | 20 4 26 29 | By Sold to R. Hall... „ „ G. Knight „ „ do. „ „ J. Pringle | 3 8 10 11 | |
| | | | 50 | | | | | 5 |

## TEA.

| 1850 | | | Chests. | 1850 | | | Day-Bk page. | Ch |
|---|---|---|---|---|---|---|---|---|
| Jan. | 6 | To Received from— William Black, Canton, per "The Mary".... | 40 | Jan. Mar | 8 30 6 9 31 | By Sold to T. Dundas „ „ G. Smith. „ „ T. Dundas „ „ G. Campbell „ On hand, forward | 2 4 8 9 | |
| | | | 40 | | | | | 4 |
| Apr. | 1 | „ On Hand .......... | 8 | | | | | |

# STOCK-BOOK.

*Goods on Hand, March* **31**, 1850.

| | | | | £ | s | d |
|---|---|---|---|---|---|---|
| 10 Pieces | Superfine Black Cloth, 200 yards 14/6 | | | 145 | 0 | 0 |
| 6 „ | Printed Cotton, 180 „ 7d. | | | 5 | 5 | 0 |
| 3 „ | French Merino, 92 „ 4/10 | | | 22 | 4 | 8 |
| 2 „ | Crimson Velvet, 60 „ 12/6 | | | 37 | 10 | 0 |
| 12 „ | Irish Linen, 362 „ 1/6 | | | 27 | 3 | 0 |
| Sundries | (In actual business all the particulars are given.) | | | 1595 | 5 | 10 |
| This sum is entered in the Ledger under " Goods." | | | | 1832 | 8 | 6 |
| Coffee—6 Tierces, 32 cwt. 2 qrs. @ £7, 4s. 8d. | | | | 235 | 1 | 8 |
| This is entered in the Ledger under " Coffee." | | | | | | |
| Wine—2 Pipes ..................... @ £68 | | | | 136 | 0 | 0 |
| This is entered in the Ledger under " Wine." | | | | | | |

The Coffee and Wine are entered by themselves, because separate accounts are kept for them in the Ledger.

*Books on Commission from J. Wilson, London— on Hand, March* 31, 1850.

| | £ | s | d |
|---|---|---|---|
| 2 Brown's Moral Philosophy, 8vo............. 12/ | 1 | 4 | 0 |
| 3 Campbell's Poems, 18mo..................... 3/4 | 0 | 10 | 0 |
| 2 Russell's Modern Europe, 4 vols. 8vo...... 30/6 | 3 | 1 | 0 |
| Sundries...................................... | 85 | 4 | 2 |
| These goods are entered to the *Dr.* of J. Wilson's account in the Ledger, to show the balance due to him; but are not included in the Inventory of Hamilton and Boyd's own goods, as they belong not to **them** but to J. Wilson. | 89 | 19 | 2 |

The chests of Tea on hand (see Warehouse-Book) are not included in the Inventory, **as** they belong to the parties who sent them on sale.

# LEDGER.

---

## INDEX.

## James Arnold, London.

| 1850. | | | | | | | 1850. | | | | | | |
|---|---|---|---|---|---|---|---|---|---|---|---|---|---|
| Jan. | 1 | To Goods..... | 1 | 369 | 10 | 0 | Jan. | 3 | By Cash....... | 1 | 351 | 0 | 0 |
| Feb. | 18 | „ do. ...... | 6 | 24 | 13 | 0 | „ | „ | „ Discount.. | „ | 18 | 10 | 0 |
| Mar. | 4 | „ do.* ..... | 8 | 10 | 18 | 0 | Mar. | 20 | „ 3 Bills* ... | 1 | 380 | 13 | 0 |
| | 18 | „ do. ...... | 10 | 335 | 2 | 0 | | | | | | | |
| | „ | „ do.† Mar. 4 under posted | | 10 | 0 | 0 | | | * The dates are left out for want of space. | | | | |
| | | | | 750 | 3 | 0 | | | | | 750 | 3 | 0 |

\* Posted incorrectly, to show the mode of rectifying the error.
† The error of March 4 is rectified by making this entry, as soon as the mistake is discovered.

## John Turner, 10 Charlotte Street.

| 1850. | | | | | | | 1850. | | | | | | |
|---|---|---|---|---|---|---|---|---|---|---|---|---|---|
| Jan. | 2 | To Goods ..... | 1 | 25 | 12 | 6 | Jan. | 5 | By Cash....... | 1 | 25 | 0 | 0 |
| Mar. | 14 | „ do. ...... | 9 | 252 | 0 | 0 | „ | „ | „ Discount. | „ | 0 | 12 | 6 |
| | 26 | „ do. ...... | 11 | 53 | 9 | 0 | Mar. | 31 | „ Balance*.. | | 305 | 9 | 0 |
| | | | | 331 | 1 | 6 | | | | | 331 | 1 | 6 |
| Mar. | 31 | To Balance. § | | 305 | 9 | 0 | | | * or, Balance forward. | | | | |

## James Pringle, Dublin.

| 1850. | | | | | | | 1850. | | | | | | |
|---|---|---|---|---|---|---|---|---|---|---|---|---|---|
| Jan. | 3 | To Goods ..... | 1 | 222 | 0 | 0 | Jan. | 4 | By Cash....... | 1 | 210 | 18 | 0 |
| | 12 | „ do. ...... | 1 | 495 | 4 | 6 | „ | „ | „ Discount. | „ | 11 | 2 | 0 |
| Mar. | 14 | „ do. ...... | 9 | 50 | 6 | 4 | Feb. | 1 | „ Cash....... | 3 | 470 | 9 | 0 |
| | | | | | | | „ | „ | „ Discount. | „ | 24 | 15 | 6 |
| | | *to page* 4 | | 767 | 10 | 10 | | | *to page* 4 | | 717 | 4 | 6 |
| | | Carried to page 4, as this space is filled up. | | | | | | | | | | | |

## James Edwards, 20 Princes Street.

| 1850. | | | | | | | 1850. | | | | | | |
|---|---|---|---|---|---|---|---|---|---|---|---|---|---|
| Jan. | 5 | To Goods..... | 1 | 13 | 8 | 9 | Jan. | 9 | By Cash....... | 1 | 3 | 5 | 6 |
| | | This is posted £10 too much: the error is rectified by making an entry on the other side of the account, as soon as the mistake is discovered. | | | | | „ | „ | „ Discount. | „ | 0 | 3 | 3 |
| | | | | | | | „ | „ | „ Goods, Jan. 5, overposted.. | | 10 | 0 | 0 |
| | | | | 13 | 8 | 9 | | | | | 13 | 8 | 9 |

§ In business, it is unnecessary to balance off unsettled accounts in this way. It is sufficient merely to add up the columns, marking the Dr. or Cr. balances in a temporary way with a pencil, and ruling off the accounts only when they are actually settled.

## Thomas Dundas, Manchester.

| 1850. | | | | | | 1850. | | | | | | |
|---|---|---|---|---|---|---|---|---|---|---|---|---|
| Jan. | 8 | To Goods..... | 2 | 107 | 16 | 6 | Jan. | 10 | By 2 Bills...... | 1 | 107 | 16 | 6 |
| | 17 | „ do.* ..... | 3 | 13 | 5 | 5 | | 17 | „ Goods— posted in error, carried to John Addison's a/c | 2 | 13 | 5 | 5 |
| | | *This is supposed to be posted by mistake to T. Dundas instead of to J. Addison: the error is rectified by an entry on the other side. | | | | | | 7 | „ Cash....... | 5 | 84 | 11 | 3 |
| | | | | | | | Mar. | 31 | „ Balance... | | 238 | 5 | 8 |
| Mar. | 6 | To Goods..... | 8 | 84 | 11 | 3 | | | | | | | |
| | 16 | „ do. ...... | 10 | 238 | 5 | 8 | | | | | | | |
| | | | | 443 | 18 | 10 | | | | | 443 | 18 | 10 |
| Mar. | 31 | To Balance... | | 238 | 5 | 8 | | | | | | | |

## Francis Milner, Dundee.

| 1850. | | | | | | | 1850. | | | | | | |
|---|---|---|---|---|---|---|---|---|---|---|---|---|---|
| Jan. | 10 | To Goods...... | 2 | 200 | 16 | 1 | Jan. | 15 | By Cash....... | 1 | 190 | 15 | 0 |
| Feb. | 19 | „ do. ....... | 6 | 243 | 2 | 1 | | „ | „ Discount. | „ | 10 | 1 | 1 |
| | | | | | | | Feb. | 26 | „ Bill due Mar. 23... | 1 | 243 | 2 | 1 |
| | | | | 443 | 18 | 2 | | | | | 443 | 18 | 2 |

## Alexander Gregory, Calcutta.

| 1850. | | | | | | | 1850. | | | | | | |
|---|---|---|---|---|---|---|---|---|---|---|---|---|---|
| Jan. | 16 | To Goods..... (or Sundries.) | 2 | 200 | 19 | 9 | Mar. | 30 | By Cash— Drawback.. | 5 | 63 | 16 | 10 |
| Feb. | 18 | „ Goods ..... | 6 | 265 | 12 | 6 | | 31 | „ Balance... | „ | 402 | 15 | 5 |
| | | | | 466 | 12 | 3 | | | | | 466 | 12 | 3 |
| Mar. | 31 | To Balance... | | 402 | 15 | 5 | | | | | | | |

## John Addison, Glasgow.

| 1850. | | | | | | | 1850. | | | | | | |
|---|---|---|---|---|---|---|---|---|---|---|---|---|---|
| Jan. | 17 | To Goods...... | 3 | 13 | 5 | 5 | Jan. | 20 | By Cash....... | 1 | 12 | 19 | 0 |
| Feb. | 4 | „ do....... | 5 | 386 | 16 | 8 | | „ | „ Discount.. | „ | 0 | 6 | 5 |
| | | | | | | | Feb. | 25 | „ Cash....... | 3 | 200 | 0 | 0 |
| | | | | | | | Mar. | 22 | „ Cash— Composition | 5 | 93 | 8 | 4 |
| | | | | | | | | „ | „ Balance carried to Bad Debts | 13 | 93 | 8 | 4 |
| | | | | 400 | 2 | 1 | | | | | 400 | 2 | 1 |

I

## WALTER FORBES, George Street.

| 1850. | | | | | | | 1850. | | | | | | | |
|---|---|---|---|---|---|---|---|---|---|---|---|---|---|---|
| Jan. | 17 | To Goods...... | 3 | 1 | 5 | 8 | Feb. | 14 | By Bill due | | | | | |
| Feb. | 14 | ,, do......... | 5 | 115 | 16 | 2 | | | May 17 ... | 1 | 115 | 16 | 2 |
| | | | | | | | Feb. | 2 | ,, Cash........ | 3 | 1 | 4 | 6 |
| | | | | | | | ,, | ,, Discount.. | ,, | 0 | 1 | 2 |
| | | | | 117 | 1 | 10 | | | | | 117 | 1 | 10 |

## RICHARD HALL, Leeds.

| 1850. | | | | | | | 1850. | | | | | | |
|---|---|---|---|---|---|---|---|---|---|---|---|---|---|
| Jan. | 20 | To Goods...... | 3 | 212 | 7 | 11 | Jan. | 31 | By Bill due | | | | |
| Feb. | 27 | ,, do...... | 7 | 24 | 10 | 2 | | | April 1 ... | 1 | 212 | 7 | 11 |
| | | | | | | | Mar. | 31 | ,, Balance carried to BadDebts | 13 | 24 | 10 | 2 |
| | | | | 236 | 18 | 1 | | | | | 236 | 18 | 1 |

## GEORGE CAMPBELL, Liverpool.

| 1850. | | | | | | | 1850. | | | | | | |
|---|---|---|---|---|---|---|---|---|---|---|---|---|---|
| Jan. | 25 | To Goods...... | 4 | 249 | 1 | 8 | Mar. | 20 | By Bill due | | | | |
| Mar. | 9 | ,, do. ...... | 9 | 133 | 7 | 0 | | | May 20 ... | 1 | 182 | 0 | 2 |
| | | | | | | | | | ,, Bill due June 20... | ,, | 200 | 8 | 6 |
| | | | | 382 | 8 | 8 | | | | | 382 | 8 | 8 |

## GEORGE SMITH, Bristol.

| 1850. | | | | | | | 1850. | | | | | | |
|---|---|---|---|---|---|---|---|---|---|---|---|---|---|
| Jan. | 30 | To Goods..... | 4 | 136 | 19 | 2 | Feb. | 14 | By Bill due | | | | |
| Feb. | 9 | ,, do........ | 5 | 75 | 9 | 1 | | | March 17 | 1 | 136 | 19 | 2 |
| | | | | | | | 20 | ,, Cash........ | 3 | 71 | 13 | 6 |
| | | | | | | | ,, | ,, Discount.. | ,, | 3 | 15 | 7 |
| | | | | 212 | 8 | 3 | | | | | 212 | 8 | 3 |

### Robert Ireland, London.

| 1850. | | | | | | | 1850. | | | | | |
|---|---|---|---|---|---|---|---|---|---|---|---|---|
| Feb. | 1 | To Goods...... | 5 | 109 | 12 | 9 | Feb. | 9 | By Cash....... | 3 | 104 | 3 | 0 |
| Mar. | 22 | „ do........ | 10 | 49 | 2 | 10 | | | „ „ Discount... | „ | 5 | 9 | 9 |
| | | | | | | | Mar. | 31 | „ Balance... | | 49 | 2 | 10 |
| | | | | 158 | 15 | 7 | | | | | 158 | 15 | 7 |
| Mar. | 31 | To Balance ... | | 49 | 2 | 10 | | | | | | | |

### James Pringle, Dublin.

| 1850. | | | | | | | 1850. | | | | | |
|---|---|---|---|---|---|---|---|---|---|---|---|---|
| | | *from page* 1 | | 767 | 10 | 10 | | | *from page* 1 | | 717 | 4 | 6 |
| Mar. | 19 | To Goods.... | 10 | 293 | 8 | 4 | Mar. | 15 | By Cash...... | 5 | 47 | 16 | 0 |
| | 29 | „ do...... | 11 | 265 | 16 | 10 | | | „ „ Discount | „ | 2 | 10 | 4 |
| | | | | | | | | 31 | „ Balance.. | | 559 | 5 | 2 |
| | | | | 1326 | 16 | 0 | | | | | 1326 | 16 | 0 |
| **Mar.** | 31 | To Balance.. | | 559 | 5 | 2 | | | | | | | |

### Archibald Logan, Newcastle.

| 1850. | | | | | | | 1850. | | | | | |
|---|---|---|---|---|---|---|---|---|---|---|---|---|
| Feb. | 7 | To Goods...... | 5 | 297 | 0 | 0 | Feb. | 20 | By Bill due May 21...... | 1 | 297 | 0 | 0 |

### Thomas Simpson, Belfast.

| 1850. | | | | | | | 1850. | | | | | |
|---|---|---|---|---|---|---|---|---|---|---|---|---|
| Feb. | 20 | To Goods...... | 6 | 76 | 0 | 0 | Mar. | 2 | By Bill due April 4... | 1 | 76 | 0 | 0 |

## WILLIAM JERDAN, Queen Street.

| 1850. | | | | | | 1850. | | | | | | |
|---|---|---|---|---|---|---|---|---|---|---|---|---|
| Mar. | 1 | To Goods...... | 8 | 106 | 7 | 2 | Mar. | 7 | By Bill due | | | |
| | 28 | ,, do. ...... | 11 | 290 | 9 | 8 | | | July 11... | 1 | 106 | 7 | 2 |
| | | | | | | | | 31 | ,, Balance... | ,, | 290 | 9 | 8 |
| | | | | 396 | 16 | 10 | | | | | 396 | 16 | 10 |
| Mar. | 31 | To Balance... | | 290 | 9 | 8 | | | | | | | |

## WILLIAM THOMSON, Aberdeen.

| 1850. | | | | | | 1850. | | | | | | |
|---|---|---|---|---|---|---|---|---|---|---|---|---|
| Mar. | 1 | To Goods...... | 8 | 18 | 5 | 8 | Mar. | 4 | By Cash........ | 5 | 17 | 16 | 6 |
| | 16 | ,, do. ...... | 9 | 20 | 3 | 6 | | ,, | ,, Discount.. | ,, | 0 | 9 | 2 |
| | | | | | | | | 31 | ,, Balance... | ,, | 20 | 3 | 6 |
| | | | | 38 | 9 | 2 | | | | | 38 | 9 | 2 |
| Mar. | 31 | To Balance... | | 20 | 3 | 6 | | | | | | | |

## GEORGE KNIGHT, Birmingham.

| 1850. | | | | | | 1850. | | | | | | |
|---|---|---|---|---|---|---|---|---|---|---|---|---|
| Mar. | 4 | To Goods...... | 8 | 278 | 7 | 0 | Mar. | 30 | By Cash........ | 5 | 298 | 4 | 7 |
| | 11 | ,, do. ...... | 9 | 19 | 17 | 7 | | 31 | ,, Balance... | ,, | 664 | 11 | 8 |
| | 26 | ,, do. ...... | 10 | 664 | 11 | 8 | | | | | | | |
| | | | | 962 | 16 | 3 | | | | | 962 | 16 | 3 |
| Mar. | 31 | To Balance... | | 664 | 11 | 8 | | | | | | | |

## JOHN WATSON, Edinburgh.

| 1850. | | | | | | 1850. | | | | | | |
|---|---|---|---|---|---|---|---|---|---|---|---|---|
| Jan. | 4 | To Cash........ | 2 | 491 | 16 | 6 | Jan. | 1 | By Goods...... | 1 | 517 | 14 | 0 |
| | ,, | ,, Discount. | ,, | 25 | 17 | 6 | | 16 | ,, do.......... | 2 | 383 | 5 | 0 |
| | 10 | ,, Bill due | | | | | | | | | | | |
| | | Jan. 23... | 3 | 300 | 0 | 0 | | | | | | | |
| | 25 | ,, Cash ...... | 2 | 79 | 2 | 0 | | | | | | | |
| | ,, | ,, Discount. | ,, | 4 | 3 | 0 | | | | | | | |
| | | | | 900 | 19 | 0 | | | | | 900 | 19 | 0 |

### Thomas Johnston, Leeds.

| 1850. | | | | | | | 1850. | | | | | | |
|---|---|---|---|---|---|---|---|---|---|---|---|---|---|
| Jan. | 20 | To 2 Bills... | 3 | 741 | 8 | 0 | Jan. | 1 | By Goods.... | 1 | 741 | 8 | 0 |
| Feb. | 1 | „ do. due Mar. 4 | „ | 250 | 0 | 0 | Mar. | 13 | „ do. ..... | 5 | 757 | 17 | 6 |
| | „ | „ do. due Apr. 4 | „ | 300 | 0 | 0 | | | | | | | |
| Mar. | 31 | „ Balance | | 207 | 17 | 6 | | | | | | | |
| | | | | 1499 | 5 | 6 | | | | | 1499 | 5 | 6 |
| | | | | | | | Mar. | 31 | By Balance.. | | 207 | 17 | 6 |

### James Irving & Co., Oporto.

| 1850. | | | | | | | 1850. | | | | | | |
|---|---|---|---|---|---|---|---|---|---|---|---|---|---|
| | | | | | | | Jan. | 1 | By Goods.... (or Sundries.) | 1 | 359 | 7 | 6 |

### John Wilson, London.

| 1850. | | | | | | | 1850. | | | | | | |
|---|---|---|---|---|---|---|---|---|---|---|---|---|---|
| Mar. | 31 | To Goods on hand— forward.. *This sum is taken from the Stock-Book.* | | 89 | 19 | 2 | Jan. | 6 | By Goods.... | 1 | 7 | 10 | 2 |
| | | | | | | | Feb. | 17 | „ do. ..... | 4 | 25 | 19 | 6 |
| | | | | | | | Mar. | 4 | „ do. ..... | 5 | 86 | 19 | 6 |
| | „ | To Commission. | 12 | 3 | 0 | 0 | | | | | | | |
| | „ | „ Cash...... | 6 | 27 | 0 | 0 | | | | | | | |
| | | | | 119 | 19 | 2 | | | | | 119 | 19 | 2 |
| | | | | | | | Apr. | 1 | By Goods on hand* | | 89 | 19 | 2 |

* This is not entered in the " Account-Book " as a debt, J. Wilson's account having been settled up to the end of March. The goods on hand are not payable, or due, until they are sold. See Goods on Commission, page 138.

### William Graham, Kingston, Jamaica.

| 1850. | | | | | | | 1850. | | | | | | |
|---|---|---|---|---|---|---|---|---|---|---|---|---|---|
| Mar. | 3 | To 2 Bills, at 30 & 60 days' sight........ | 3 | 400 | 0 | 0 | Jan. | 12 | By Goods.... | 2 | 504 | 12 | 8 |
| | 31 | „ Balance.. | | 420 | 4 | 7 | Feb. | 12 | „ do. ..... | 4 | 315 | 11 | 11 |
| | | | | 820 | 4 | 7 | | | | | 820 | 4 | 7 |
| | | | | | | | Mar. | 31 | By Balance.. | | 420 | 4 | 7 |

### D. Mortimer and Son, Manchester.

| 1850. | | | | | | 1850. | | | | | | |
|---|---|---|---|---|---|---|---|---|---|---|---|---|
| Jan. | 25 | To Bill due | | | | Jan. | 15 | By Goods...... | 2 | 572 | 3 | 6 |
|  |  | Feb. 28... | 3 | 572 | 3 6 | Feb. | 1 | „ do. ...... | 4 | 142 | 17 | 1 |
| Feb. | 8 | „ Bill due | | | | Mar. | 26 | „ do. ...... | 5 | 98 | 13 | 4 |
|  |  | Mar. 11... | „ | 100 | 0 0 | | | | | | | |
|  | 28 | „ Cash........ | 4 | 40 | 15 0 | | | | | | | |
|  | „ | „ Discount.. | „ | 2 | 2 1 | | | | | | | |
| Mar. | 31 | „ Balance... | | 98 | 13 4 | | | | | | | |
| | | | | 813 | 13 11 | | | | | 813 | 13 | 11 |
| | | | | | | Mar. | 31 | By Balance... | | 98 | 13 | 4 |

### Marine Insurance Company.

| 1850. | | | | | | | 1850. | | | | | | |
|---|---|---|---|---|---|---|---|---|---|---|---|---|---|
| Jan. | 18 | To Cash....... | 2 | 5 | 14 | 0 | Jan. | 16 | By Insurance | 2 | 5 | 14 | 0 |

### James Reid, London.

| 1850. | | | | | | | 1850. | | | | | | |
|---|---|---|---|---|---|---|---|---|---|---|---|---|---|
| Feb. | 1 | To Cash....... | 4 | 111 | 11 | 0 | Jan. | 18 | By Goods...... | 2 | 117 | 8 | 6 |
|  | „ | „ Discount.. | „ | 5 | 17 | 6 | Feb. | 16 | „ do. ...... | 4 | 124 | 14 | 6 |
|  | 20 | „ Bill due | | | | | Mar. | 1 | „ do. ...... | 5 | 283 | 13 | 6 |
|  |  | May 23... | 3 | 124 | 14 | 6 | | 20 | „ do. ...... | „ | 146 | 6 | 8 |
| Mar. | 4 | „ Cash....... | 6 | 142 | 10 | 0 | | | | | | | |
|  | „ | „ Discount. | „ | 7 | 10 | 0 | | | | | | | |
|  | 31 | „ Balance... | | 280 | 0 | 2 | | | | | | | |
| | | | | 672 | 3 | 2 | | | | | 672 | 3 | 2 |
| | | | | | | | Mar. | 31 | By Balance... | | 280 | 0 | 2 |

### Alexander Robertson & Co., Glasgow.

| 1850. | | | | | | | 1850. | | | | | | |
|---|---|---|---|---|---|---|---|---|---|---|---|---|---|
| Feb. | 2 | To Bill due | | | | | Jan. | 25 | By Goods...... | 3 | 234 | 14 | 8 |
|  |  | April 5... | 3 | 234 | 14 | 8 | Feb. | 6 | „ do. ...... | 4 | 206 | 7 | 6 |
| Mar. | 23 | „ Cash....... | 6 | 201 | 4 | 0 | | | | | | | |
|  | „ | „ Discount.. | „ | 5 | 3 | 6 | | | | | | | |
| | | | | 441 | 2 | 2 | | | | | 441 | 2 | 2 |

### John Anderson, Glasgow.

| 1850. | | | | | | 1850. | | | | | |
|---|---|---|---|---|---|---|---|---|---|---|---|
| Mar. | 10 | To Bill due April 13... | 3 | 73 | 6 | 7 | Feb. | 24 | By Goods...... | 4 | 73 | 6 | 7 |

### Robert Cunningham, Leeds.

| 1850. | | | | | | 1850. | | | | | |
|---|---|---|---|---|---|---|---|---|---|---|---|
| Mar. | 31 | To Amount forward... | | 123 | 15 | 9 | Mar. | 16 | By Goods...... | 5 | 123 | 15 | 9 |
| | | | | | | | Mar. | 31 | By Amount forward... | | 123 | 15 | 9 |

### James Cameron, Demerara.

| 1850. | | | | | | 1850. | | | | | |
|---|---|---|---|---|---|---|---|---|---|---|---|
| | | | | | | | Mar. | 31 | By Sugar— nett proceeds due April 20.. | 11 | 643 | 7 | 5 |
| | | | | | | | | | This is brought from the a/c for "Sugar," p. 140. | | | | |

### William Black, Canton.

| 1850. | | | | | | 1850. | | | | | |
|---|---|---|---|---|---|---|---|---|---|---|---|
| | | | | | | | Mar. | 31 | By Tea— nett proceeds due April 6.. | 11 | 158 | 1 | 11 |
| | | | | | | | | | This is brought from the a/c for "Tea," p. 140. | | | | |

## Union Bank.

| 1850. | | | | | | |
|---|---|---|---|---|---|---|
| Jan. | 1 | To Cash......................................... | 2 | 2700 | 0 | 0 |
| | 11 | ,, do. ..................................... | ,, | 123 | 0 | 0 |
| | 15 | ,, do. ..................................... | ,, | 180 | 0 | 0 |
| Feb. | 1 | ,, do. ..................................... | 4 | 390 | 0 | 0 |
| | 2 | ,, do. ..................................... | ,, | 80 | 0 | 0 |
| | 17 | ,, do. ..................................... | ,, | 75 | 0 | 0 |
| | 25 | ,, do. ..................................... | ,, | 350 | 0 | 0 |
| Mar. | 1 | ,, do. ..................................... | 6 | 100 | 0 | 0 |
| | 20 | ,, do. ..................................... | ,, | 150 | 0 | 0 |
| | 22 | ,, do. ..................................... | ,, | 100 | 0 | 0 |
| | 31 | ,, do. ..................................... | ,, | 316 | 0 | 0 |
| | ,, | ,, Interest.................................. | 11 | 21 | 10 | 0 |
| | | | | 4585 | 10 | 0 |
| Mar. | 31 | To Balance.................................. | | 2180 | 10 | 0 |
| | | This is the Amount of Cash in the Bank. | | | | |

## Bills Receivable.

| 1850. | | | | | | |
|---|---|---|---|---|---|---|
| Jan. | 31 | To Amount received from Sundries... | 1 | 320 | 4 | 5 |
| Feb. | 28 | ,, do. do. ... | ,, | 792 | 17 | 5 |
| Mar. | 31 | ,, do. do. ... | ,, | 945 | 8 | 10 |
| | | | | 2058 | 10 | 8 |
| Mar. | 31 | To Balance.................................. | | 926 | 8 | 10 |
| | | This is the Amount of Bills on hand due to Hamilton & Boyd. | | | | |

## Bills Payable.

| 1850. | | | | | | |
|---|---|---|---|---|---|---|
| Jan. | 31 | To Cash—paid Sundry Bills............ | 2 | 300 | 0 | 0 |
| Feb. | 28 | ,, do. do. ............ | 4 | 1313 | 11 | 6 |
| Mar. | 31 | ,, do. do. ............ | 6 | 350 | 0 | 0 |
| | ,, | ,, Balance forward...................... | | 1132 | 15 | 9 |
| | | | | 3096 | 7 | 3 |

The *Dr.* and *Cr.* sides of the accounts are placed on the same page in the preceding part of this Ledger, as is usual in merchants' books; but in the accounts above, and

### UNION BANK.

| 1850. | | | | | | | |
|---|---|---|---|---|---|---|---|
| Jan. | 6 | By Cash......................................... | 1 | 150 | 0 | 0 |
| | 12 | ,, do. ........................................ | ,, | 200 | 0 | 0 |
| | 23 | ,, do. ........................................ | ,, | 375 | 0 | 0 |
| Feb. | 12 | ,, do. ........................................ | 3 | 50 | 0 | 0 |
| | 23 | ,, do. ........................................ | ,, | 600 | 0 | 0 |
| | 28 | ,, do. ........................................ | ,, | 350 | 0 | 0 |
| Mar. | 4 | ,, do. ........................................ | 5 | 375 | 0 | 0 |
| | 11 | ,, do. ........................................ | ,, | 75 | 0 | 0 |
| | 23 | ,, do. ........................................ | ,, | 230 | 0 | 0 |
| | 31 | ,, Balance forward...................... | ,, | 2180 | 10 | 0 |
| | | | | | | |
| | | | | 4585 | 10 | 0 |

### BILLS RECEIVABLE.

| 1850. | | | | | | | |
|---|---|---|---|---|---|---|---|
| Jan. | 31 | By Cash and Discount..................... | 1 | 107 | 16 | 6 |
| Feb. | 28 | ,, do. ..................... | 3 | 708 | 5 | 4 |
| Mar. | 31 | ,, do. ..................... | 5 | 316 | 0 | 0 |
| | ,, | ,, Balance forward....................... | | 926 | 8 | 10 |
| | | | | 2058 | 10 | 8 |

### BILLS PAYABLE.

| 1850. | | | | | | | |
|---|---|---|---|---|---|---|---|
| Jan. | 31 | By Amount granted to Sundries....... | 3 | 1613 | 11 | 6 |
| Feb. | 28 | ,, do. do. ........ | ,, | 1009 | 9 | 2 |
| Mar. | 31 | ,, do. do. ........ | ,, | 473 | 6 | 7 |
| | | | | 3096 | 7 | 3 |
| Mar. | 31 | By Balance...................................... This is the Amount of Bills due by Hamilton & Boyd. | | 1132 | 15 | 9 |

those that follow, the *Dr.* and *Cr.* sides **are** placed on opposite **pages,** as the space is too small for making the entries conveniently.

## GOODS—General Account.

### (*Bought.*)

| 1850. | | | | Credit. | | | Cash. | | | | | | |
|---|---|---|---|---|---|---|---|---|---|---|---|---|---|
| Jan. | 31 | To Purchases............... | | 1431 | 0 | 0 | 25 | 17 | 0 | | 1456 | 17 | 0 |
| Feb. | 28 | „ do. ............... | | 547 | 5 | 8 | 34 | 5 | 0 | | 581 | 10 | 8 |
| Mar. | 31 | „ do. ............... | | 1410 | 6 | 9 | 16 | 14 | 0 | | 1427 | 0 | 9 |
| | | | | 3388 | 12 | 5 | 76 | 16 | 0 | | | | |
| | „ | „ Balance, profit—carried to Profit and Loss.... | 14 | | | | | | | | 302 | 12 | 10 |
| | | | | | | | | | | | 3768 | 1 | 3 |
| Mar. | 31 | To Goods on Hand.................................... | | | | | | | | | 1832 | 8 | 6 |

## GOODS on Commission.

| 1850. | | | | | | | |
|---|---|---|---|---|---|---|---|
| Jan. | 6 | To Amount received from J. Wilson............... | 1 | | 7 | 10 | 2 |
| Feb. | 17 | „ do. do. ............... | 4 | | 25 | 19 | 6 |
| Mar. | 4 | „ do. do. ............... | 5 | | 86 | 9 | 6 |
| | 31 | „ Balance, profit—carried to Profit and Loss.. | 14 | | 18 | 19 | 9 |
| | | | | | 138 | 18 | 11 |
| Apr. | 1 | To Goods on Hand....................................... | | | 89 | 19 | 2 |

These goods are not entered in the Balance-sheet, as they belong to J. Wilson, who sent them on sale. See his account, page 133.

## PAPER.

| 1850. | | | | | | | |
|---|---|---|---|---|---|---|---|
| Jan. | 1 | To Amount bought from J. Watson............... | 1 | | 517 | 14 | 0 |
| | 15 | „ do. do. ............... | 2 | | 383 | 5 | 0 |
| | 31 | „ Balance, profit—carried to Profit and Loss... | 14 | | 256 | 3 | 0 |
| | | | | | 1157 | 2 | 0 |

## Goods—General Account.

### (Sold.)

| 1850. | | | Credit. | | | Cash. | | | | | |
|---|---|---|---|---|---|---|---|---|---|---|---|
| Jan. | 31 | By Sales..................... | 240 | 19 | 8 | 57 | 1 | 9 | 298 | 1 | 5 |
| Feb. | 28 | „    do. ..................... | 712 | 4 | 10 | 41 | 16 | 7 | 754 | 1 | 5 |
| Mar. | 31 | „    do. ..................... | 860 | 1 | 9 | 23 | 8 | 2 | 883 | 9 | 11 |
| | | | 1813 | 6 | 3 | 122 | 6 | 6 | | | |
| | „ | „ Goods on Hand,* forward........................ | | | | | | | 1832 | 8 | 6 |
| | | * This sum is taken from the Stock-Book. | | | | | | | 3768 | 1 | 3 |

## Goods on Commission.

| 1850. | | | | | | |
|---|---|---|---|---|---|---|
| Jan. | 5 | By Amount sold to J. Edwards..................... | 1 | 3 | 8 | 9 |
| Feb. | 18 | „    do.       J. Arnold..................... | 6 | 24 | 13 | 0 |
| Mar. | 4 | „    do.          do.    .................. | 8 | 20 | 18 | 0 |
| | 31 | „ Goods on Hand,* forward........................ | | 89 | 19 | 2 |
| | | * This sum is taken from the Stock-Book. | | 138 | 18 | 11 |

## Paper.

| 1850. | | | | | | |
|---|---|---|---|---|---|---|
| Jan. | 1 | By Amount sold to J. Arnold........ ............... | 1 | 369 | 10 | 0 |
| | 16 | „    do.       A. Gregory..................... | 2 | 195 | 0 | 0 |
| Feb. | 18 | „    do.          do.    ..................... | 6 | 257 | 10 | 0 |
| Mar. | 18 | „    do.       J. Arnold..................... | 10 | 335 | 2 | 0 |
| | | | | 1157 | 2 | 0 |

## PORT

| 1850. | | | | | | |
|---|---|---|---|---|---|---|
| Jan. | 1 | To Amount bought from Irving & Co........... | 1 | 350 | 0 | 0 |
| „ | | „ Cash—duty, freight, &c. ...................... | 2 | 345 | 10 | 6 |
| „ | | „ Balance, profit—carried to Profit and Loss... | 14 | 35 | 9 | 6 |
| | | | | 731 | 0 | 0 |
| Mar. | 31 | To 2 Pipes on Hand.................................... | | 136 | 0 | 0 |

## SUGAR (On Consignment from J. Cameron, Demerara).

| 1850. | | | | | | |
|---|---|---|---|---|---|---|
| Jan. | 1 | To Cash—duty, freight, &c. ........................... | 2 | 695 | 3 | 2 |
| Mar. | 31 | „ Interest.............................................. | 12 | 11 | 11 | 8 |
| „ | | „ Commission ........................................ | „ | 71 | 1 | 2 |
| „ | | „ J. Cameron—nett proceeds,* due April 20 ...... | 8 | 643 | 7 | 5 |
| | | * This is carried to the Cr. of J. Cameron's account, page 135. The Sugar sold to the various parties was payable at different dates, and April 20 is supposed to be the average of the whole. | | 1421 | 3 | 5 |

## TEA (On Consignment from W. Black, Canton).

| 1850. | | | | | | |
|---|---|---|---|---|---|---|
| Jan. | 6 | To Cash—duty, freight, &c. ........................... | 2 | 277 | 19 | 10 |
| Mar. | 31 | „ Interest.............................................. | 12 | 3 | 9 | 6 |
| „ | | „ Commission ........................................ | „ | 23 | 2 | 8 |
| „ | | „ W. Black—nett proceeds,* due April 6........... | 8 | 158 | 1 | 11 |
| | | * This is carried to the Cr. of W. Black's account, page 135. The nett proceeds are stated to be due April 6, being the supposed average of the different dates at which the tea was payable. | | 462 | 13 | 11 |

## COFFEE.

| 1850. | | | | | | |
|---|---|---|---|---|---|---|
| Jan. | 12 | To Amount received from W. Graham............ | 2 | 491 | 10 | 2 |
| „ | | „ Cash—duty, freight, &c............................... | 2 | 202 | 8 | 6 |
| | 25 | „ Amount received from Robertson & Co....... | 3 | 234 | 14 | 8 |
| Feb. | 12 | „ do. „ „ W. Graham............. | 4 | 306 | 13 | 5 |
| „ | | „ Cash—duty, freight, &c. ............................... | 4 | 129 | 4 | 10 |
| Mar. | 31 | „ Balance, profit—carried to Profit and Loss... | 14 | 389 | 12 | 4 |
| | | | | 1754 | 3 | 11 |
| Mar. | 31 | To 6 Tierces on Hand.................................... | | 235 | 1 | 8 |

### WINE.

| 1850. | | | | £ | s. | d. |
|---|---|---|---|---|---|---|
| Jan. | 3 | By Amount sold to J. Pringle | 1 | 222 | 0 | 0 |
| Feb. | 7 | „ do. „ A. Logan | 5 | 297 | 0 | 0 |
| | 20 | „ do. „ T. Simpson | 6 | 76 | 0 | 0 |
| Mar. | 31 | „ 2 Pipes on Hand*—forward | | 136 | 0 | 0 |
| | | * This is taken from the Stock-Book. | | | | |
| | | | | 731 | 0 | 0 |

### SUGAR.

| 1850. | | | | £ | s. | d. |
|---|---|---|---|---|---|---|
| Jan. | 20 | By Amount sold to R. Hall | 3 | 212 | 7 | 11 |
| Mar. | 4 | „ do. „ G. Knight | 8 | 278 | 7 | 0 |
| | 26 | „ do. „ do. | 10 | 664 | 11 | 8 |
| | 29 | „ do. „ J. Pringle | 11 | 265 | 16 | 10 |
| | | | | 1421 | 3 | 5 |

### TEA.

| 1850. | | | | £ | s. | d. |
|---|---|---|---|---|---|---|
| Jan. | 8 | By Amount sold to T. Dundas | 2 | 107 | 16 | 6 |
| | 30 | „ do. „ G. Smith | 4 | 136 | 19 | 2 |
| Mar. | 6 | „ do. „ T. Dundas | 8 | 84 | 11 | 3 |
| | 9 | „ do. „ G. Campbell | 9 | 133 | 7 | 0 |
| | | | | 462 | 13 | 11 |

### COFFEE.

| 1850. | | | | £ | s. | d. |
|---|---|---|---|---|---|---|
| Jan. | 12 | By Amount sold to J. Pringle | 2 | 495 | 4 | 6 |
| | 25 | „ do. „ G. Campbell | 4 | 249 | 1 | 8 |
| Feb. | 19 | „ do. „ F. Milner | 6 | 243 | 2 | 1 |
| Mar. | 16 | „ do. „ T. Dundas | 10 | 238 | 5 | 8 |
| | 19 | „ do. „ J. Pringle | „ | 293 | 8 | 4 |
| | 31 | „ 6 Tierces on Hand*—forward | | 235 | 1 | 8 |
| | | * This is taken from the Stock-Book. | | | | |
| | | | | 1754 | 3 | 11 |

## Counting-House

| 1850. | | | | | | |
|---|---|---|---|---|---|---|
| Jan. | 1 | To Cash........................................ | 2 | 125 | 0 | 0 |
| | | *This is the sum paid for the furniture.* | | | | |
| | | | | 125 | 0 | 0 |
| Mar. | 31 | To Balance................................. | | 118 | 15 | 0 |

## Cash.

| 1850. | | | | | | |
|---|---|---|---|---|---|---|
| Jan. | 31 | To Amount received from Sundries............. | 1 | 5683 | 4 | 3 |
| Feb. | 28 | ,,    do.    ,,    do.  ............. | 3 | 2593 | 16 | 7 |
| Mar. | 31 | ,,    do.    ,,    do.  ............. | 5 | 1623 | 3 | 2 |
| | | | | 9900 | 4 | 0 |
| Mar. | 31 | To Balance................................. | | 51 | 12 | 0 |
| | | *This is the amount of cash on hand.* | | | | |

## Discount.

| 1850. | | | | | | |
|---|---|---|---|---|---|---|
| Jan. | 31 | To Amount allowed to Sundries................. | 1 | 41 | 6 | 9 |
| Feb. | 28 | ,,    do.    ,,    do.  .................. | 3 | 37 | 17 | 4 |
| Mar. | 31 | ,,    do.    ,,    do.  .................. | 5 | 4 | 18 | 0 |
| | ,, | ,, Amount estimated on unsettled *a/cts*, carried forward | | 30 | 0 | 0 |
| | | *The discount on the accounts owing by and owing to Hamilton and Boyd is supposed to be estimated, and £30 to be the difference between the discount on the Dr. and Cr. accounts.* | | 114 | 2 | 1 |

## Interest.

| 1850. | | | | | | |
|---|---|---|---|---|---|---|
| Mar. | 31 | To Amount, profit—carried to Profit and Loss. | 14 | 36 | 11 | 2 |

## FURNITURE.

| 1850. | | | | | | | |
|---|---|---|---|---|---|---|---|
| Mar. | 31 | By Depreciation, 5 % carried to Trade Expenses | 13 | 6 | 5 | 0 | |
| " | " | " Balance forward............................. | | 118 | 15 | 0 | |
| | | | | 125 | 0 | 0 | |

## CASH.

| 1850. | | | | | | | |
|---|---|---|---|---|---|---|---|
| Jan. | 31 | By Amount paid to Sundries..................... | 2 | 5637 | 4 | 6 | |
| Feb. | 28 | " do. " do. .................. | 4 | 2603 | 10 | 7 | |
| Mar. | 31 | " do. " do. .................. | 6 | 1607 | 16 | 11 | |
| " | " | " Balance forward....................... | | 51 | 12 | 0 | |
| | | | | 9900 | 4 | 0 | |

## DISCOUNT.

| 1850. | | | | | | | |
|---|---|---|---|---|---|---|---|
| Jan. | 31 | By Amount allowed by Sundries................... | 2 | 30 | 0 | 6 | |
| Feb. | 28 | " do. " do. ................ | 4 | 7 | 19 | 7 | |
| Mar. | 31 | " do. " do. ................ | 6 | 12 | 13 | 6 | |
| " | " | " Balance, loss—carried to Profit and Loss.... | 14 | 63 | 8 | 6 | |
| | | | | 114 | 2 | 1 | |
| Mar. | 31 | By Amount estimated—brought forward......... | | 30 | 0 | 0 | |

This is entered in the Balance Sheet, to make allowance for the discount on unsettled accounts.

## INTEREST.

| 1850. | | | | | | | |
|---|---|---|---|---|---|---|---|
| Mar. | 31 | By Amount received from Bank.................. | 11 | 21 | 10 | 0 | |
| " | " | " do. " Tea.................... | 12 | 3 | 9 | 6 | |
| " | " | " do. " Sugar.................. | " | 11 | 11 | 8 | |
| | | | | 36 | 11 | 2 | |

## INSURANCE.

| 1850. | | | | £ | s | d |
|---|---|---|---|---|---|---|
| Jan. | 1 | To Amount charged by Irving & Co............... | 1 | 8 | 18 | 6 |
| | 12 | ,, do. ,, W. Graham............... | 2 | 12 | 10 | 0 |
| | 16 | ,, do. ,, Marine Insurance Co.... | 2 | 5 | 14 | 0 |
| Feb. | 12 | ,, do. ,, W. Graham............... | 4 | 8 | 10 | 0 |
| | 18 | ,, Cash—Insurance on Goods to A. Gregory.... | 4 | 7 | 14 | 9 |
| | | | | 43 | 7 | 3 |

## COMMISSION.

| 1850. | | | | £ | s | d |
|---|---|---|---|---|---|---|
| Jan. | 1 | To Amount charged by Irving & Co............... | 1 | 0 | 9 | 0 |
| | 12 | ,, do. ,, W. Graham............... | 2 | 0 | 12 | 6 |
| Feb. | 12 | ,, do. ,, do. ............... | 4 | 0 | 8 | 6 |
| Mar. | 31 | ,, Balance, profit—carried to Profit and Loss... | 14 | 96 | 7 | 4 |
| | | | | 97 | 17 | 4 |

## BAD DEBTS.

| 1850. | | | | £ | s | d |
|---|---|---|---|---|---|---|
| Mar. | 22 | To J. Addison's a/c—balance......................... | 2 | 93 | 8 | 4 |
| | 31 | ,, R. Hall's a/c—balance............................. | 3 | 24 | 10 | 2 |
| | | | | 117 | 18 | 6 |

## TRADE

| 1850. | | | Rent & Taxes | | | Salaries | | | Sundries | | | | | £ | s | d |
|---|---|---|---|---|---|---|---|---|---|---|---|---|---|---|---|---|
| Jan. | 31 | To Cash................... | 5 | 7 | 6 | 21 | 2 | 0 | 4 | 3 | 6 | 2 | | 30 | 13 | 0 |
| Feb. | 28 | ,, do. ................... | 2 | 9 | 6 | 22 | 17 | 0 | 1 | 2 | 0 | 4 | | 26 | 8 | 6 |
| Mar. | 31 | ,, do. ................... | 85 | 0 | 0 | 28 | 9 | 0 | 0 | 19 | 11 | 6 | | 114 | 8 | 11 |
| | ,, | ,, Counting-House Furniture— depreciation......... | | | | | | | | | | 12 | | 6 | 5 | 0 |
| | ,, | ,, Insurance.............. | | | | | | | | | | 13 | | 29 | 18 | 6 |
| | | | 92 | 17 | 0 | 72 | 8 | 0 | 6 | 5 | 5 | | | 207 | 13 | 11 |

In this account is shown the manner of entering some of the particulars of the Trade Expenses, which may be done more or less minutely, according to circumstances. The sum-total of each month is the amount of the columns in the Cash-Book for Trade Expenses, the particulars being noted on a piece of paper and entered as above. Care must be taken to see that the amount of the particulars agrees with the sum-total.

INSURANCE.

| 1850. | | | | | | |
|---|---|---|---|---|---|---|
| Jan. | 16 | By Amount charged to A. Gregory.................. | 2 | 5 | 14 | 0 |
| Feb. | 18 | „     do.         „         do.     ................. | 6 | 7 | 14 | 9 |
| Mar. | 31 | „  Balance to Trade Expenses........................ | 13 | 29 | 18 | 6 |
| | | | | | | |
| | | | | 43 | 7 | 3 |

COMMISSION.

| 1850. | | | | | | |
|---|---|---|---|---|---|---|
| Jan. | 16 | By Amount charged to A. Gregory.................. | 2 | 0 | 5 | 9 |
| Feb. | 18 | „     do.     „         do.     ................. | 6 | 0 | 7 | 9 |
| | „ | „     do.     „     J. Wilson................... | 12 | 3 | 0 | 0 |
| Mar. | 31 | „     do.     „     Tea........................... | „ | 23 | 2 | 8 |
| | „ | „     do.     „     Sugar....................... | „ | 71 | 1 | 2 |
| | | | | 97 | 17 | 4 |

BAD DEBTS.

| 1850. | | | | | | |
|---|---|---|---|---|---|---|
| | | | | | | |
| Mar. | 31 | By Amount, loss—carried to Profit and Loss..... | 14 | 117 | 18 | 6 |

EXPENSES.

| 1850. | | | | | | |
|---|---|---|---|---|---|---|
| | | | | | | |
| Mar. | 31 | By Amount, loss—carried to Profit and Loss... | 14 | 207 | 13 | 11 |

## TRIAL BALANCE.

| 1850. | | | | | |
|---|---|---|---|---|---|
| Mar. | 31 | To Amount of page 1...................................... | 305 | 9 | 0 |
| | | do.           2........................................ | 641 | 1 | 1 |
| | | do.           3........................................ | 0 | 0 | 0 |
| | | do.           4........................................ | 608 | 8 | 0 |
| | | do.           5........................................ | 975 | 4 | 10 |
| | | do.           6........................................ | 0 | 0 | 0 |
| | | do.           7........................................ | 0 | 0 | 0 |
| | | do.           8........................................ | 0 | 0 | 0 |
| | | do.           9........................................ | 3106 | 18 | 10 |
| | | do.           10....................................... | 4486 | 6 | 7 |
| | | do.           11....................................... | 2060 | 2 | 1 |
| | | do.           12....................................... | 284 | 9 | 1 |
| | | do.           13....................................... | 327 | 2 | 5 |
| | | do.           14....................................... | 0 | 0 | 0 |
| | | do.           15....................................... | 190 | 0 | 0 |
| | | | | | |
| | | | 12,985 | 1 | 11 |

The Trial Balance (see page 91) is drawn up before making the various entries for *Profit and Loss* and *Goods on Hand*, in the accounts from pages 10 to 15 of the Ledger; **in** adding these pages, therefore, all such entries must be omitted, and the accounts **in** which they occur, understood as not balanced off at this stage.

## PROFIT AND LOSS.

| 1850. | | | | | | |
|---|---|---|---|---|---|---|
| Mar. | 31 | To Loss—Discount........................................ | 12 | 63 | 8 | 6 |
| | | „      „      Bad Debts............................... | 13 | 117 | 18 | 6 |
| | | „      „      Trade Expenses........................... | „ | 207 | 13 | 11 |
| | | „  Balance forward..................................... | | 746 | 15 | 0 |
| | | These entries on each side are transferred from the accounts under their respective heads. | | | | |
| | | | | 1135 | 15 | 11 |
| Mar. | 31 | To J. Hamilton—Interest on £2000, January to March | 15 | 25 | 0 | 0 |
| | | „      „          „      Profit—his half-share,    „      „ | „ | 348 | 7 | 6 |
| | | „      „  Robert Boyd—Interest on £2000,    „      „ | „ | 25 | 0 | 0 |
| | | „      „          „      Profit—his half-share,    „      „ | „ | 348 | 7 | 6 |
| | | | | 746 | 15 | 0 |
| | | Interest on the capital of each partner is entered as above, for the reason mentioned under " Profit," page 20. | | | | |

## TRIAL BALANCE.

| 1850. | | | | | |
|---|---|---|---|---|---|
| Mar. | 31 | By Amount of page 1.......................................... | 0 | 0 | 0 |
| | | do.          2.......................................... | 0 | 0 | 0 |
| | | do.          3.......................................... | 0 | 0 | 0 |
| | | do.          4.......................................... | 0 | 0 | 0 |
| | | do.          5.......................................... | 0 | 0 | 0 |
| | | do.          6.......................................... | 1077 | 8 | 9 |
| | | do.          7.......................................... | 378 | 13 | 6 |
| | | do.          8.......................................... | 925 | 5 | 1 |
| | | do.          9.......................................... | 1132 | 15 | 9 |
| | | do.          10.......................................... | 3141 | 14 | 6 |
| | | do.          11.......................................... | 2114 | 2 | 3 |
| | | do.          12.......................................... | 117 | 4 | 9 |
| | | do.          13.......................................... | 97 | 17 | 4 |
| | | do.          14.......................................... | 0 | 0 | 0 |
| | | do.          15.......................................... | 4000 | 0 | 0 |
| | | | 12,985 | 1 | 11 |

The Profit and Loss Account, page 14, and Balance Sheet, page 15, are supposed not to be entered at all; and the accounts of J. Hamilton and R. Boyd to contain only the sums paid into or drawn from the business.

## PROFIT AND LOSS.

| 1850. | | | | | | |
|---|---|---|---|---|---|---|
| Mar. | 31 | By Profit—Goods (general account).............. | 10 | 302 | 12 | 10 |
| | | "    "    Goods on Commission.................... | " | 18 | 19 | 9 |
| | | "    "    Paper ..................................... | " | 256 | 3 | 0 |
| | | "    "    Port Wine................................. | 11 | 35 | 9 | 6 |
| | | "    "    Coffee..................................... | " | 389 | 12 | 4 |
| | | "    "    Commission................................ | 13 | 96 | 7 | 4 |
| | | "    "    Interest................................... | 12 | 36 | 11 | 2 |
| | | | | 1135 | 15 | 11 |
| Mar. | 31 | By Balance................................................ | | 746 | 15 | 0 |
| | | | | 746 | 15 | 0 |

It will be useful, as a check on the accuracy of this account, also to ascertain the Profit by the method described at page 29.

## BALANCE SHEET.

*Dr.*                    HAMILTON AND BOYD.

| 1850. | | | | | | |
|---|---|---|---|---|---|---|
| Mar. | 31 | To Bills Payable............................................. | 9 | 1132 | 15 | 9 |
| | | „ Accounts due by Hamilton & Boyd............. | | 2291 | 8 | 2 |
| | | This is the sum-total of the accounts in the Ledger : the particulars are entered in the " Account-Book," page 150. | | | | |
| | | „ Discount (estimated) on unsettled Accounts. | 12 | 30 | 0 | 0 |
| | | | | 3454 | 3 | 11 |
| | | „ BALANCE—NETT CAPITAL*........................ | | 4556 | 15 | 0 |
| | | | | 8010 | 18 | 11 |
| | | * The one half of the capital belongs to J. Hamilton, and the other half to R. Boyd. | | | | |

### JAMES HAMILTON.

| 1850. | | | | | | |
|---|---|---|---|---|---|---|
| Jan. | 30 | To Cash................................................... | 2 | 30 | 0 | 0 |
| Feb. | 17 | „ do. ................................................... | 4 | 30 | 0 | 0 |
| Mar. | 5 | „ do. ................................................... | 6 | 35 | 0 | 0 |
| | 31 | „ Balance forward.................................... | | 2278 | 7 | 6 |
| | | | | 2373 | 7 | 6 |

### ROBERT BOYD.

| 1850. | | | | | | |
|---|---|---|---|---|---|---|
| Jan. | 30 | To Cash.................................................. | 2 | 25 | 0 | 0 |
| Feb. | 10 | „ do. ................................................... | 4 | 15 | 0 | 0 |
| Mar. | 5 | „ do. ................................................... | 6 | 40 | 0 | 0 |
| | 31 | „ do. ................................................... | „ | 15 | 0 | 0 |
| | „ | „ Balance forward.................................... | | 2278 | 7 | 6 |
| | | | | 2373 | 7 | 6 |

## BALANCE SHEET.

### HAMILTON AND BOYD.                    *Cr.*

| 1850. | | | | | | |
|---|---|---|---|---|---|---|
| Mar. | 31 | By Goods on Hand (general account).............. | 10 | 1832 | 8 | 6 |
| | | „  Port Wine........................................... | 11 | 136 | 0 | 0 |
| | | „  Coffee............................................... | „ | 235 | 1 | 8 |
| | | „  Counting-House Furniture....................... | 12 | 118 | 15 | 0 |
| | | | | 2322 | 5 | 2 |
| | | „  Accounts due to Hamilton & Boyd. See "Account-Book." | | 2530 | 2 | 11 |
| | | „  Bills Receivable................................... | 9 | 926 | 8 | 10 |
| | | „  Union Bank (viz. Cash in Bank).................. | 9 | 2180 | 10 | 0 |
| | | „  Cash (viz. Cash on Hand)........................ | 12 | 51 | 12 | 0 |
| | | | | 8010 | 18 | 11 |

The entries on each side are taken from the accounts
under their respective heads in the Ledger.

### JAMES HAMILTON.

| 1850. | | | | | | |
|---|---|---|---|---|---|---|
| Jan. | 1 | By Cash.......................................................... | 1 | 2000 | 0 | 0 |
| Mar. | 31 | „  Interest, Jan. to March, brought from Profit & Loss | 14 | 25 | 0 | 0 |
| | „ | „  Profit,      „   ½ share   „    „      do. | „ | 348 | 7 | 6 |
| | | | | 2373 | 7 | 6 |
| Mar. | 31 | By Balance................................................ | | 2278 | 7 | 6 |

This is J. Hamilton's half of the capital belonging to the
firm of Hamilton and Boyd.  See Balance Sheet.

### ROBERT BOYD.

| 1850. | | | | | | |
|---|---|---|---|---|---|---|
| Jan. | 1 | By Cash...................................................... | 1 | 2000 | 0 | 0 |
| Mar. | 31 | „  Interest, Jan. to March, brought from Profit & Loss | 14 | 25 | 0 | 0 |
| | | „  Profit,      „   ½ share   „    „      do. | „ | 348 | 7 | 6 |
| | | | | 2373 | 7 | 6 |
| Mar. | 31 | By Balance................................................ | | 2278 | 7 | 6 |

This is R. Boyd's half of the capital belonging to the firm
of Hamilton and Boyd.  See Balance Sheet.

# ACCOUNT-BOOK.

Accounts **owing by** HAMILTON & BOYD, March 31, 1850.

| | | | £ | s | d | | | | | |
|---|---|---|---|---|---|---|---|---|---|---|
| T. Johnston | Leeds | 6 | 207 | 17 | 6 | | | | | |
| Irving & Co. | Oporto | ,, | 359 | 7 | 6 | | | | | |
| W. Graham. | Kingston | ,, | 420 | 4 | 7 | | | | | |
| D. Mortimer & Son | Manchester | 7 | 98 | 13 | 4 | | | | | |
| J. Reid. | London | ,, | 280 | 0 | 2 | | | | | |
| R. Cunningham | Leeds | 8 | 123 | 15 | 9 | | | | | |
| J. Cameron | Demerara | ,, | 643 | 7 | 5 | | | | | |
| W. Black | Canton | ,, | 158 | 1 | 11 | | | | | |
| | | | 2291 | 8 | 2 | | | | | |

The names, when numerous, should be
arranged alphabetically.

Accounts owing to HAMILTON & BOYD, March 31, 1850.

| | | | £ | s | d | | | | | |
|---|---|---|---|---|---|---|---|---|---|---|
| J. Turner | Charlotte Street | 1 | 305 | 9 | 0 | | | | | |
| T. Dundas | Manchester | 2 | 238 | 5 | 8 | | | | | |
| A. Gregory | Calcutta | ,, | 402 | 15 | 5 | | | | | |
| R. Ireland | London | 4 | 49 | 2 | 10 | | | | | |
| J. Pringle | Dublin | ,, | 559 | 5 | 2 | | | | | |
| W. Jerdan | Queen Street | 5 | 290 | 9 | 8 | | | | | |
| W. Thomson. | Aberdeen | ,, | 20 | 3 | 6 | | | | | |
| G. Knight. | Birmingham | ,, | 664 | 11 | 8 | | | | | |
| | | | 2530 | 2 | 11 | | | | | |

The Account-Book contains a list of all the
Accounts owing to and by Hamilton and
Boyd, as ascertained from the various Accounts in the Ledger. When any of these
are paid, the sums are entered in the outer
money columns here left blank: it can
thus be seen at a glance what accounts are
settled.

# APPENDIX.

## SPECIMENS OF ACCOUNTS, EXPLANATIONS OF MERCANTILE TERMS, TRANSACTIONS, &c.

---

ABBREVIATIONS.—The following contractions are in common use :—

| | | | | |
|---|---|---|---|---|
| A/c, a/c, | Account. | Ulto | The last month. |
| Cr. | Creditor. | d/d | Days after date. |
| Dr. | Debtor. | d/s | Days after sight. |
| Ditto, do. | The same. | m/d | Months after date. |
| E. E. | Errors excepted. | %o | per cent. |
| I. O. U. | I owe you. | @ | at. |
| Inst | The present month. | ⅌ | per. |
| Proxo | The next month. | | |

ACCOUNT.—A statement showing the amount due by one person to another for goods, cash, &c. Accounts are kept under their several titles in the Ledger, from which they are copied when required.

### Examples.

Account copied from a *Wholesale* **Ledger.**

Mr GEORGE KNIGHT, *Birmingham.*

To HAMILTON & BOYD, *London.*

| 1850. | | | | | |
|---|---|---|---|---|---|
| Mar. | 4 | Goods ................................................................ | 278 | 7 | 0 |
| | 11 | do. ................................................................ | 19 | 17 | 7 |
| | 26 | do. ................................................................ | 664 | 11 | 8 |
| | | | 962 | 16 | 3 |
| | 30 | By Cash................................................................ | 298 | 4 | 7 |
| | | | 664 | 11 | 8 |

In rendering this account, it is unnecessary to give the particulars of the entries. When the goods were forwarded, *invoices*, containing the particulars, were either sent along with the goods, or separately by post; and in making out the account, only the dates and sums require to be stated. The above is copied from Hamilton & Boyd's Ledger, page 132.

## Account copied from a *Retail* Ledger.

Mr JOHN ALISON, *Frederick Street.*

To JOHN ADAMS, *Edinburgh.*

| 1850. | | | | | | |
|---|---|---|---|---|---|---|
| Feb. | 20 | 2 Pair Blankets............................... 17/6 | | 1 | 15 | 0 |
| | „ | 10 Yards Superfine Black Cloth.................... 18/6 | | 9 | 5 | 0 |
| | „ | 5 „ Doeskin............................. 5/6 | | 1 | 7 | 6 |
| Mar. | 12 | 6 lbs. Green Tea............................. 5/6 | | 1 | 13 | 0 |
| | „ | 8 „ Black do............................. 4/ | | 1 | 12 | 0 |
| | „ | 6 „ Loaf Sugar............................. 8d. | | 0 | 4 | 0 |
| | | | | 15 | 16 | 6 |

In copying this account, all the particulars require to be given, as no invoice or account of these was sent when the goods were got. This is taken from J. Adams's Ledger, page 60. The Ledger contains only the sums-total of each entry; the particulars are ascertained by referring to the Day-Book.

If a note of the account requires again to be sent to John Alison, it is written out in this way:—

Mr JOHN ALISON, *Frederick Street.*

To JOHN ADAMS, *Edinburgh.*

| 1850. | | | | | |
|---|---|---|---|---|---|
| Mar. | 12 | Account rendered................................... | 15 | 16 | 6 |

When wages or salaries are not paid in full to the parties at stated times, but by partial payments at irregular times, the sums are entered in the Cash-Book, not under the head of Trade Expenses, but under the names of the different persons who receive the salaries. The sums are then posted to their several accounts, and afterwards transferred to an account for Salaries. Thus—

JAMES BROWN.

| 1850. | | | | | | | 1850. | | | | | | |
|---|---|---|---|---|---|---|---|---|---|---|---|---|---|
| Jan. | 14 | To Cash......... | 2 | 5 | 0 | 0 | | | | | | | |
| Mar. | 31 | „ do. ......... | 6 | 7 | 0 | 0 | | | | | | | |
| | | | | | | | Mar. | 31 | By Salary, carried to Salary a/c | 8 | 12 | 0 | 0 |
| | | | | 12 | 0 | 0 | | | | | | | |

## A. SMITH.

| 1850. | | | | | | | 1850. | | | | | |
|---|---|---|---|---|---|---|---|---|---|---|---|---|
| Jan. | 19 | To Cash......... | 2 | 4 | 0 | 0 | | | | | | |
| Feb. | 14 | „   do. ......... | 4 | 6 | 0 | 0 | | | | | | |
| Mar. | 31 | „   Balance forward.... | | 5 | 0 | 0 | Mar. | 31 | By Salary, carried to Salary a/c | 8 | 15 | 0 | 0 |
| | | | | 15 | 0 | 0 | | | | | | |
| | | | | | | | Mar. | 31 | By Balance...... | | 5 | 0 | 0 |

A. Smith's salary amounts to £15; but as he has drawn only £10, the balance of £5 is carried forward to the *Cr.* of his account.

## SALARIES.

| 1850. | | | | | | | 1850. | | | | | |
|---|---|---|---|---|---|---|---|---|---|---|---|---|
| Mar. | 31 | To J. Brown's Salary | 7 | 12 | 0 | 0 | | | | | | |
| | „ | „ A. Smith's Salary | 9 | 15 | 0 | 0 | | | | | | |
| | | | | | | | Mar. | 31 | By Amount carried to Trade Expenses | 10 | 27 | 0 | 0 |
| | | | | 27 | 0 | 0 | | | | | | |

Accounts are kept in the Ledger not only for individuals, but also for the various branches of a merchant's property. The details of such accounts vary according to the nature of the case, but the following will serve as specimens:—

## WAREHOUSE BUILDINGS.

| 1850. | | | | | | | 1850. | | | | | |
|---|---|---|---|---|---|---|---|---|---|---|---|---|
| Jan. | 1 | To Cash...... | 1 | 1000 | 0 | 0 | | | | | | |

.The warehouse is supposed to have cost £1000. This sum is entered in the Cash-Book when paid, and posted from thence to an account to be opened in the Ledger under whatever title will best describe the property. If the building becomes deteriorated in value from any cause, an entry requires to be made similar to that in the account for Machinery given in next page.

Interest 5 per cent. on the value requires to be charged to the "Trade Expenses," or to whatever department of the business it belongs, also any payments for repairs, &c.

### PRINTING MACHINERY.

| 1850 | | | | | | | 1850 | | | | | | | | |
|---|---|---|---|---|---|---|---|---|---|---|---|---|---|---|---|
| Jan. | 1 | To Cash...... | 1 | 1000 | 0 | 0 | Dec. | 31 | By Tear & Wear 5 ꝑ cent. carried to Printing-Office a/c | 8 | 50 | 0 | 0 | | |
| | | | | | | | | | „ Balance forward. | | 950 | 0 | 0 | | |
| | | | | 1000 | 0 | 0 | | | | | 1000 | 0 | 0 | | |
| 1851 | | | | | | | | | | | | | | | |
| Jan. | 1 | To Balance. | | 950 | 0 | 0 | | | | | | | | | |

The machinery is supposed to cost £1000, and to undergo a yearly deterioration of 5 per cent. off the cost price. This deterioration (£50) is carried every year to the *Dr.* of the Printing-Office account, reducing the value of the machinery by this sum annually.

### PRINTING-OFFICE.

| 1850 | | | | | | | |
|---|---|---|---|---|---|---|---|
| Dec. | 31 | To Interest on Machinery, 5 % | 9 | 50 | 0 | 0 | |
| | | „ Tear & Wear of do.—— from " Machinery" a/c | 7 | 50 | 0 | 0 | |
| | | | | 100 | 0 | 0 | |

The Printing-Office requires to be charged yearly with the interest on the value of the machinery, and with the tear and wear.

ACCOUNT CURRENT.—An account in which is drawn out in *Dr.* and *Cr.* columns, a statement of the transactions that have taken place **between** two parties during a certain time.

Example.

*Dr.*     J. BLACK, Edinburgh, in account **with** T. SMITH, London.     *Cr.*

| 1850. | | | | | | | 1850. | | | | | | |
|---|---|---|---|---|---|---|---|---|---|---|---|---|---|
| Jan. | 1 | To Goods...... | 12 | 14 | 6 | | Jan. | 5 | By Goods...... | 24 | 3 | 2 | |
| Feb. | 7 | „ do. ...... | 37 | 19 | 3 | | | 20 | „ do. ...... | 30 | 7 | 6 | |
| | 10 | „ do. ...... | 45 | 16 | 8 | | Feb. | 3 | „ do. ...... | 12 | 8 | 2 | |
| Mar. | 4 | „ do. ...... | 30 | 8 | 2 | | Mar. | 2 | „ do. ...... | 40 | 6 | 3 | |
| | 15 | „ do. ...... | 72 | 4 | 2 | | | 30 | „ Balance— forward. | 91 | 17 | 8 | |
| | | | 199 | 2 | 9 | | | | | 199 | 2 | 9 | |
| Mar. | 30 | To Balance... | 91 | 17 | 8 | | | | | | | | |
| | | This is the balance due by John Black to Thomas Smith. | | | | | | | | | | | |

ACCOUNT-SALES. — An account drawn out by a commission agent, showing the sales he has made of goods on account of another party. It contains a statement of the quantities sold, and the prices, also the charges for freight, commission, &c.

Example.

Account-Sales of 50 hhds. Sugar, per **"The Jane,"** consigned by James Cameron, Demerara.

| 1850. | | | | |
|---|---|---|---|---|
| Jan. | 30 | 6 Hhds. J. C. 1 to 6, (@ 72 days.) | | |
| | | cwt. qr. lbs.   cwt. qr. lbs.   cwt. qr. lbs. | | |
| | | gross 98 2 **27**, tare 7 2 24, nett 91 0 3, @ 46/8 | 212 | 7 11 |
| Mar. | 4 | 16 Hhds. J. C. 7 to 22, (@ 26 days.) | | |
| | | gross 245 0 16, tare 17 1 12, nett 227 3 4, @ 42/ | 278 | 7 0 |
| | 26 | 20 Hhds. J. C. 23 to 42, (@ 1 month.) | | |
| | | gross 311 1 0, tare 26 1 20, nett 284 3 8, @ 46/8 | 664 | 11 8 |
| | 29 | 8 Hhds. J. C. 43 to 50, (@ 1 month.) | | |
| | | gross 131 1 9, tare 11 1 17, nett 119 3 **20**, @ 44/4 | 265 | 16 10 |
| | | | 1421 | 3 5 |
| | | CHARGES. | | |
| | | cwt. qr. lbs. | | |
| Jan. | 1 | Duty on 723 2 7...............£506 9 10 | | |
| | | Freight....................177 15 0 | | |
| | | Shore dues, &c...................... 2 3 4 | | |
| | | Cooperage, porterage, &c............. 8 15 0 | | |
| Mar. | 31 | Interest on cash paid for duty, freight, &c. 11 11 8 | | |
| | | Commission 5 % on Sales (£1421, 3s. 5d.) 71 1 2 | 777 | 16 0 |
| | | Besides the above, there are generally charges for rent, insurance, &c. | | |
| | | Nett proceeds, due April 20............... | 643 | 7 5 |
| | | E. E.         *London,* | | |
| | | HAMILTON & BOYD. | | |

The **above** is taken from the **account in the Ledger** under Sugar, page 140: the amounts only are given in the Ledger, **but** the particulars of the entries will be found in the Day-Book and Cash-Book **at** the dates marked. A book termed **an** "Account Sales-Book" is generally used for entering sales of goods on commission such as the above.

The **proceeds are stated** to be due on **April** 20, being the supposed average of the various dates at which the sugar is **payable.** The letters E. E. mean "Errors Excepted."

ADVENTURE.—A term applied to shipments of goods **to** or from some particular place. Thus if a merchant shipped a quantity of goods to Calcutta, the shipment might be termed "Adventure to Calcutta," and under this title an account would be kept in the Ledger of the proceeds and expenses, showing how much was gained or lost.

AFFIDAVIT.—An oath or declaration as to the truth of a fact. In cases of bankruptcy, or when a debtor dies, persons on lodging their claims or accounts require to send their affidavits along with them. Thus—

### ENGLISH FORM.

**In the Matter of *Edward Lindsay, Silk Mercer*, 139 *Strand, London*, a Bankrupt.**

*John Douglas of the city of London, Silk Mercer,* maketh oath and saith that the said *Edward Lindsay, Silk Mercer*, in 139 *Strand, London,* the person against whom a Fiat in Bankruptcy hath been late awarded and issued, and is now in prosecution, *was* at and before the date and issuing forth of the said Fiat, and still *is* justly and truly indebted to this Deponent (or if there is a partner, *and to his* partner *in trade, James Hamilton,*) in the Sum of *one hundred and twenty pounds, for goods sold and delivered by this deponent (and his said partner*), *in the months of August and September* 1849, for which said sum or any part thereof, he this deponent, hath not (nor hath *his said partner*), nor any other person or persons by *this deponent's* order, or for *his (or their)* use to this Deponent's knowledge or belief, had or received any security or satisfaction whatsoever.                    *John Douglas.*

{ Sworn at **London** in the County of *Middlesex*, this *sixth* day of **January**, one thousand eight hundred and *fifty*.
       Before me, *Thomas Smith*,
           a Master Extraordinary in Chancery.

### SCOTCH FORM.

At Edinburgh, the *tenth* day of *January*, Eighteen Hundred and *fifty*, in presence of *James* **Anderson, *Esq.*,** one of Her Majesty's Justices of the Peace for the *city* of *Edinburgh*, compeared *John Adams* (or if there are partners, *John Adams of the firm of John and Thomas Adams*), who being solemnly sworn and interrogated, Depones, That, *George Brown, Draper,* 12 *George Street, Edinburgh*, is justly indebted and resting owing to the Deponent (or, *to the company of which Deponent is a partner*) the sum of *twenty pounds ten shillings*, being the Amount of *the annexed account.* Depones that no part of said sum has been paid or compensated ; nor does the Deponent (*or his said partner*) hold any other Person than the said *George Brown* bound for the Debt, or any security for the same. All which is truth, as the Deponent shall answer to God.

                 *John Adams.*
                 *James Anderson*, **J. P.**

The affidavit is usually a printed form filled up with writing. The words in *Italics* are those commonly written.

ASSETS.—A term used to denote the property of every description belonging to an individual.

BANKRUPTCY.—When a person becomes unable to pay his debts, he is said to be insolvent ; and when his insolvency is legally announced, or gazetted, he is termed a Bankrupt. By the process of bankruptcy in the law of England, termed *Fiat in Bankruptcy* (similar to that of Sequestration in the law of Scotland), if the creditors to a certain amount concur in petitioning for a *fiat*, the causes of the insolvency are investigated; and if there has been no fraud, the individual is relieved from all previous obligations, on giving up his entire property. It is only persons in trade that are entitled to the benefit of this process of bankruptcy, all others being excluded. In the event of persons not in trade becoming insolvent, they must submit to the ordinary laws respecting debtors. The persons to whom the realisation, management, and distribution of the estate of a bankrupt are committed, are termed his *Assignees* or *Trustees.* (See INSOLVENCY.)

BANK CHEQUE.—An order on a banker to pay a certain sum of money when the order is presented, drawn out by a person who has money deposited with the banker. A bank cheque is usually a printed form filled up with writing.

## Examples.

No. 324.

No. 324.      EDINBURGH, *January* 1, 1850.

*Jan.* 1, 1850.

To the Treasurer of the Bank of Scotland.

*G. Bruce.*

Pay to *Mr George Bruce,* - - - or Bearer,

- - - -     *One hundred pounds* - - - - - - - Sterling.

£100.

£100.      *James Campbell.*

BANK OF SCOTLAND.

---

No. 171.

No. 171.      LONDON, *January* 1, 1850.

*Jan.* 1, 1850.

The London Joint Stock Bank, Princes Street, Mansion-House.

*Jas. Russell.*

Pay to *Mr James Russell,* - - - or Bearer,

- - - -     *One hundred pounds* - - - - - - - Sterling.

£100.

£100.      *John Anderson.*

* This part of the cheque is retained by the person who draws it out.

† The cheque is cut or torn through here when sent to the bank.
The words in Italics are those usually in writing; the others are printed.

BILLS.—A Bill, or more properly speaking, a Bill of Exchange, is an agreement written on stamped paper, in which a debtor agrees to pay to his creditor on a certain day a specified sum of money which he is owing to him.

Bills are used for the settlement of accounts or debts. They are drawn at various dates, but in trade the usual term is from two to nine months.

A Bill is termed an " Acceptance," or a " Promissory-Note," according to the form in which it is drawn out. The term *bill* is, however, sometimes applied more strictly to an " Acceptance."

### AN ACCEPTANCE.

£100.          *due Nov. 8.*          *London, 5th August* 1850.

*Three months after date, pay to me* **or my** *order the sum of one hundred pounds, value received.*

                                        *John Wilson.*

    *To Mr Thomas Arnold, Merchant,*
          *Strand, London.*

The bill being **drawn** by Mr Wilson in this form, **Mr** Arnold, on whom it is drawn, *accepts* it, by writing his name either below that of Mr Wilson, or across the face of the writing. Hence he is termed the acceptor of the bill. The bill, when accepted, will appear thus—

£100.          *due Nov. 8.*          *London, 5th August* 1850.

*Three* **months after date, pay** *to me or my order the sum of one hundred* **pounds, value received.**

                             *John Wilson.*
                             *Thomas Arnold.*

    *To Mr Thomas Arnold, Merchant,*
          *Strand, London.*

The banking-house at which the bill is payable is also sometimes stated by the acceptor.

If **Mr** Wilson, who is called the drawer of the bill, wishes to make use of it, he indorses the bill—that is, writes his name *across* the back of it—and thus it becomes negotiable paper. It may be paid away to a **third party**; and he indorsing it below Wilson's name, may pay it away to a **fourth;** who indorsing it in the same manner, may pay it away to a **fifth; and so on.** Thus the bill may pass from hand to hand, on each occasion liquidating a debt of £100, till the day of payment by the original acceptor arrives, when it is duly presented by the last holder.

*Discounting Bills.*—**Instead** of running this course, the bill may at any period be *discounted* by a bill-broker or banker. The discounting of a bill consists in giving the money for it, less a certain sum for *interest.* Five **per cent.** is the highest legal interest chargeable in the United Kingdom on all debts or loans in ordinary circumstances; but for discounting bills or promissory-notes, a larger per-centage may be legally taken. When a bill for £100 for three months (or fourth part of a year) is discounted at 5 per cent. interest, a charge equal to the fourth part of £5 is made by the discounter, and this is his profit for the loan of the money for that period.

*Presentment for Acceptance.*—"An Acceptance," to render it complete, requires to be duly presented to the party on whom it is drawn, that he may *accept* of it. This is not necessary in a " Promissory-Note."

*Presentment for Payment.*—All bills require to be presented for payment on the exact day they become due—that is, on the last *day of grace* (see next page): if not presented, they cease to have the peculiar privileges of bills, and become mere evidences of debt.

*Noting and Protesting.*—When a bill is not duly paid on presentation, the holder applies to a notary-public, who again presents the bill. If not paid, he *notes* its non-payment, and afterwards draws out a formal *protest* on stamped paper, that legal steps may be taken for recovering the amount. The bill should be *noted* on the day it falls due: the *protest* may be written out afterwards. When the acceptor of a bill fails to pay the amount, the holder can fall back for payment on the drawer, or on any of the indorsers, provided he gives them the earliest notice possible of its non-payment. In England, the noting and protest are necessary only for foreign (including Scotch and Irish) bills: inland—that is, English bills—do not require to be protested, although it is common to *note* them. In Scotland, the noting and protest are indispensable in the case of all bills, foreign and inland. A bill may be protested for non-acceptance as well as for non-payment.

### A PROMISSORY-NOTE.

£100.    *due Nov. 8.*    *London, 5th August* 1850.

*Three months after date, I promise to pay to Mr James Brown, or order, the sum of one hundred pounds, value received.*

*Robert Hamilton.*

The banking-house at which the bill is payable is also sometimes stated. No signature is written across the front of the promissory-note; it is complete in itself, and only requires to be indorsed by the holder of it (in the above case, James Brown) when he wishes to make use of it, or to pay it away. Promissory-notes are in every respect liable to the same regulations as acceptances. Both promissory-notes and acceptances must be written on stamps of the proper price; if on stamps of an inferior value, they are not negotiable, and cannot be protested.

Bills are sometimes drawn at *sight*, or at so many days after sight; for example:—

£50.    *London, 5th August* 1850.

*Ten days after sight, pay me or my order the sum of fifty pounds, value received.*

*John Thomson.*

*To Mr Thomas Jones,*
*Castle Street, Liverpool.*

A bill of this kind is usually drawn by a person at a distance from his debtor; and on writing it out and indorsing it, he transmits it to an agent in the town in which the debtor resides. The agent sends it to the debtor to be *sighted;* which consists in the debtor—as, for instance, the above Mr Jones—accepting it by signing his name, and marking the day on which he has done so. The bill is now a negotiable instrument, and on the third day after the day specified it is presentable for payment.

It is common to draw foreign bills of exchange at so many days after sight. These bills are of precisely the same nature as inland or home bills of exchange; but for the sake of security in transmission, they are drawn in sets of three. The following is a common form:—

FOREIGN BILL.

*Exchange for £100 sterling.*               *Philadelphia, Jan.* 1, 1850.

*No.* 479.            *Sixty days after sight of this* FIRST *of* EXCHANGE *(second and third of same tenor and date unpaid), pay to the order of John Robertson the sum* **of one** *hundred pounds sterling, value received.*

**James** *Anderson.*

*To Messrs Brown & Jones,*
  *Merchants, Liverpool.*

This bill being indorsed by Mr Robertson, is transmitted to England (probably in liquidation of a debt of the same amount), and is presented to *Messrs Brown and Jones to be sighted*, or seen by them. When it becomes due, it is *presented* to them for payment accordingly. The agent or individual to whom it is sent, receives by the next packet the second bill of the same tenor. Should the first have been lost by shipwreck, this second is available, but otherwise it is of no use, and may be destroyed. The third bill of the same tenor is retained by the drawer till he learn whether the first or second has been received; if both have been lost, it is transmitted. Bills of this description are rarely sent by the actual drawer. They are usually paid away or sold on the spot to another party, who transmits them to a creditor of his own, and he negotiates the payment.

*Days of Grace.*—According to a practice of old standing, bills are not presentable for payment till the third day after that which is specified for them to fall due. The three days allowed are called the *days of grace.* Thus a bill drawn on the 5th of August, at three months, is not legally due till noon of the 8th of November. In some countries the period of grace is much longer than three days. If the day on which a bill falls due happens to be a Bank holiday or a Sunday, the bill is payable the day previous.

Bills of exchange serve three useful purposes in commerce. 1. A bill puts a debt in a tangible form: for example, instead of leaving a debt of £100 to be paid at an indefinite period, so as to protract its settlement, if it be put in the shape of a promise to pay, the creditor possesses the power to compel payment at a certain and not very distant period. 2. A bill is a negotiable instrument. If the parties be trustworthy, it may be discounted for cash; and thus, while the creditor will receive his money, less a trifle for discount, the debtor is left unmolested till the final day of payment. 3. A bill is a convenient representative of money, which may be sent from place to place in a letter; and if accidentally lost, its payment may be stopped and a new bill forwarded to its destination.

BILL OF ENTRY.—A list of goods entered at the Customhouse.

BILL OF LADING.—A receipt on stamped paper (usually a printed form filled up with writing), given by the master of a vessel for goods that have been shipped with him. Three copies are usually drawn out—one for the use of the master, another to be retained by the shipper of the goods, and the third to be sent to the party to whom the goods are forwarded. The shipper gives the party to whom he sends the bill the right to receive the goods. A bill of lading, like a bill of exchange, may be indorsed over to another person, who thus acquires the right to the goods. The following is a common form. The words in *Italics* are those usually written :—

J. BROWN, Ship Broker, Birchin Lane Cornhill.

Shipped in good Order and well conditioned, by *Messrs Hamilton and Boyd*, in and upon the good ship called the " *Wellington*," whereof is master for this present Voyage, *Wm. Crosby*, and now lying in the RIVER THAMES, and bound for *Hobart Town, Van Diemen's Land.*

A. C. H.

1 *Case.*

*One Case of Printed Books*, being marked and numbered as in the Margin, and are to be delivered in the like good Order and well conditioned at the aforesaid Port of *Hobart Town, V. D. L.* (the Act of God, the Queen's Enemies, Fire, and all and every other Dangers and Accidents of the Seas, Rivers, and Navigation, of whatever Nature or Kind soever, save risk of Boats so far as Ships are liable thereto, excepted) unto *Mr Jones*, or to his Assigns, Freight for the said Goods to be PAID IN LONDON, Ship lost or not lost, with Primage and Average accustomed, In Witness whereof the Master or Purser of the said Ship hath affirmed to *Three* Bills of Lading, all of this Tenor and Date ; the one of which Bills being accomplished, the others to stand void.

Dated in London, the 25*th* day of *May* 1850.
Contents unknown to

*W. Crosby.*

BILL OF PARCELS.—A list or account of goods that have been sold, sent by the seller to the buyer. It is nearly the same as an invoice.

BONDED GOODS.—Imported goods deposited in a government warehouse until the duty is paid.

BROKERAGE.—A charge of so much per cent. made by persons termed Brokers, for assisting merchants or others in buying or selling goods, or for transferring property from one person to another.

CAPITAL.—The nett amount of property belonging to a merchant after deducting the debts that he is owing. This term is more strictly applied, either to the sum of money which he has embarked in his business at first, or to the available sum he may afterwards have at command for carrying it on.

CARRIERS.—Persons who undertake to convey goods from one place to another, whether by land or water, are carriers. " Carriers are bound to receive and carry the goods of all persons, for a reasonable hire or reward; to take proper care of them in their passage; to deliver them safely, and in the same condition as they were received (excepting only such losses as may arise from *the act of God or the king's enemies*); or in default thereof, to make compensation to the owner for whatever loss or damage the goods may have received while in their custody that might have been prevented. Hence a carrier is liable, though he be robbed of the goods, or they be taken from him by irresistible force. On the same principle, a carrier has been held accountable for goods accidentally consumed by fire while in his warehouse."—*M'Culloch.* Violent storms, tempests, and lightning, are considered to be " the act of God," or such as no human precaution could have averted, and no fraudulent intention could have produced.

CASH-BOOK. — The following example is given to show the form commonly used in business, the dates being placed in the centre of the page. In the preceding *Cash-Books*, pages 44 and 114, the dates are placed on the margin, as the form shown here would have

### Cash Received.

| Jan. 1, 1850. | Discount. | | | Cash. | | |
|---|---|---|---|---|---|---|
| Cash on Hand...................................... | | | | 20 | 5 | 6 |
| Goods—Cash Sales................................ | | | | 7 | 10 | 6 |
| James Arnold, London........................... | 18 | 10 | 0 | 351 | 0 | 0 |
| | | | | | | |
| | | | | 378 | 16 | 0 |
| —Jan. 2.— | | | | | | |
| Union Bank........................................ | | | | 150 | 0 | 0 |
| James Edwards, Princes Street............... | 0 | 3 | 3 | 3 | 5 | 6 |
| Bills Receivable, No. 1......................... | 0 | 4 | 0 | 49 | 16 | 0 |
| | | | | | | |
| | | | | 581 | 17 | 6 |
| —Jan. 31.— | | | | | | |
| James Pringle, Dublin.......................... | 24 | 15 | 6 | 470 | 9 | 0 |
| Goods—Cash Sales............................... | | | | 6 | 15 | 0 |
| | | | | | | |
| | | | | 1059 | 1 | 6 |

CESSIO BONORUM.—A legal process in the law of Scotland, according to which, persons not engaged in trade who have become insolvent, or traders who have been refused a Sequestration, give up their whole property to their creditors. On doing so, they are released from prison, and left at liberty to pursue any line of industry : the property, however, which they may accumulate, is liable to be seized upon by their creditors, until their claims are settled in full.

CLEARING A VESSEL.—Entering her name and an account of her cargo in the Customhouse books, on her leaving port.

COMMISSION.—A charge of so much per cent. made by an agent for selling goods on account of another.

COMPANY.—Two or more individuals engaged in carrying on a business constitute a company or copartnery, each being termed a partner. Companies are of two kinds—private and public. A private company is formed by a private arrangement among the parties, each having certain duties to perform, and receiving such a share of the profits as may be agreed upon. In companies of this description no individual can leave the concern at his own pleasure. He can withdraw only after giving a reasonable warning, that time may be allowed to wind up the concern, or place it in a condition to pay him back the capital which he has risked, or the profits which are his due. No partner, however, can been inconvenient, owing to the small number of entries on each day.

In this example is also shown a convenient method of balancing the Cash-Book daily.

*Cash Paid.*

| Jan. 1, 1850. | Discount. | | | Cash. | | |
|---|---|---|---|---|---|---|
| Union Bank............................................... | | | | 250 | 0 | 0 |
| Goods—Cash Purchases............................. | | | | 6 | 15 | 0 |
| Trade Expenses—Carriages ...................... | | | | 0 | 17 | 9 |
| James Watson, Edinburgh......................... | 5 | 0 | 0 | 95 | 0 | 0 |
| Cash on Hand £26, 3s. 3d.* | | | | " | " | " |
| * This is marked here merely as a memorandum, to show that the two sides balance when the *cash on hand* is taken into account. | | | | | | |
| | | | | 352 | 12 | 9 |
| —Jan. 2.— | | | | | | |
| Bills Payable, No. 1................................... | | | | 200 | 0 | 0 |
| Cash on Hand £29, 4s. 9d. | | | | " | " | " |
| | | | | 552 | 12 | 9 |
| —Jan. 31.— | | | | | | |
| Union Bank............................................... | | | | 500 | 0 | 0 |
| Cash on Hand........................................... | | | | 6 | 8 | 9 |
| The cash on hand is noted every day as above; but the sum is not extended to the money columns till January 31, when the Cash-Book is finally balanced for the month. | | | | 1059 | 1 | 6 |

transfer his share to another person, by which a new member would be introduced into the firm, without the consent of the partners. Whatever be the share which individual partners have in a concern, the whole are equally liable for the debts incurred by the company, because the public give credit only on the faith that the company generally is responsible. He who draws the smallest fraction of profit, failing the others, may be compelled to pay the whole debts. On this account every partner, on leaving a company, should be careful to advertise in the Gazette and newspapers that he no longer belongs to the firm of which he was a member; he is then responsible for no debts incurred subsequent to the announcement.

Public companies are very different: they consist of a large body of partners, or proprietors of shares, the aggregate amount of which forms a joint stock; hence such associations are called *joint-stock companies.* They are public, from being constituted of all persons who choose to purchase shares; and these shares or rights of partnership are also publicly saleable at any time without the consent of the company. Unless specially provided for in the deed of copartnery, every member of a joint-stock company is liable in his whole personal property or fortune for the debts of the concern. In some instances this liability is obviated by the provisions of an act of parliament, or parliamentary charter, establishing the company. Joint-stock companies are managed by directors appointed by the shareholders.

COMPOSITION.—A payment of so much a pound by a bankrupt to his creditors, they agreeing to receive the sum as a composition for the full amount of the debts.

CONSUL.—A government officer, who resides in some foreign country in order to take charge of the commercial affairs of his nation.

CONVERSION OF MONEY.—Every nation has its own peculiar money; that of the United Kingdom consisting of pounds, shillings, and pence, established at a certain standard value, known by the name *sterling.*

*British Colonies.*—In the British colonies it is usual to reckon money also by pounds, shillings, and pence; but the value of these denominations of money fluctuates, and to distinguish it from sterling, it is called *currency.* In Canada, Nova Scotia, and other British colonies in America, one of the most common standards is that of Halifax, according to which the English sovereign or pound is considered equivalent to 25 shillings currency, and the English shilling equivalent to 1s. 3d. currency.

*United States.*—In the United States of North America, the standard money is *dollars* and *cents.* Each dollar contains 100 cents. The dollar is equal to about 4s. 2d. sterling, the cent to an English halfpenny. $ is the sign of the dollar.

*France.*—In France, the standard money is *francs* and *centimes.* Each franc contains 100 centimes. The franc is usually reckoned to be equal to 10d. in English money; therefore, 10 centimes are equal to an English penny.

With respect to all foreign monies, there is usually a *premium* for or against, in making the exchange. Thus a person taking a sovereign to Paris, will in reality get 25 instead of 24 francs for it, or a premium of 1 franc. In purchasing bills in the colonies drawn on parties in England, a premium is generally exacted according to the demand for such bills; therefore, although £125 currency is equal to £100 sterling, it may happen that the purchaser of a £100 bill on England may have to pay for it £130 or £135. When no premium is exacted, the course of exchange is said to be at *par.*

COUNTING-HOUSE.—The office in which a merchant's correspondence, book-keeping, and other business is conducted.

CREDIT.—To give credit, or to sell on credit, is to sell goods on trust; that is, without requiring the person buying them to pay them at the time. In Book-keeping, to credit a person is to enter his name in your books as "*Cr. By*" the goods or cash you have received from him.

CREDITOR.—A person to whom another is in debt for money or goods. When you receive goods from a person without paying for them at the time, he is said to be your "Creditor" for the amount.

CUSTOMS—EXCISE.—The duties or taxes imposed upon goods entering or going out of the country are called *customs*, and those imposed upon goods at the period of their manufacture in the country are called *excise duties.*

DEBENTURE.—The certificate given at the Customhouse to the exporter of goods, entitling him to receive payment of the drawback allowed on goods being exported. It is usually a shipping agent who gets the certificate, and acts in the matter on behalf of the exporter.

**The** word "debenture" has another application: it signifies a certificate of mortgage or loan on railway or other public works. Debentures of this class are documents briefly and simply expressed, conveying authority to the holder to seize the property impledged, in the event of the obligations of the deed not being fulfilled. Along with these debentures are given a sheet of separate orders to receive payment of interest at appointed terms. These orders being cut off for presentation for payment, are called *coupons*.

DEBIT.—To debit a person, in Book-keeping, is to enter his name in your books as "*Dr. To*" the goods or cash he has received from you.

DEBTOR.—A person who is in debt to another for money or goods. When a person receives goods from you without paying for them at the time, he is said to be your debtor for the amount.

DISCOUNT.—An allowance made to bankers or others for advancing money upon bills before they become due. For an explanation of the discounting of bills, see "BILLS."

This term is also applied to the allowance or deduction frequently made at the settlement of accounts. Thus a person who is owing an account of £100, on settling it, may receive an allowance of 2½ per cent.; he would therefore pay only £97, 10s. 0d., the remaining £2, 10s. 0d. being allowed as discount.

DIVIDEND.—When a person becomes unable to pay his debts, and makes a composition with his creditors, he may agree to pay them 15s. in the pound, in three equal instalments, at intervals of two or three months. Each of these payments is termed a dividend.

This term is also applied to the profits divided among the proprietors of joint-stock companies, &c.

DRAWBACK.—A term applied to those duties of Customs or Excise which are repaid by government after a certain period, when goods on which they have previously been levied, are exported. This repayment is made to enable the exporter to sell his goods in the foreign market unburdened with duties. Before the goods are packed, notice must be sent to the Excise officer of the district; he sees them weighed, and sends a note of the gross and nett weight and tare to the Excise Office at the port where the goods are to be shipped. After the goods are packed, the gross weight, the tare, and the nett weight of each box or package, require to be marked on the outside. The Excise officer requires twenty-four hours' notice.

**FORM OF NOTICE.**

*Edinburgh, Jan.* 1, 1850.

*Notice to pack books for exportation, January* 2, 12 *noon,* to be *shipped from the port of Liverpool.*

*James Allan.*

*To the Officer of*
*the 3d Division of Excise.* }

DUTCH AUCTION.—In common auction, the highest bidder by competition is the purchaser; but according to the process of sale called Dutch Auction, the article is put up at a certain nominal price, which is gradually lowered; and the first who speaks, and offers the sum mentioned by the auctioneer, is at once knocked down as the purchaser.

FIRM.—The term applied to the name or names under which persons carry on business.

FOLIO.—A word frequently used instead of *page* in mercantile books. The word page, however, being more easily understood, has been employed in the preceding sets of books.

GOODS.—A general name for all kinds of merchandise.

GOODS ON COMMISSION, CONSIGNMENT, OR, ON SALE.—Goods sent by one party to another, to be sold on his account—a commission of so much per cent. being charged by the person to whom they are sent, for selling them.

INDORSATION.—When a person in whose favour a bill has been drawn, writes his name on the back of it, he is said to indorse the bill, and his signature is termed the indorsation (see BILLS).

INSOLVENCY—INSOLVENT.—When a person becomes unable to pay his debts in full, he is said to be insolvent. If he has been engaged in business, his affairs, with a certain consent of creditors, are examined according to the process of Bankruptcy by the law of England, or Sequestration by the law of Scotland. If not engaged in business, or, if a trader whose creditors have refused to concur in a Fiat of Bankruptcy or a Sequestration, he may take the benefit of the Insolvent Act in England, or process of Cessio Bonorum in Scotland; by which, on giving up all his property for the benefit of his creditors, he is relieved from prison, and left at liberty to pursue any line of industry. Any property he may accumulate, however, is at all times liable to be seized upon by his creditors, until their claims are paid in full.

INSURANCE.—A contract by which certain persons or insurance offices engage to make good to the party insuring, any loss he may sustain of ships or their cargoes at sea, or of houses or goods by fire. The parties who take upon themselves the risk are called the *insurers*, or *underwriters*; the person protected is called the *insured*; the sum paid to the insurers is called the *premium*; and the paper on which the contract is written is called the *policy of insurance*.

INTEREST.—The sum charged by the person who lends money, to the party to whom he lends it. The interest charged is at the rate of so much per cent. on the sum lent. The sum lent is called the *principal*, and the allowance for lending it the *interest*. If £100 were lent for a year at the rate of 5 per cent., the interest at the end of the year would be £5.

INVOICE.—A list or account of goods that have been sold or sent on a certain day by one person to another, stating all the particulars and the prices. The invoice is sent by the seller to the buyer, either along with **the** goods, **or** separately by post. In the case of inland transactions, when the invoice is not forwarded by post, the purchaser is not liable if the goods should be lost by the way. It is the seller in that case that must have recourse upon the carriers for the **recovery** of the loss (see CARRIERS).

An invoice has nearly the same signification as *Bill of Parcels.*

Examples.

MANCHESTER, *January* 1, 1850.

MR JOHN ADAMS,
  *Edinburgh.*                  *Bought of* EDWARD JOHNSTON **& Co.**
                                    Manufacturers.

Terms 2½ % discount for Cash, or Bill @ 3 months.

| | £ | s. | d. |
|---|---|---|---|
| 26 Pieces Printed Cotton, 825 yards............ 7d. | 24 | 1 | 3 |
| 2 ,, do. do. 120 ,, ............ 8d. | 4 | 0 | 0 |
| 12 ,, Twilled do. 504 ,, ............ 7d. | 14 | 14 | 0 |
| Wrapper............................... | 0 | 2 | 6 |
| | 42 | 17 | 9 |

per Rail.

It is common to mark the terms on which the goods are sold, and the conveyance by which they are sent. The date may be placed either at the top of the invoice or on the margin, and the form used may be either " *Bought of* E. Johnston & Co.," or, " *To* E. Johnston & Co."

MR GEORGE SMITH,
  *Leeds.*
                        *To* JAMES REID,
                          41 *Strand, London.*

| 1850. | | | | £ | s. | d. |
|---|---|---|---|---|---|---|
| Mar. | 1 | 15 Pieces Black Silk, 720 yards........... 3/2 | | 114 | 0 | 0 |
| | | 8 ,, do. Satin, 248 ,, ........... 4/3 | | 52 | 14 | 0 |
| | | 6 ,, Silk Velvet, 180 ,, ........... 12/6 | | 112 | 10 | 0 |
| | | 2 Dozen Satin Stocks.............. 38/ | | 3 | 16 | 0 |
| | | Packing, &c............... | | 0 | 13 | 6 |
| | | | | 283 | 13 | 6 |

Invoices of goods exported may also be drawn out as on the previous page; in extensive export transactions, however, they are commonly made out more formally.   The following is an example:—

Invoice of six hogsheads of tobacco, shipped on board the "Triton," **James** Duncan, master, for Hamburg, on account and risk of James **Green,** merchant there.

| J. G. 1 to 6 | No. cwt. qrs. lbs.      cwt. qrs. lbs. | £ | s. | d. |
|---|---|---|---|---|
| | 1.  18  0  23 gross.  1  2  11 tare. | | | |
| | 2.  19  1  12 ...    1  3  5 ... | | | |
| | 3.  18  3  15 ...    1  2  26 ... | | | |
| | 4.  18  1  26 ...    1  2  19 ... | | | |
| | 5.  19  2  24 ...    1  3  24 ... | | | |
| | 6.  12  2  17 ...    1  2  17 ... | | | |
| | 107  1   5 gross.  10  1  18 tare. | | | |
| | 10  1  18 tare. | | | |
| | 96  3  15 nett, at 7d. per lb. .    .    . | 316 | 9 | 9 |
| | CHARGES. | | | |
| | Bond and Custom-house entry,   .    £0 10  6 | | | |
| | Cost of empty hogsheads, .   .    4 16  0 | | | |
| | Lighterage and small charges,   .    1  8  0 | | | |
| | Bills of Lading, .   .   .   .    0  2  6 | | | |
| | Brokerage on £316, 9s. 9d. at ½ ⅌ cent.  1 11  8 | 8 | 8 | 8 |
| | Commission on £324, 18s. 5d. at 2 ⅌ cent. 6  9 11 | | | |
| | Insurance on £350 at 42s. ⅌ cent.   .   7  7  0 | | | |
| | Commission on £350 at ½ ⅌ cent.   . 1 15  0 | | | |
| | Policy duty,    .   .   .    .    1  1  0 | 16 | 12 | 11 |
| | Errors excepted. | 341 | 11 | 4 |
| | *London, 13th February* 1847. | | | |
| |          ANDREW SMITH. | | | |

*Note.*—The letters J. G. **on** the left of this invoice are the letters marked on the hogsheads. Merchants generally write *errors excepted* to every account which they subscribe, that they may not be precluded from the correction of errors afterwards, if any be discovered.

LEASE or TACK.—An agreement for a specified time between two parties, in reference to the occupancy of houses, shops, land, &c.

LEDGER.—The following is a form of the Ledger often used by retail dealers, in which the *Dr.* and *Cr.* money columns are placed together, instead of on the opposite sides of each page, as in a wholesale Ledger. The object of this is to give more space for writing the particulars of the entries :—

| JOHN SIMPSON, Esq. George Street. | | | | *Dr.* | | | *Cr.* | | |
|---|---|---|---|---|---|---|---|---|---|
| 1850. Jan. | 8 | To 1 cwt. Sago............... | 2 | 0 | 18 | 0 | | | |
| | ,, | ,, 1 Box Preserved Fruit.............. | ,, | 0 | 12 | 6 | | | |
| | 17 | ,, Various small articles.............. | 4 | 0 | 4 | 6 | | | |
| | 21 | ,, 10 lbs. of best Sugar.............. | 6 | 0 | 8 | 4 | | | |
| Feb. | 11 | ,, 12 lbs. Wax Candles............... 2/6 | 7 | 1 | 10 | 0 | | | |
| Mar. | 7 | ,, 6 lbs. Congou................ 4/6 | 9 | 1 | 7 | 0 | | | |
| | ,, | ,, 1 lb. Hyson................ | ,, | 0 | 6 | 0 | | | |
| April | 6 | By Cash................ | 10 | | | | 2 | 0 | 0 |
| May | 1 | To Half cwt. Sago............ 18/ | 12 | 0 | 9 | 0 | | | |
| June | 16 | ,, 1 Cheese................ | 13 | 3 | 11 | 0 | | | |
| | ,, | By Cash................ | ,, | | | | 2 | 10 | 0 |
| July | 1 | ,, Cash................ | 14 | | | | 4 | 16 | 4 |
| | | | | 9 | 6 | 4 | 9 | 6 | 4 |

LETTER OF ATTORNEY, or POWER OF ATTORNEY.—A legal document, by which one party is authorised to act on behalf of another in some matter of business.

LETTER OF CREDIT.—A letter or order sent by one banker to another, authorising him to pay the bearer of the letter a certain sum specified, in consideration of the same sum having been paid to the banker who grants the letter.

LLOYD'S.—The name given to a set of rooms in London, used by the Society of Underwriters or Marine Insurers there as their office. Lloyd's is not only a centre point in the metropolis for all sea-insurance business, but is the place to which every species of intelligence respecting shipping is forwarded from all parts of the world; and this information is exhibited in one of the rooms for public inspection. The lists made up and exhibited at Lloyd's furnish authentic information for the use of merchants and shippers of goods all over the United Kingdom.

MANIFEST.—A document containing a specific description of a ship, with a list of the names of the passengers, and of the packages, &c. forming her cargo. It is signed by the master at the place of lading.

ORDERS.—An order is a request from one dealer to another to supply certain goods. An order, when in writing, should be plain and explicit, and ought to contain no more words than are necessary to convey the sense in a simple, courteous manner. Studied abbreviations should be avoided—such as " have just received" for " I have just received," "amt." for "amount," " recd." for "received," &c.

PARTNERSHIP.—When two or more individuals associate together to carry on a business, they are said to be in partnership. Each partner receives such a share of the profits as may be agreed upon, according to the nature of the partnership and the amount of capital that each has embarked in the business (see COMPANY).

PER CENT.—A contraction of Per Centum, meaning per hundred, and is applied to rates of interest, discount, &c. Thus interest at 5 per cent. means interest at five pounds for every hundred pounds. Per cent. is in business frequently written % as a contraction. Thus 5 per cent. would **be written** 5 %.

PERMIT.—A license given by the Excise Office to permit the removal of exciseable goods from one place to another.

PETTY CASH-BOOK.—This book **is** often used for entering small sums received and paid, see page 45.

Example.

| Cash Received. | | | | | | Cash Paid. | | | | | |
|---|---|---|---|---|---|---|---|---|---|---|---|
| 1850. | | | | | | 1850. | | | | | |
| Jan. | 1 | Sundries................ | 0 | 4 | 6 | Jan. | 1 | Carriage................ | 0 | 1 | 6 |
| | 3 | do. | 0 | 7 | 8 | | 2 | Washing Shop...... | 0 | 1 | 0 |
| | 7 | do. | 0 | 9 | 3 | | 5 | Twine................ | 0 | 3 | 3 |
| | 31 | do. | 0 | 7 | 6 | | 31 | Coals................ | 0 | 12 | 6 |
| | | Goods—cash sales entered in Cash-Book.. | 1 | 8 | 11 | | | Trade Expenses— entered in Cash-Book.. | 0 | 18 | 3 |

The sums received and paid are transferred to the "Cash-Book," either daily, weekly, or monthly, according to circumstances.

POSTAGE.—Inland letters are charged 1d. if not above half an ounce, 2d. if not above one ounce, 4d. if not above 2 ounces, 6d. if not above 3 ounces, and so on.

POST-OFFICE ORDER.—An order granted at the Post-Office for sums not exceeding five pounds. A person wishing to transmit money to a distance pays the amount to the nearest Post-Office, and receives a Post-Office order, payable at the Post-Office where the person resides who is to receive the money. Orders are granted at the principal Post-Offices throughout the kingdom. The charge is 3d. for sums not exceeding £2, and 6d. for sums above £2.

POSTING.—Copying or transferring into the Ledger the entries made in the Day-Book, Invoice-Book, Cash-Book, and Bill-Book.

PRICE CURRENT.—The technical term for a list showing the market prices of commodities.

PRINCIPAL.—The term applied to money when lent out at interest.

**PROTESTING** BILLS.—See **Bills.**

RECEIPT.—An acknowledgment of a certain sum of money having been received. The following are common forms :—

£25 3 6. *Edinburgh, January* 1, 1850.

    *Received from Mr John Brown, London, the sum of twenty-five pounds three shillings and sixpence, in payment of account rendered (or of annexed account).*

                          *James Wilson.*

**London, March** 31, 1850. *Received from Mr James Russell, the sum of seventy-five pounds eight shillings, in payment of account to this date.*

£75 8 0.                         *Robert Thomson.*

When the sum received **is above** five pounds, **the** receipt, **in** order to be legally valid, requires **to be** written on stamped paper. The price of the stamp varies **according** to the sum.

If **a** stamp is not required, an account may be marked as settled by the person who receives the money writing at the bottom of it " paid " or " received payment," and then subscribing his name, thus—

*Mr* **W.** *Hunter.*

        *To John Adams, George Street, Edinburgh.*

1850.

Mar. **31.**   *Account rendered*..................................£10 **16** 2

               *May 2. Paid, John Adams.*

When one person receives money **on** behalf of another, he signs thus:

*Paid,* **John** *Adams*   **or**   *Paid, Thomas Smith*
*per Thomas Smith.*       *for John Adams.*

SALVAGE.—When **a** ship or its cargo has been saved from shipwreck or loss at sea by uninterested parties, the persons saving the vessel or goods are entitled to remuneration **from** the owners. The sum paid is termed the *salvage.*

SEQUESTRATION.—The term used **in the** law of Scotland to denote the form of process by which, if the creditors to a certain amount concur in petitioning for it, an insolvent's affairs are legally **investigated, and his whole property** officially taken possession of or sequestrated for behoof of his creditors. By the process of sequestration, if there has been **no** fraud, he is relieved from all his previous obligations. It is only persons in trade that are entitled to the benefit of this legal process. See CESSIO BONORUM and INSOLVENCY. Sequestration has nearly the same meaning as " Fiat in Bankruptcy " in the law of England.

STAMP DUTIES.—The following are the duties on bills and receipts:—

*Inland.*  BILLS.  *Foreign.*

| Not exceeding Two Months after date, or Sixty Days after Sight. | | Longer period. | Drawn singly, same as Inland Bills. | |
|---|---|---|---|---|
| | s. d. | s. d. | When in *sets*, then for every bill of each set not exceeding - - £100 | s. d. |
| For £2 & not above £5, 5s. | 1 0 | 1 6 | | 1 6 |
| Above 5, 5s. ... 20 | 1 6 | 2 0 | Above £100 & not above 200 | 3 0 |
| 20 ... 30 | 2 0 | 2 6 | ... 200 ... 500 | 4 0 |
| 30 ... 50 | 2 6 | 3 6 | ... 500 ... 1000 | 5 0 |
| 50 ... 100 | 3 6 | 4 6 | ... 1000 ... 2000 | 7 6 |
| 100 ... 200 | 4 6 | 5 0 | ... 2000 ... 3000 | 10 0 |
| 200 ... 300 | 5 0 | 6 0 | ... 3000 | 15 0 |
| 300 ... 500 | 6 0 | 8 6 | | |
| 500 ... 1000 | 8 6 | 12 6 | | |
| 1000 ... 2000 | 12 6 | 15 0 | | |
| 2000 ... 3000 | 15 0 | 25 0 | | |
| 3000 ... | 25 0 | 30 0 | | |

RECEIPTS

|  |  |  |  | s. d. |
|---|---|---|---|---|
| For money amounting to £5 and under £10 | - | - | - | 0 3 |
| ... ... 10 ... 20 | - | - | - | 0 6 |
| ... ... 20 ... 50 | - | - | - | 1 0 |
| ... ... 50 ... 100 | - | - | - | 1 6 |
| ... ... 100 ... 200 | - | - | - | 2 6 |
| ... ... 200 ... 300 | - | - | - | 4 0 |
| ... ... 300 ... 500 | - | - | - | 5 0 |
| ... ... 500 ... 1000 | - | - | - | 7 6 |
| ... ... 1000 or upwards, | - | - | - | 10 0 |
| For any sum acknowledged to be in full of all demands, | | | - | 10 0 |

TERMS.—The following are the terms for leases, &c. :—

| *England and Ireland.* | | | *Scotland.* | | |
|---|---|---|---|---|---|
| Lady Day, - | - | March 25 | Candlemas, | - | February 2 |
| Midsummer, | - | June 24 | Whitsunday, - | - | May 15 |
| Michaelmas Day, | - | September 29 | Lammas, - | - | August 1 |
| Christmas, | - | December 25 | Martinmas, - | - | November 11 |

TARIFF, OR TARIF.—The term applied to a table of the articles subject to Customhouse and Excise duties, with their respective rates.

UNDERWRITER.—The name given to those who follow the profession of marine insurers: they undertake the risk of the insurance, and subscribe—that is, write their names under the policy or deed expressing this—hence the term underwriter.

VENDUE.—A colonial phrase, used instead of *public auction.* To sell goods at vendue is to dispose of them at auction.

VOUCHER.—A document shown in proof of some payment having been made. Thus an account marked *paid* in the hands of a person, is a voucher that the sum mentioned in the account has been paid.

EDINBURGH: PRINTED BY W. & R. CHAMBERS.

www.ingramcontent.com/pod-product-compliance
Lightning Source LLC
Chambersburg PA
CBHW020543270326
41927CB00006B/697